◇ RIVERS *of the* UPPER ◇
OTTAWA VALLEY

MYTH, MAGIC AND ADVENTURE

*This edition is a tribute to all the expedition leaders and tour companies
who have dedicated time, money and passion to keeping these rivers pristine.*

A BOSTON MILLS PRESS BOOK

Published by Boston Mills Press, 2004
132 Main Street, Erin, Ontario N0B 1T0
Tel: 519-833-2407 Fax: 519-833-2195
e-mail: books@bostonmillspress.com
www.bostonmillspress.com

In Canada:
Distributed by Firefly Books Ltd.
66 Leek Crescent
Richmond Hill, Ontario, Canada L4B 1H1

In the United States:
Distributed by Firefly Books (U.S.) Inc.
P.O. Box 1338, Ellicott Station
Buffalo, New York 14205

National Library of Canada Cataloguing in Publication

Wilson, Hap, 1951-
Rivers of the Upper Ottawa Valley : myth, magic and adventure /
compiled and illustrated by Hap Wilson.

Includes bibliographical references.
ISBN 1-55046-438-8

1. Canoes and canoeing—Ottawa River Valley (Quebec and
Ont.)—Guidebooks. 2. Ottawa River Valley (Quebec and Ont.)—Guidebooks. I. Title.

GV776.15.O8W54 2004   797.1'22'097138   C2004-900045-4

Publisher Cataloging-in-Publication Data   (U.S.)

Wilson, Hap, 1951-
Rivers of the Upper Ottawa Valley : myth, magic and adventure /
compiled and illustrated by Hap Wilson.
[144] p. : photos., ill., maps ; cm.
Includes bibliographical references.
Summary: A guide to canoeing the rivers of the Upper Ottawa Valley. Contains outfitting, camping,
canoeing and safety tips, as well as notes on the region's history, geography, archaeology, flora and fauna.
ISBN 1-55046-438-8 (pbk.)
1. Canoes and canoeing — Ottawa River Valley (Quebec and
Ont.) — Guidebooks. 2. Ottawa River Valley (Quebec and Ont.) — Guidebooks. I. Title.
797.1'22'09713 22   GV776.15. O8W56 2004

The publisher acknowledges for their financial support of our publishing program,
the Canada Council, the Ontario Arts Council and the Government of Canada
through the Book Publishing Industry Development Program (BPIDP).

Photography, maps, illustrations by Hap Wilson
Cover design by Gillian Stead

Printed in Canada

Disclaimer: The author/publisher of this book accepts no responsibility for misguided expeditions, injury or loss of life
while using the information in this publication. *Rivers of the Upper Ottawa Valley* is intended for use as reference only;
it is the sole responsibility of the paddler, etc., to determine whether or not he/she is qualified to safely navigate any
fast water situations, trails and road conditions, to accurately assess present conditions in relation to published material.
Whitewaterists: Before choosing to run any rapid you must evaluate for yourself: water volume, water and air temperature,
skills, fatigue, amount of freeboard, value and waterproofness of load, isolation, feasibility of rescue and risk to your equipment.

RIVERS *of the* UPPER OTTAWA VALLEY

MYTH, MAGIC AND ADVENTURE

COMPILED AND ILLUSTRATED BY
HAP WILSON

The BOSTON MILLS PRESS

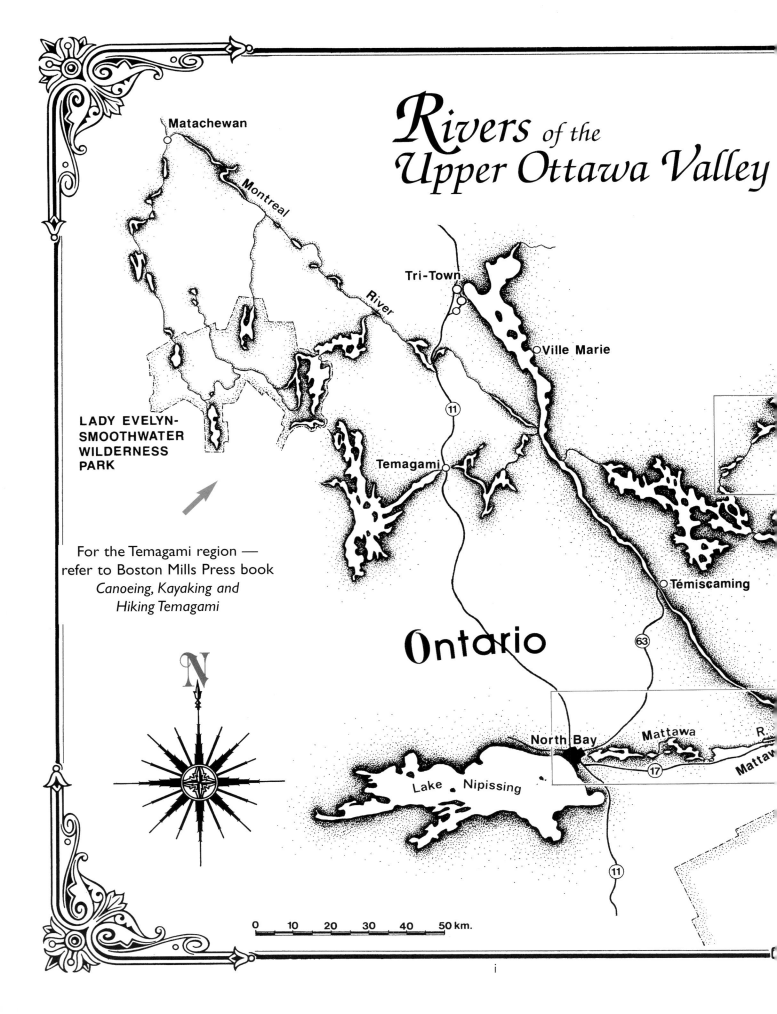

Rivers of the Upper Ottawa Valley

Matachewan

Montreal

River

Tri-Town

Ville Marie

LADY EVELYN-
SMOOTHWATER
WILDERNESS
PARK

Témiscaming

For the Temagami region —
refer to Boston Mills Press book
*Canoeing, Kayaking and
Hiking Temagami*

Temagami

11

63

Ontario

N

North Bay

Mattawa

R.

17

Mattawa

Lake   Nipissing

11

0   10   20   30   40   50 km.

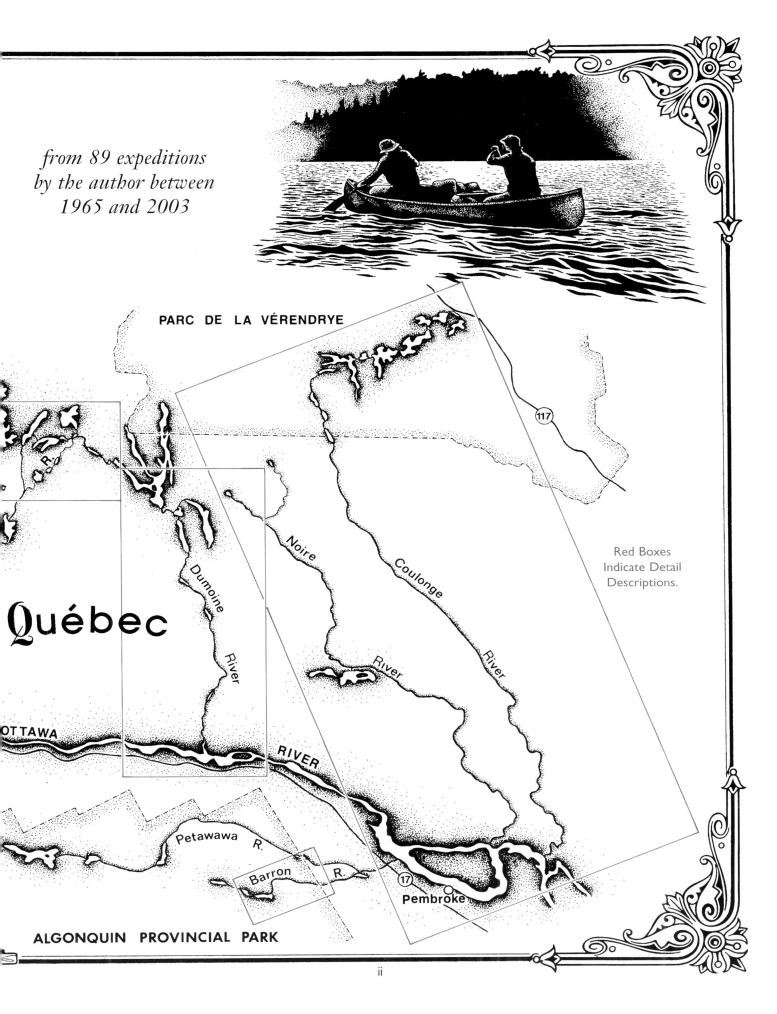

*from 89 expeditions
by the author between
1965 and 2003*

PARC DE LA VÉRENDRYE

117

Red Boxes
Indicate Detail
Descriptions.

Noire

Coulonge

Dumoine

River

River

River

Québec

OTTAWA

RIVER

Petawawa   R.

Barron   R.

17

Pembroke

ALGONQUIN   PROVINCIAL   PARK

Preface

When my canoe overturned while running rapids at the base of Snake Creek, I very nearly became another statistic. It was late March 1980, and the creek was swollen where it emptied into the Ottawa River. Like many other canoeing enthusiasts, the moment open water appears, I must ceremoniously inaugurate my canoe in the spring freshet. The water was bitter cold, and great slabs of ice prevented easy access to the shores. Sheer stubbornness saved me, and the fact that I willingly broke the Canadian Red Cross Society's number-one rule of canoe safety: *Stay with your canoe!* I didn't. My canoe was being drawn out into the expansive Ottawa. I was on the Quebec side of the river, where there was no development — no people to save me — yet I managed to save my own life and that of my fourteen-year-old brother-in-law.

In a way, it was an event that would bring about a change not only in the way I sought out wilderness adventure, but also foreshadow an evolution in the outdoor industry in general.

The modern paddler has become more mature and demands better equipment and revised techniques to optimize both experience and safety. Also, there has been a gradual "softening" of the psyche: the well-dressed, well-outfitted adventurer of the New Millennium has a patent distaste for portaging. They also prefer to know where they are going and how to get there. Holidays and free time have become a precious commodity not to be wasted on second-rate canoe routes. This time-conscious planning gave rise to the "playboat" genre of paddlers who, with creative verve, could whittle down the number of carries by maneuvering their canoes through once forbidden rapids and chutes.

People eventually realized that adventure canoeing was dangerous fun if you didn't really know what you were getting yourself into. Eighteen years ago I made my first trip down the Dumoine River and watching the general confusion among paddlers along the course of its many rapids. Derelict canoes stood along its rocky shores as grim reminders of the potential hazards. It was on this trip that I decided to create a detailed route guide to illustrate and classify the river's rapids. The original Dumoine River guidebook became so popular that in 1993 I decided to expand the scope of the book to include the major rivers of the upper Ottawa Valley. Rivers like the Noire and Coulonge were threatened by hydro-development, and I knew that if attention were focused on these rivers, recreational paddlers, as economic contributors to the region, could effectively quash plans for unnecessary exploitation by industry. And expanding the number of paddleable routes would relieve much of the pressure on the heavily used Dumoine River.

Some river guides and paddling purists refused to patronize the guidebook (though some were spotted by their clients and friends secretly referring to a well-concealed copy each time they came to the head of a rapid). Most paddlers, however, realize that a good guidebook reduces risk and works as an instrument for environmental and recreational awareness.

Other guidebooks followed. And, like when I swam away from my overturned canoe, I broke yet another rule, albeit an unwritten one. This "rule" governed the secrecy of the wilderness trail. Certain paddlers had their own private destination points, and to them the guidebook appeared to be a commercial exploitation of their largely unknown canoeing spots. They were right. Resource exploitation is the inherent result of this and every other guidebook I publish. But most would agree that it is much better to exploit the river for sustainable adventure-tourism than to see another power dam built.

Aside from a few obvious changes to the appearance of the book, I present *Rivers of the Upper Ottawa Valley* as it originally appeared when it was released a decade ago. Where change in technology has benefited the paddler, any change to the river landscape is usually irreparable. The rivers found within these pages will continue to taunt, tantalize and teach us. Enjoy these rivers, but please respect their spirit and purpose.

Hap Wilson
2004

Contents

Maps

Foreword

This excellent guidebook that you are about to purchase describes in accurate and artistic detail four of the Ottawa Rivers best canoeable tributaries: the Kipawa, Dumoine, Coulonge and the Noire.

The Ottawa River's watershed is over 1,700 km long and transports a volume of water to the St. Lawrence that ranks it third in the world in terms of volume. But the Ottawa River is much, much more, as Hap suggests.

The Ottawa was the highway for east, west and north migration and trade for over 6,000 years. The mouth of the Dumoine, Coulonge, Noire and Kipawa rivers were campsites, fort sites or access routes into the interior for every era of economic history that fueled the early economy of Canada, from Native trading to coureurs de bois, to the Northwest or Hudson's Bay Company, to the prospectors, lumber barons, and finally the adventure recreation companies of today. Through the early morning mists of the mid-1600s paddled Iroquois war parties whose terrifying tactics drove the Huron of Algonquin out of the Ottawa Valley for several decades. In March of 1686, one of the most challenging and successful commando raids ever executed in North America was accomplished by French troops, Canadian irregulars and Native guides led by the Chevalier de Troyes. With two young officers, Pierre de Moyne d'Iberville and his brother Jacques de Sainte Helene (de Moyne possibly the root name of the Dumoine) led their troops from Montreal to James Bay in "eighty two days over unchartered territory" and captured the Hudson's Bay Company posts on the bay.

Today there is a movement to have "the Route of de Troyes," the Ottawa River from its mouth near Montreal to the height of land and beyond to James Bay, recognized as a Canadian Heritage River. There is probably no other river in Canada that possesses such outstanding cultural, recreational, historic and natural heritage values. Unfortunately the responsibility for establishing these credentials falls upon a volunteer committee. Given that the Ottawa River is a provincial boundary and one of Canada's largest rivers, it will take a lot of documentation, lobbying and a large body of literature, such as this excellent guidebook from Hap Wilson, to sway our politicians. Nothing influences a politician more than a direct letter from you, the voter. Please take the time to express your support for the Ottawa River as a candidate for inclusion into the Canadian Heritage Rivers System (CHRS). Write or email your provincial and federal representative as well as CHRS within Parks Canada.

Thank you,

Wally Schaber
Director, Trailhead

*P*reamble — *"fulfilling the quest"*

The Ottawa is truly a great world river. Geographically it personifies the Canadian spirit of strength and vitality; historically it has provided a thoroughfare for exploration and discovery; culturally it embodies the very character of our heritage by delineating two distinct societies by political boundary. No other river has bestowed so much through an evolution of trade, battle, greed and exploitation, providing us with the high standard of living we so often take for granted.

In the name of progress, over a span of four centuries, we have managed to displace its aboriginal heirs, denude its shores of the greatest pine stands found on this earth, drown its rapids, native and historic sites, subdue its vitality under huge man-made reservoirs, and in final indignation, taint its water with innumerable agricultural and industrial toxins.

Yet the Ottawa river remains humbly stoic, often demure in temperament, except where we have gratuitously allowed it to express itself in tumultuous chutes along the Grand Calumet; but it has survived the great fur-trade era, the timber drives and hydro-electric developments, oddly enough. Virtually tamed but not quiet – the spirit of the Ottawa lives on...charged with the energy of its high-country tributaries – the Coulonge, Dumoine, Petawawa, Montreal, and numerous other tertiary rivers, all compelling and capable of capturing our hearts and commandeering our souls as we follow their paths.

This book is about those rivers; from the Grand Calumet northwest four-hundred kilometers to the rock knob uplands of the Temagami wilds, to the source-waters of the Coulonge, Noire and Dumoine rivers, born of heavy snow and spring rains that descend upon the folds of the Laurentian highlands - the world's oldest mountain range.

Canadian Shield rivers...fast, turbulent and always unpredictable; each with its own rogue characteristics that taunt and tantalize whitewater paddlers. Topographic contour lines that meld shorelines into precipitous escarpments, allowing headwaters to spill through granitic chasms with canoe-eating ferocity; and boulder gardens that exhibit no forgiving empathy to the unskilled or

foolhardy. Tepid, summer water tumbling recklessly to the Ottawa, a tributary of the ocean-bound St. Lawrence.

Along with the rapidly growing throngs of whitewater enthusiasts, I too possess that insatiable appetite for water in its mobile state. If it's deep enough to float a canoe and littered with ample boulders and ledges, chances are you'll probably see me there pondering the improbable. With adventure trends ferrying to whitewater sports, however, the northern rivers are being deluged with neophytes looking for the adrenalin rush. This book was not published in order to entice the inexperienced or make running rapids any easier for the unskilled. Its primary design is to function as a reference tool only, and by those who are well versed in reading fast-water situations. The focus on detail illustrates the inherent complexities and potential hazards of remote river tripping.

"In the woods we return to reason and faith"
(Emerson)

The Ottawa valley is a very special place to me; not for the singular reason of having provided avenues of escape and adventure...or a place to bump and grind my canoe down its many corridors; but for a more enduring relationship that I have enjoyed with the land itself.

I homesteaded in the valley for eight years; built a cabin, nurtured a garden, fought off marauding black bears, black flies and poachers.lived, breathed and touched the very essence of the river and its people. I was married then and life was sometimes harsh; twenty kilometers from the nearest neighbour and you spend a lot of time soul searching and talking to yourself. But the river was my friend, my mentor...particularly when I subjugated the laws and the will of Nature. The river did allow me to live after my canoe overturned in the icy March water and I made it to shore on the Quebec side. I should have died – hundreds of others were not quite so

fortunate. I gained a deep respect for the river, not just the Ottawa but for all rivers I chance to float my canoe down.

Although it is the quality and extent of the white-water that seduces our passion for aqueous pleasures, I have learned from my experiences that there exists other inherent qualities of the river that transcend the familiar parameters that we tend to build around experiences. Rivers are more than just water flowing over and around rocks, or a theatre to fulfill vain accomplishments reserved for the attack, survive and defeat genre of canoeists. Like the water we are only passing through; if we concentrate only on the magic of the water then we distance ourselves from the land - the very embodiment that created the spirit of the river. To know the land is an exploration of our own persona. Our vision is strengthened by our own perceptions, our ability to observe and accept the how and why until we are rewarded with abundant pleasures for our efforts. In a few words...if we suffice in only absorbing water – we remain forever wet behind the ears!

In order to maximize our perceptions of the river we often expose or mirror our own sensitivities. And, as we allow our curiosity to probe and explore we become infatuated with a living, flowing entity. By becoming a congruous part of the river we embellish that experience. We are totally and inexorably mesmerized by the pulsating, rhythmic undulations of the current, much similar to the hypnotic stare into the flickering tongues of flame that dance above the embers of our campfire...we ride our brain impulses down a neurotic class-three rapids in search of ourselves.

Familiarity compels us to expect adventure only along those rivers with an acknowledged reputation, usually attributed to its notoriety or trendiness. As with the Dumoine, the Icon of intermediate whitewater rivers, it has become fashionable to answer its challenge simply because everyone else is doing it. And what are the consequences? We cram too many bodies down a river that can't support the traffic – ethically or environmentally.

Indeed, recreational paddling has changed considerably over the past twenty years, evolving past the canoeing is for men only

Du Fond House – Mattawa, 1864. Vintage architecture is one of the main attractions throughout the Upper Ottawa Valley

era and enveloping the interests of a much broader genre of adventure seekers. We still come for the same challenge yet in true technological methodology we have busied ourselves to make life easier along the trail; lighter canoes, better packs, tastier food and so on. There was just one thing missing... better route information.

In 1992, while canoeists were taking numbers and lining up at the Dumoine portages and rapids, I paddled for five weeks on the Noire and Coulonge and met only two other canoe parties! Why is that? Simple...we don't have enough information on alternative choices. So what do we do...we embrace the familiar.

But now we do have other options, equally as inspiring as the popular Dumoine. There are twelve rivers in this book, each individually introduced, some in more detail than others in order to facilitate the needs of the serious whitewaterist; all in all, an attempt at improving or creating a wider range of recreational possibilities...and not solely for the ardent canoeist. I've included choice hiking trails, mountain bike routes and even motor routes that blend soft wilderness with accessibility.

I have also added a personal touch to each chapter and route with my own cerebral wanderings, anecdotes and ramblings in order to make this book rise above the ordinary ranks of "how-to" mundaness. There exists a plethora of books devoted to the histories of the Ottawa Valley – the wellspring of facts and information available is overwhelming. I have searched far and wide for the more bizarre trivia and resolved to only briefly skim over the usual stuff we learned in grade school. In composing this book I chose to include the upper Ottawa valley only in order to minimize the size and scope of the publication; also because of the associated wilderness values still compatible to the desires of todays adventurer found more commonly within this region.

I have had the good fortune of being able to paddle all of these rivers, some many times, over a period of twenty-seven years.

Discounting my other meanderous sojourns into the wilds peripheral to the valley routes, this would include 38 expeditions of a notorious sort...adventures easily recounted for some notable quirk or mishap or circumstance.

This book is an accumulation of many miles paddled against wind and current and innumerable portages ascended with oftentimes Herculean loads. Blisters well-earned and a few extra lines about the eyes fashioned from the hours of squinting at the strobe-like reflection of the sun as it danced upon wave and rapid. It's all in this book, about rivers, about that insuperable desire to thrust our bodies into wild chaos and physical abuse, that compelling need to know ourselves through adventure and the fulfillment of the quest...an awakening of that primordial spirit that lives within us all.

Quintessentially, a river imbues a story or legend; a modest but honourable quality albeit less tangible than the physical presence of thrashing waves over precambrian ledges. Nonetheless, involvement allows us to peer beyond the depths of the water demon and into the realm of total experiential freedom... outdoor nirvana if you dare. Enjoy the rivers as I have, respect wilderness values and preserve the experience for others to enjoy. Keep the open side up!

Hap Wilson, January 1993

2

– Section I –
A View of the Past

*"What are most histories of the world, but lies?
Lies immortalized and consigned over as a perpetual abuse
and a flaw upon prosperity."*

– South

*An Algonquin encampment: many of these ancient village sites, some dating back 6,000 years,
have been flooded by hydro-electric power developments.*

The Physical Setting – "faultlines and folklore"

Legend tells us that a long time ago, the baby of a young Indian girl was carried off by a very large bird that lived at the top of Oiseaux Rock. To save her child the mother scaled the mammoth six-hundred foot rock face to the very top. Ever since, Indians travelling along the river were obligated to make offerings in return for safe passage.

Oiseaux Rock...just one of many impressive escarpments indicative of the physical melange of the valley landscape–powerful, demonstrative of some gigantic terrestrial upheaval, towering above our canoes and validating our insignificance.

The evolution of the earth's skin, the physiography of the Upper Ottawa has been a determining factor in man's intercourse with the land. The rugged promontories and monolithic outcroppings have long since been the source and subject of folklore and legend, burial and religious rites and the place for vision-questing to the various Algonkian cultures. Faultlines have also been used ingeniously as natural travel-ways or nastawgan routes.

The north district, Temagami in particular, has a collection of 1,300 native nastawgan trails, most of which are still used by canoeists today. The greatest of these routes follows a natural faultline 115 kilometers from Ishpatina Ridge (highest point in Ontario and headwater area of the Montreal River), east to the Ottawa River along the Ottertail Creek–a dogsled trail once used to deliver mail between Temiskaming and Temagami in the early part of this century.

Most of these prominent faultline escarpments run in north/south or northwest to southeast patterns–much the same lineature taken by glacial movements. These landforms of the Upper Ottawa region lie within the "Grenville Province" of the Canadian Shield–a specific geological zone that reveals ancient mountains and granite ridges. The geological character-building process began a mere 1 to 2.5 billion years ago when the valley crust was an elastic metamorphic mix of granite, syenite and other igneous rocks, underlaid by gneiss (pronounced "nice").

The Precambrian age began 2,000 million years ago and lasted for 1,400 million years. During this period when chrystalline rocks first began to harden, at the same time sandwiching folds of sedimentary rock, volcanic thrusts formed chrystalline domes and dykes. Through various stages of tilting, faulting and erosion, the "shield" was reduced to a region of composite features or what is known as an uplifted peneplain.

What gives the upper valley rivers their megalithic personality are granitic intrusions, deposits of conglomerates and graywackes. Look at any escarpment, especially along the Dumoine, and you'll notice the obvious layered,

> *". . . the Indian here make their offerings, throwing arrows over, to the end of which they attach a little bit of tobacco."*
>
> (French explorer De Troyes at Oiseaux Rock, 1686)

wave-pattern of compressed and twisted metamorphic rock, often veined with quartz.

The Rock-Knob Uplands of the Temagami interior are comprised of a series of north/south ridges–the highest in the province of Ontario. Ishpatina Ridge, Maple and Florence Mountain are all remnants of this precambrian mountain-building process.

At one time ancient seas covered most of the valley imprisoning fossil and marine animals in the "Chaudiere Limestone."

Finally, the landscape was depressed under 3 kilometers of glacial ice. Four advances, ending 12,000 years ago, further etched the surface features to its present state by wind, ice and water action. The dumping of ground and end-moraines along with snake-like eskers are notable features throughout this entire region. The parabolic dunes of Lady Evelyn Lake are prime examples of unique regional features.

As glaciers retreated northward, meltwaters followed depressions and fault-lines. The Fossmill drainage pattern that emptied glacial Lake Algonquin (an expanded Lake Huron) descended through the Petawawa and Barron River canyons flowing in to the Champlain Sea which, at one time, covered the entire lower Ottawa valley up to Pembroke.

Precambrian thrusting also exposed valuable minerals that led to the discovery of precious metals and the development of specific ore-rich areas scattered through the valley. Cobalt, Gowganda, Temagami and Rouyn/Noranda have depleted much of their available ore in only half a century. Unlike trees, rocks will never grow back.

Soils and Vegetation:

One other obvious geographical feature of the upper drainage area is the Temiskaming Clay Belt, a glacial bed of deep, sandy soils which have produced some of the finest farms in Ontario and Quebec. The belt follows the north side of the Montreal River, rounds the head of Lake Temiskaming and south to the Kipawa River. Soils elsewhere are either non-existent or thin and acidic, comprised chiefly of forest duff with a leached under-layer. Belts of gravel and deep sands are scattered but most prevalent on a south-eastward course across the Petawawa and over to the Noire and Coulonge rivers. Just remember about soils when you go to pitch your tent on bedrock campsites–free-standing varieties are highly recommended.

Before exploitation the entire upper Ottawa watershed supported the most extensive red and white pinery ever known. Giant trees, 40 meters in height, almost two meters thick, numbering 400 to the acre and three to four centuries old, once lined the banks and hills of all valley rivers. The fight to save Temagami's Last Stands of old-growth pine at least forced the Ontario government to adopt a policy (borrowed from the U.S.), on old-growth forests.

Today, throughout the watershed, a second growth of mixed deciduous and coniferous hold dominance as far north as the Mattawa basin. Sugar maple, beech, white and yellow-birch, hemlock, black and white spruce are complimented by just enough of the red and white pine monarchs left to add an ambiance of majesty–archaic symbols of a defiant royalty over man and the forest.

Above the Mattawa valley the transitional warm-boreal forest replaces many of the hardwoods with coniferous species such as balsam and tamarack–pine still dominates the forest cover although massive clear-cutting has reduced much of the traditional forest in the northern zones. Throughout the clay-belt, massive fires in the early 1900s and the clearing of land for agriculture has left scattered belts of poplar and birch mixed with balsam and spruce.

Fall Colours:

Fall trips designed to take in the explosion of colours are best planned for late September up to the second week in October. There is about a two week difference in colour-peak times from Pembroke to New Liskeard. Colours also intensify as you travel southeast. The southern "canopy" vegetation is a spectacular blend of brilliant reds and oranges, mostly oak and maple, while the northern complexion is more subtle; the subdued golds and yellows of the forest canopy are highlighted by splashes of carmine and ochre of the bedrock shrubbery.

Wetlands:

Canoeists should also take the opportunity to appreciate the various wetland communities and the indigenous wildlife that exists there. Weedbeds, marshes, fringe and scrubland, floating bogs and black-spruce bogs are an integral part of the landscape and provide the highest potential for wildlife viewing.

Weather:

The upper watershed is affected by the east maritime, microthermal climate - that means generally warm summers and cold winters. July and August temperatures range from 15 to 20 degrees celsius with occasional 28 degree fluctuations. Water temperatures rise quickly following break-up in late April and the various rivers are warm enough to swim in (sans wet or dry suits) by mid-June with an average summer water temperature of 16 to 18 degrees celsius.

Unsettled weather prevails after break-up to mid June; those planning polar bear runs should be prepared for the occasional snow squall and freezing temperatures. Extra care must be employed because of the extreme cold river water. This includes fall trips beginning mid-September.

Average monthly rainfall during the summer months is 10 cm. and July and August are notorious for brewing up severe wind and thunderstorms that can develop in a matter of minutes. Canoeists should keep a sharp eye for storm clouds especially in late afternoon when the humidity peaks and be prepared to head for shelter at the first sign of trouble. Tents should not be pitched near tall, dead or outstanding trees during these storms.

During the seemingly endless winters both the Polar and Atlantic air masses are at work dumping an average of 200 plus centimeters of snow annually. Temperatures range from minus 15 degrees celsius to minus forty. It's a land, some say, that suffers ten months of winter and two months of black flies!

Stephen Leacock once stated that, "winter consists of preparing for, suffering and recovering from." Succinctly put and needless to comment further on the harshness of winter on early settlers and bushwhackers. Indians would gauge the ferocity of the coming winter by the size of white-mans woodpile. It was the great depths of snow in the uplands and the subsequent April meltwaters that allowed the exodus of timber down the rivers during the spring rush.

Temperature and weather variance, from Pembroke to New Liskeard can differ by five degrees in the summer, and as much as fifteen to twenty degrees in winter. Although summer weather is generally consistent, winter rain in Chalk River could be powder snow in Temiskaming. The high country receives substantially more snow than does the lower valley.

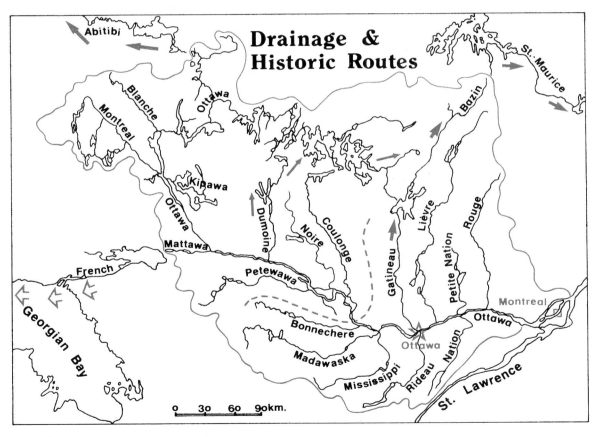

Voyageur Route from Montreal

Main trade route to Quebec used to avoid Iroquois war parties

Route To James Bay and Hudsons Bay Company posts

Trade route used to by-pass toll-collection at Morisson Island

Drainage:

Because of the unique geological faulting that created spillways for the Ottawa valley watershed rivers, a valuable and diverse man-travelled network of trade and commerce routes were established. When white-man arrived it was a celebrated route for exploration, discovery and exploitation – the shaky foundation to which this country is built upon.

The total drainage area of the Ottawa River covers an area larger than the British Isles or 57,000 square miles with a calculated flow of 70,000 cu. ft./sec. (a valuable bit of trivia to know when calculating whether there is enough water to float your canoe or not – 1 cu.ft./sec. is ample creek mire to get you through). Within this book we cover the upper half of the total Ottawa drainage area as indicated on the accompanying map.

The 1,120 km. Ottawa River originates in Lake Capimichigama, about 200 km. north of Ottawa, and within the La Verandrye Provincial Park. From here it flows westward 480 km. dropping 200 meters to Lake Temiskaming through a series of lakes, many of which are now dammed. From Lake Temiskaming to Mattawa, another 160 km., the river drops another 28 meters and finally, descends an additional 120 meters over the 320 km. trek to the city of Ottawa.

The Temagami district rivers originate within the Lady Evelyn-Smoothwater Wilderness Park – the highest plateau features in Ontario. At one time, Lake Temagami itself also drained northward into the Lady Evelyn system but this outlet was blocked by a permanent burm built to maintain water height to float logs down the lake.

The larger tertiary rivers in the valley region – the Montreal, Noire, Petawawa and Coulonge, each over 200 km. in length, draw from an average 1,500 square miles while the smaller rivers drain areas somewhat smaller. After break-up in April, water levels on rivers may exceed their high-water mark by several feet for a short period of time. This would effectively negate any of the detail information I have included in this book and present extreme navigational risks during cold-water periods.

Water levels gradually recede regardless of normal spring rainfall and safe travel could commence by the second or third week in May. The Makobe River Waterway Park is the lone SPRING-ONLY whitewater run because of its small drainage basin and low summer levels. However, a torrential rainfall overnight could mean the difference of a couple of inches clearance.

The detailed information in this book is calculated at average flow levels which normally run about 2 feet below the visible high-water mark, seen as a dark line along the shores. This may fluctuate with the amount of seasonal rainfall and spring run-off.

The book acknowledges that the most popular travel time is from late June to early September - when main channels along rapids and chutes become well defined. High-water conditions do allow the use of secondary running channels and the level of technical proficiency needed is not exceedingly great, primarily because the rapids have been smoothed-out somewhat; however, the volume and cold water temperature may bump the classification of a rapids up to a higher degree of challenge and risk.

Headwaters of the majority of these rivers are protected within the three provincial park reserves – Algonquin, Lady Evelyn and La Verandrye. Once outside protected boundaries all rivers are then subject to extraneous impact by man in some way or another; by hydro electric or retaining dams, bridge crossings, hunt or logging camps, but these distractions are only minimal. On rivers affected by major power dams (Montreal, Ottawa, Lower Noire), water levels may fluctuate during peak power needs on a daily basis. Just ensure that all shore duffle and gear is secured or brought up to higher ground before retiring for the night. One morning while camped below Temiskaming I awoke to find all my pots and fire grill under a meter of water...my canoe, although tethered to shore, was floating aimlessly in the bay.

$\mathcal{N}$ative History – "Shamans, Sorcerers and the Everlasting Leaf"

Ne-bene-gwun-e or "feathers all over", who's totem was caribou, stood at the foot of the great falls of the men-jama-goseebi and contemplated. He was dressed only in rawhide leggings and breech-cloth and a thick pair of moosehide moccasins were wrapped tightly around his ankles. Over his shoulder hung a skin pouch; in it were all his worldly possessions...some sweetgrass for his clay pipe, a small wooden bow and drill for making fires, some cornmeal that was bartered for with the Hurons in exchange for dried fish; there was a slab of jerked venison too, and a handful of dried berries and some ga-gi-gay-bug for brewing tea and to make his headaches go away.

Ne-bene-gwun-e's canoe was pulled up on to the shore and a log placed over it so the wind would not carry it off. It was very light and could be carried easily over one shoulder. The wah-tuk or spruce roots that held it together needed some repair and two of the cedar ribs were broken after lodging on a rock in the fast water that very morning. He would mend it later...there was no hurry.

Wen-dok-i-gabwa-kwe or "come to earth and stand towards daylight woman" sat by the campfire throwing green leaves on the embers to make smoke. That kept the blowflies off of the drying fish that they had caught earlier by hand in the shallow rapids. Tonight they would try their luck at spearing the fish from the canoe by torch-light...

That may have been a long time ago...today we paddle our canoes on new water but the earth it travels over is still very old. The trails and the campsites are still haunted by the spirits of those who dwelled here before us, reticent perhaps and for good reason...elusive to the close-minded city person; but the signs are still there – the beaten path, the rock cairn, the old fire circle.

We must celebrate the fact that any portage trail or water route illustrated in this book had been travelled over by native Canadians thousands of years before the arrival of white-man. Those traditional routes or nastawgan once formed the most unique, inter-connecting trade and travel networks found anywhere on this continent. And what makes it all the more exceptional is the fact that we have not destroyed them all yet with our meddling. Most of these ancient trails are still intact, just the same way they had existed when only moccasined Algonkians roamed the forests of the upper Ottawa.

And after all...is it not what self-propelling is all about anyway? Canoeing, hiking, snowshoeing, camping...isn't it just an emulation of the lifestyle of our native people? Actually, it's more like a mock parody because we do it for vain reasons whereas the Indian did it as a necessity to survive.

We do, nonetheless, have a golden opportunity presented to us; a chance to enrich our own meagre explorations of wild places by learning more about the land and its people. History allows us to facilitate our imaginations – to get value-added enjoyment out of the present and to give us wise direction into the future.

Delving into the aboriginal history of the upper Ottawa, for myself, was much like reading a Stephen King novel. There were more demons, demi-gods, sprites, fairies and goblins still roaming about the north woods than any of us would really like to know about. If it isn't bad enough that many of us constantly worry about bears ravaging our campsites, or the bone-crushing rocks waiting to wear our canoes like Cheshire cat grins, we now have to worry about the flesh-eating Wendigo, or Paguk, the flying skeleton...or the May-may-quay-shi-wok– hairy, gnome-like creatures that live in the high ledges and paddle stone canoes.

To the Anishnabai these were, and still are, very real concerns and many unexplained personal mishaps are directly associated with the tricks of the various deities and demons that still plague the backwoods.

Before the coming of the white-man and the fur-trade post, these people were independent and nomadic. To the west of Lake Temiskaming through the Mattawa river basin, the Teme Augama and Nipissing anishnabai were generally of Ojibway stock while the north and east valley Anishnabai were a mix of Ojibway, Algonquin, Cree and Montagnais. There was some Iroquois influence from the south, specifically after the Iroquois wars of the mid 1600s.

They depended upon their skills at hunting, fishing and gathering. From their close association with the land there evolved a deep religious belief that everything possessed a spirit and purpose. Superstitions, legends and folklore were born out of the unexplained and the bizarre.

The Algonkians practised conservation – they would take only what they needed.
The success of the hunt could mean tribal security...or ill-fated starvation.

Anishnabai woman building a pole and bark "Wakinogan" – essential camp skills were the responsibility of the women while men had to prove their prowess at hunting and fishing.

Regions along the Ottawa watershed were divided into patronymic family groups and rigid hunting grounds or nok-i-wak-i were established. The islands on Lake Temiskaming were considered shared or common ground. The killing of any game was closely scrutinized and it was the responsibility of each family group to practice sound conservation habits. Each family possessed its own totem or clan representation – usually an animal or bird such as the Kingfisher or Caribou, etc. Individually, each family member possessed a wisana or personal guiding spirit that came to them at birth or through vision-questing. This was also an animal entity, of the opposite sex and seldom coinciding with that of the totem.

Separate family bands generally had communal village sites that were used during the coming together at summer time. These were most often located at beach sites or other significant geographic gathering points (such as Ville Marie, Bear Island, Morisson's Island, etc.). In more recent times these villages became sophisticated longhouses protected by high pallisades, but families spent more time in their skin or bark wigwams and wakinogans, deep within their hunting grounds.

Although all upper watershed Algonkians were basically a close mix of Ojibway and Algonquin, and shared the same linguistic and social nuances, there were certain dissimilarities that individualized each band, either through language, customs or personal "household" items, usually associated with the degree of inter-marriage with other native groups such as the Huron, Cree or Iroquois.

They practiced a form of democratic oligarchy whereby a chief was elected simply by a show of hands and nods. Only the men were allowed to hold council and vote. There were generally two chiefs equal in rank that performed specific duties and planned for the whole band. Inter-action with adjoining bands, battle, punishment, etc., were all regulated by the chiefs. Polygamy was allowed and a second wife could be taken without the usual ceremony upon the whim of the man.

Religion was important and each band had its own shaman or sorcerer and conjuring was an integral part of daily functions. The dead were often buried in trees so that they could watch their relatives pass-by underneath. More often they were buried under piles of rocks to prevent animals from eating the body. In the winter the dead person was buried below the wigwam fireplace because the ground was not frozen. The wigwam was then moved to a new location.

When white-man came the natives became less dependent on traditional ways of life and began migrating to the fur-trade posts, relying on trade with the French and English. Many bands became totally displaced and scattered, some were almost annihilated after the great Iroquois wars that were prompted by French/English animosities towards each other.

The upper Ottawa is rich in native history and culture. Archaeological sites, pictographs and serpent mounds are widespread and protected by secrecy. You can still enjoy the nastawgan, the sacred escarpments, vantage points, trails and campsites just as native Canadians did for many centuries...with respect and humble appreciation.

Hunting Territories of the Upper Ottawa Algonkians

ABOUT THIS MAP: In 1913, F.G. Speck of the Geological Survey Branch of the Department of Mines, spent considerable time living amongst the upper Ottawa Anishnabai collecting information about their traits and social variations. This map is a compilation of Speck's findings and related research, outlining the indigenous family or band groups that lived in a particular geographic area as it relates to our own adventures. Specific points of historical or cultural significance are numbered in sequence.

A. MATACHEWAN BAND A mix of Algonquin-Ojibway who's main headquarters were at Lake Abitibi, 160 miles north and later site of an H.B.C. trading post. There were three family groups: Ka-tci-dji, Twen and Wa-wi-eski-sik (round eye).

B. TEMAGAMI BAND: Or Teme-Augama anishnabai ("Deep water people"). Ojibway that migrated some time ago from Sault Ste. Marie area. There were 12 family groups, four of the more common names were: Pi-ku-djick ("Pile of mud"), Misabi ("Giant man"), Wa-bi-ma-kwa ("White bear"), and Wendaban ("Coming dawn"). Entire area was under land claim and legal caution since 1972 but the band was defeated in both provincial and federal courts. They are now working co-operatively with the Ontario government under the Wendaban Stewardship Authority.

Keypoint 1. Kuka-wagami or Smooth-water Lake-scene of world transformation. It is assumed that the Teme-Augama hid here during the Iroquois wars because of its rugged, protective nature. Nenebuc or "whiskey-jack" was a trickster-transformer who, disguised in a toadskin, slew the giant lynx queen in a cave on the west side of the lake. An enveloping flood issued forth from the cave so Nenebuc built a raft and took on many different animals. After a week he sent muskrat down to bring up mud but he drowned—Nenebuc pulled muskrat up by a leather thong attached and took earth from his paws. Nenebuc dried the mud and made the world again.

Keypoint 2: Chee-bay-jing or Maple Mountain, rising over a thousand feet above the surrounding lakes it is also one of the highest points in Ontario (2,050 ft. above sea level). This was the Teme Augama burial and sacred site. In 1971 the Ontario government almost succeeded in developing the mountain as a ski resort. There is an excellent hiking trail here with a 60km. surrounding view.

Keypoint 3: Wendaban Stewardship area: Site of the 1989 road blockades (remember when Ontario premier Bob Rae was arrested?). Also site of the Wakimika Triangle—one of North America's largest remaining old-growth pine stands.

C. TEMISKAMING BAND: Known collectively as "head-of-the-lake-people", they were predominantly Algonquin with a Cree and Montagnais influence. One common family group was Mazi-ni-gi-jik or "striped coloured sky".

Keypoint 4: Devil Rock - a 320 foot vertical escarpment of native religious importance. There is an excellent foot trail to the top that can be accessed by vehicle.

Keypoint 5: Ville Marie - an early traditional native campsite, later an H.B.C. post, known as O ba-dji-wan-an Sag ehi-gan or "narrow current lake."

Keypoint 6: "Med-a-beejeewan"–or "place where 2 rivers come together". The confluence of the Montreal and Matabitchuan Rivers—a very ancient campground and site of the first French post. It was the entrance to Temagami or portage route used prior to the building of the railroad.

D. KIPAWA BAND: Ki-pawe Anishnabai or "narrows beyond which river widens people".

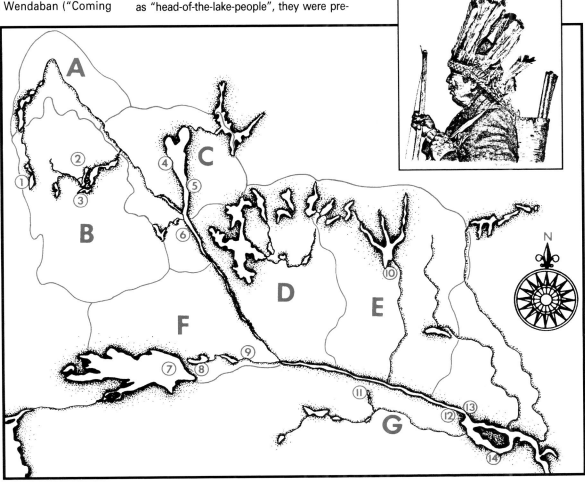

9

There were three family groups here, Mi-skoci-ma-gan or "red coated soldier" was a prominent clan.

E. DUMOINE BAND: Ki-we-gama anishnabai or "turn back lake people". There were five family groups that roamed the Dumoine Lake and upper Noire and Coulonge area. Nak-we-gi-jik or "middle of the sky" was one such family clan.

Keypoint 10: Legends of Wiske-djak (whiskey-jack or Canada Jay...Nenebuc to the Teme Augama Ojibway), originate here. Wendigo is also known to roam these woods.

F. NIPISSING BAND: Ojibway stock, very superstitious; early explorers called them "sorciers" or sorcerers. Immersed in magic, conjuring and shamanism the Mattawa river natives or Mata-wasi-bi anishnabai, the "mouth of river people", were the most widely travelled of all regional Algonkian bands, trading between the Hurons of Georgian Bay and the Cree of James Bay.

Keypoint 7: Manitou Islands–important for its native legends and folklore.

Keypoint 8: Tyyska site–ancient ceremonial grounds 6,000 years old (predates Stonehenge by 2,000 years!).

Keypoint 9: Porte de L'Enfer or "gates of hell" was a native ochre mine.

G. ALGONQUIN BAND: Kici-si-bi anishnabai or "big river people"–inter-acted with the early explorers more than other bands.

Keypoint 11: Wendigo Lake–the source of the Petawawa as acknowledged by early natives and from where the evil Wendigo hailed from.

Keypoint 12: Chalk River–this area was generally deserted by Indians on account of the devil that presided there and is still said to be seen year round. This demon comes in the shape of a huge ball of fire with an open hand in the middle. This is also the site of the first Nuclear Research station in North America (1944)!

Keypoint 13: Oiseaux Rock–a 600 foot vertical stone face and religious native site.

Keypoint 14: Morisson's Island–copper workers lived here 5,000 years ago. In the early 1600s chief Tessouat of the Kici-si-bi Anishnabai collected a toll for passage here.

$\mathcal{W}$hite History – "fur, axe and hydro power"

Four Centuries of Exploitation

I sat for days, in a quandary, just staring blankly at this title chapter without writing a single phrase. It wasn't for the lack of things to write about, quite the contrary in fact for there exists volumes upon volumes of literature devoted to the wonders of Canadian exploration, the fur-trade, timber-drives and yes, certainly the development which is born out of such adventures.

I suppose it was the manner in which I was to portray this important segment of book parts that kept the words and thoughts from flowing...at least in patronizing tones. But since I didn't have to pacify the conscience of corporate sponsors or patronize magnanimous political bureaucracies, I was able to maintain a latitude of autonomy from external influence and actually say the things that I wanted to.

The reader will, unfailingly, pick up on my penetrating cynicism in this chapter. Why? Well, remember back in grade school, how the subject of early Canadian history was wholly captivating, romantic and exciting, filled with intrigue and adventure? Sure enough...it was all of that, perfectly believable and filled with the nuances that initiate a foundation for a child to build dreams upon. It was also about nation-building and securing a comfortable way of life in the auspices of a free and democratic regime.

Regardless of all historic compliments that this country enjoys bestowing upon itself, I had to seriously question whether savaging the land and ostracizing its native people justified the high opinion we extolled upon ourselves as a benevolent nation. I scrutinized our methodology applied to getting this country to its present situation - the more I researched, the more I travelled the once secret wild places, the harder it was for me to maintain a quiet or complaisant position. It's not my nature anyway. But in the name of progress and the Alter of Mammon, and in the name of the King and Queen of France or England, and in the name of holy Christian belief and all which is good and wise and true...we built this country by taming the land. It is whether or not you believe this to be good or evil.

Knowing that in our arrogant attempt at changing the course and face of mother earth –something that took her millions of years to perfect, we, in our myopic wisdom, have in such a short time, permanently altered one of the most beautiful regions in this entire country. It was impossible for me to ramble on about the romantic endeavours of the wiley coureur de bois, the daringness of the timber driver, the religious fervour of the oblate priest without first contemplating the consequences their actions had upon the land and native Canadians. Other books may espouse the fame and fortune of the "timber kings" and their admirable accomplishments, allowing us our so-called freedoms and comfortable lifestyle as a result of their proliferation, but you won't find any praise within these pages.

I believe myself to be an optimist. I like to believe that there is hope, and justification for what we continue to do to the land. Unfortunately, being an artist and an impossible romantic I live most of my time in illusory panic, trying to make sense out of insensitivities. The truth is, we have learned nothing from history whatsoever; we continue to blunder on–only we have become more clever at masking the problems and concealing our greed in a variety of self-righteous ways. Wilderness has been re-defined so that we will accept and allow multiple-use development (with impossible "sustainable" guidelines to adhere to); clear-cut logging is now multiple-specie harvesting and so on...

Through a shroud of soft catch-words, cliches, bureaucratic bafflegab and politically-correct jargon, we continue to usurp the resources of our natural wonderlands in order to remain competitive in world trade markets...and sustain our profuse lifestyles. And as for our freedom? Who are we kidding...are we nothing more than slaves to the industrial and financial institutions that control this country? Of course we are, but we are afraid of the reality of our social manipulations.

The Ottawa Valley watershed is surprisingly resilient in lieu of the war we've raged across its back. Surprisingly beautiful too, but certainly nothing like it must have been to the moccasined Algonkian that paddled its' waterways before the dawn of the appearance of the white explorer. And it was the lure of jewels and insatiable greed that brought the explorer to the valley wilderness, in search of the northern passageway to the riches of the Orient.

In Search of "la mer du Nord"

Champlain, Brulé, Nicolet, Radisson and Groselliers, De Noyen, Galinee and Casson, Marquette and Joliet, and La Verendryes ...famous names synonymous with exploration and the "Voyageur Highway". They came to this great waterway not so much to know the land but to know what the land could yield in resources for their country...for themselves. During white-mans compulsive ventures to effect change and an obsession with the religious subjugation of the heathen savage, in all his old world wisdom could not even agree upon an appropriate title for this great river in which all travel took place.

On his premier map of the upper Ottawa, in 1613 Champlain called it "La rivière des Algonquians." After the destruction of the Huron nation in 1647-50, the Outaouais (Ottawa) Indians from upper Lake Huron and Michigan became predominant traders along the river. "Outaouais" means "to trade".

Other assorted names included; La Grande Rivière du Nord", a popular title enobled by the coureur de bois and first introduced by Galinee in 1670. Bernou in 1680 called it, "Rivière des Outouai ou des Hurons, Rivière des Outaouais ou des Prairies", in true aristocratic, seigneural flair for long titles. Alexander Henry in 1761 kept it brief but couldn't quite figure out whether it was spelled "Outaouais" or "Utawas". It eventually became "Rivière des Outaouais" or anglicized to just plain "Ottawa".

Undoubtedly, these voyageurs built the foundation for a commercial empire based on the wholesale trade of furs. Two centuries of exploration, and exploitation, began with Champlain's influence over the Hurons, Algonquins and Montagnais in a personal, self-motivated passion to secure passage to the Kingdom of China and the East Indies.

"The land of plenty isn't plenty anymore"

(song, Alabama)

The age-old war between France and England took on a shiny new coat of armour as exploration burgeoned in the New World. To claim domination over these new-found riches, native Canadians were manipulated and conscripted to fight this European war on Canadian soil. White interference eventually went awry and led to the annihilation of the Huron native population over the fight to control trade through the Ottawa valley.

The establishment of the trading post network through the H.B.C. and later N.W.C. manoeuverings, transmogrified the native-Canadian character to one of white-dependency, and a gradual migration away from traditional lifestyles and motivations.

The devious method of trade and barter between white and Indian bordered on criminal–founded on how many beaver pelts one could compact in the company fur-press, in exchange for cheap trinkets, faulty muskets and worse...cheap navy rum.

Chief Tessouat of the Kici-si-bi Anishnabai Algonquins, caught on to the white-man method of commerce and his band became quite wealthy. His band camped on Morrison Island near present day Pembroke. The chief was disgruntled because they lost their status as middlemen when the French began trading directly with the Huron. In retaliation, Tessouat began extracting a "toll" for passageway knowing that all river traffic would have to come through his camp because of the rapids surrounding the island. He would detain several groups of Hurons so that the gathering would produce lower trade prices for valuable Huron cornmeal. Huron traders eventually got wise and began using the back-country route to Quebec city by way of the Dumoine and St. Maurice rivers.

As the war with the Iroquois intensified during 1647 to 1650, much of the trade routes took advantage of tertiary river travel, although much more arduous than the Ottawa River route. Eventually, with the extermination of the Huron (New France's trading partner) so began the era of the coureur de bois who took to the backwoods with zeal, trading with whomever offered the best price for their furs.

Along the "Mast Road"

Fur trade posts along the Ottawa Valley and deep within the interior, came and went. Succumbing to battle, sickness, murder and isolation, these garrisons eventually fell upon hard times with the depletion of moose and beaver and the shift to trade routes to James Bay. A new era began with the cultivation of a new crop of Canadian resources and commercial enterprise - the log drive! It was little wonder why interests focused on a new resource by the end of the 1800s. Moose and beaver populations were seriously depleted along the heavily travelled Ottawa watershed and the familiar trade patterns were giving way to rail and steamship travel through the Great Lakes corridor. The timber trade offered to be an even greater prospect than the fur market and was soon to become

Canada's largest and most profitable resource industry.

The Napoleonic wars of 1812-14 and the war with the United States demanded ship-building timber and sawn logs for planking and masts. The Ottawa valley was rich in red and white pine that numbered an average 400 giant trees to an acre. Many were five to six feet across at waist height and towered well over a hundred feet in height. And thus began the era of the square-timber; great rafts of Canadian pine that would find their way down the mast road to the mills at Quebec city.

Licences to cut timber were initially granted to war veterans in reserves along the Ottawa held by the Royal Navy. In 1826, a system of

cutting licences was established which effectively nullified Navy reserves and opened the industry up to bidding by private firms. Huge tracts of land were acquired by an elite few; the likes of Wright, Gillies and Bryson who created small empires for themselves by cutting pine along the Ottawa valley.

Timber was cut and squared in the bush from late September to mid March. It was then hauled by horse-drawn sleigh to the various river headwaters and dumped on the ice. Spring thaw in April would flush the logs down to the Ottawa River where the timbers were joined together to form huge cribs. Several cribs composed of up to 2,400 pine logs, would comprise a "raft", upon which the rafting crew would pitch camp and sail the craft down the Ottawa with the aid of oar and sail. Rafting of timbers went on for a century, the last one reaching the Ottawa mill in 1909. Riding the voluminous rapids and man-made sluices on these rafts was considered great sport, but like the occupation of driving logs down the tributary rivers in April and May, constituted enormous risk - especially for the unskilled.

Thomas C. Keefer, civil engineer, related in an address to the Mechanics Institute of Montreal in 1854:

> "There is scarcely a portage, a cleared point, jutting out into the the river where you do not meet with wooden crosses, on which are rudely carved the initials of some unfortunate victim of the restless waters...," he goes on to say, "In a prosperous year about ten thousand men are afloat on loose timber, or in frail canoes, and as many as eighty lives have been lost in a single spring..Some of the eddies in high water become whirlpools, tearing a bark canoe into shreds and engulfing every soul in it."

By mid century, Great Britain once again began to purchase cheaper timber from the Baltic through a policy of free trade. The Canadian forest industry, until then, was enjoying the benefit of heavy tariffs charged to foreign markets. At the same time, the United States timber machine had virtually stripped the northeast clean of quality pine and were now eyeing the Canadian forests with covetous expectations.

Doors were soon thrown wide open to U.S. investors and company men–the Reciprocity Treaty of 1854 allowed a free grab at Canadian resources by U.S. based companies who took advantage by quickly setting up bases along the Ottawa valley. E.B. Eddy migrated to Bytown (Ottawa) from his native Vermont in the 1850s as did J.R. Booth, Rochester, Perley, Bronson, Weston, Baldwin and the Walsh Brothers. Bronson was the first of these American timber barons to run logs through from above Pembroke and Des Joachims.

Not only did Canada sell out to the U.S. but they sold out dirt cheap! Timber rights, as in the case of William MacKay in 1861, were purchased for four-dollars an acre. He bought a 100 square mile cutting parcel for $400.00. He turned around and sold the same parcel back to J.R. Booth in 1902 for $665,000. But it was in the last half of that century when the great forests fell to the axe–by 1900 there were few pine left along the valley.

J.R. Booth, known as the "lumber king" and probably the best known of the valley barons, had, at the peak of his career, more than 4,000 square miles of timber rights in the Ottawa valley watershed. This included licences to cut along the Dumoine, Noire and Coulonge rivers. He had a "shantyman" working for each square mile of licence, working an area larger than Prince Edward Island.

"The Raftsmen"

When mealtime comes, the men all say
It's pork and beans again today.

Their axes sharp with no delay,
They swing and strike, the tall trees sway.

The logs they trim and drag away
To drive down when the ice gives away.

In spring they draw their winter's pay,
And go back home on holiday.

To greet them come their ladies gay
Who help them spend their hard-earned pay.

(folksong)

"Agents" or company bosses kept the woodland operations running efficiently. There were no safety regulations, or for that matter, precautions taken to reduce risk while running logs down the rivers. The "green hands", many of them runaway kids, were often killed beneath tons of logs or drowned in the rapids. Hasty crosses or rock cairns would serve, not as a commemorative marker for the dead, but as a stern reminder to those living to mind their ways. Boots of the dead were nailed to a prominent tree; those who needed good boots often exchanged their own for those of the dead man's.

Even with the abrogation of the Reciprocity Treaty in 1866 and the reimposition of trade tariffs, the New England based companies continued to control the Ottawa valley timber resources by building key rail lines directly to their Canadian mills. "Digley" tariffs, imposed in 1890 by Washington Republicans were established to protect the U.S. logging industry. This affected trade with Canada considerably, particularly as new timber resources were discovered in the Pacific northwest states; but then most of the high-class pine had been eliminated in the Ottawa valley as far north as Lake Temiskaming and the Montreal River.

E.B. Eddy and J.R. Booth soon saw the potential for processing pulp to answer the demand for newsprint in the blossoming paper industry in the United States. Mills quickly moved upstream and closer to the tertiary rivers, connected by rail and road, development and support industry matured as forests disappeared.

Logs were no longer squared and sub-species such as spruce, balsam and jackpine were now being cut along with what remained of the great pine stands. Spring river drives employed valley farmers, a mixture of French, Irish and Scottish, most of them leaving home in the fall and not returning until after the spring drive...or not returning at all.

The decimation of valley timber was a blatant example of waste and greed by both government and industry. There were no controls, unjust licencing and absolutely no regard for environmental or aesthetic integrity. Slopes denuded of timber were left bristling with stumps and unsightly debris - much of which was attributed to the incredible wildfires that ravaged much of the valley interior in the latter part of the 1800's.

The Coulonge river saw the last timber drive in 1984. E.B. Eddy pulled the plug and abandoned its Lake Pomponne camp a disgraceful blemish on the side of the lake. At many of the chutes and rapids you can see the obvious waste of timber washed up on the banks and beached along the shores..enough probably to feed a small town logging mill for ten years. The river is slowly winning its old face back and it is now safe to make canoe runs down without being sucked under a log jam; but it is also good to see the negative aspects of man's inter-action with nature here so that we can never let it happen again.

"Dona Naturae Pro Populo Sunt"

The gifts of nature are for the people.

Ontario Hydro motto

The 1940s and 50s saw the development of hydro-electric power throughout the Ottawa valley watershed. Forever changing the nature of the river, rapids and chutes were drowned along with innumerable archaeological or historic sites without hue or cry from the Canadian public. No environmental impact studies. The Northern Ontario Power Company built plants on the Montreal to service the Cobalt mines while Quebec dammed the upper Ottawa above Lac des Quinze to supply Rouyn and Noranda mines with electricity.

White Canadian history is one founded upon a self-serving policy of rapacious hunger for power and dominance over nature... a chronology of continued land abuse and public manipulation that still goes on today, albeit in more sedentary ways.

Provincial governments still deny the river its essential requirement to remain isolated and insulated from man's probings. Forests continue to be cut close to the shores, roads provide easy access to the gun and rod toting mechanized sportsperson, resources are dispatched and the perpetrators simply move on when it's gone.

And we remain silent...

Being Prepared: Things you should know

> " *C*onsider well what your strength is equal to,
> and what exceeds your ability."
>
> – **HORACE**

Nipissing Shaman: They had their own way of dealing with emergencies

INTRODUCTION:
THINGS YOU SHOULD KNOW

It was hard to contain my enthusiasm in this section–I could drone on till the cows came home and have ventured into the twilight zone of preparatory topics...insect pests, lightweight food, canoeing skills and so on. But I didn't...there are enough books published on the subject already to warrant another one to join the ranks of "how to" redundancy.

The selection of topics I adhered to were simply the more consequential items of discussion – those that would form the substratum of any prospective wilderness trek as it pertains to the inherent environment within these pages, and, that are necessary for you to know. You can still get down the river with a lousy food menu or a disaffection for black flies; and if you can't already perform the required basic canoe strokes then you have no right paddling any fast-water – until you do. On the other hand, waterproofed food and gear packed in to a serviceable canoe, will at least get you down river in a better mood – just remember this equation:

DRY PACKS + SERVICEABILITY = INNER PEACE.

No Trace Camping

In the attempt to quell whatever primitive urge that compels us to seek the sanctity of the outdoors, there will always be those who disregard ethical, moral and environmental responsibilities by despoiling our wilderness trails. It's our nature to create garbage...and our foible not to know where to put it.

During the spring of '92 I made my annual pilgrimage to Maple Mountain in Temagami. It's a challenging five kilometer climb with a 60 kilometer panorama in all directions at the summit. In the summer you can find the world's best blueberries there, but it gets pretty busy with canoeists – that's why I prefer spring treks because you know you'll be alone.

As I reached the 30 meter vertical cliff that embraces you at the apex, I noticed that someone had spray-painted their names in meter high letters across the face of the rock, no less in fluorescent orange! Who would do such a thing? Probably some pimpled-face, pubescent from some ill-organized canoe camp who was trying to impress the pretty girl in the group. "Skip loves Gloria" will still be there for my great-grandchildren to enjoy. Isn't it nice to know that some things do last a lifetime? I'm sure the Teme Augama Anishnabai are grateful for the decoration, being a religious burial site and all...anyway, it was far too grey up there.

It did make me think... and ask myself whether I really wanted to help people enjoy, participate and experience the rewards of our wild places? To subject honest, respectful trippers and a beautiful landscape to an onslaught of degenerate slobs? Maybe we should just join the other industrial and recreational fraternities who use the same woods to cut, dig, flood, shoot, trap and hook the last remnants of the wild forest...teach us a lesson perhaps?

As soon as we step across that "civilized" boundary and climb into our canoes, or walk that forest trail, we have an individual responsibility to uphold the "unwritten" laws and ethical codes of the wilderness. Those that do not should be subjected to some form of medieval trial by ordeal; a public flogging will do nicely.

As we continue to make wilderness more accessible to "multiple-use" groups by building roads, or allowing local fish and game clubs to construct illegal ones, the desecration of our wilderness will continue unchecked. Little or no money from government coffers goes toward maintaining crown land outside of Provincial Parks so it is up to us to keep the wild places clean.

From 1977 to 1984 I worked as Interior Ranger for the Temagami District Natural Resources Parks department. During that tenure, (along with various crews), I removed over 1,000 bags of compressed garbage each year from interior campsites! Granted most of the refuse originated at fly-in related campsites and lakes that were accessible by boat and vehicle sportspeople, but...there was ample litter left behind by canoeists and hikers along the more remote routes that make them no less guilty of breaking the rules. Canoeists are simply more discreet about where they leave their droppings. Where anglers and hunters just make their garbage obvious wherever they go by dumping it copiously and generously over the landscape – the self-propellist will at least conceal it under a log or rock, sometimes char it in the fire or even bury it if they're not in too much of a hurry. This is all very disconcerting.

I love to get to a campsite after a hard day on the river. The only luxury I look forward to, more than a pair of dry socks, is a hot cup of java. Always, there are bits of tin foil, egg shells, globs of gooey oatmeal, melted shoes and other lesser known substances lying in wait for my bare hands within the confines of the fire pit. Half the time someone has carried the fire pit rocks back to the tent sites so I usually spend a good deal of time arranging an orderly place to prepare meals.

GARBAGE: No Trace Camping is a simple term to understand. That means ALL refuse should be packed out! Campsites, beaches, portage trails and lunch spots should show no evidence of you being there. Seasoned campers and responsible paddlers or hikers always pick up garbage left behind by the more unrefined adventurer, displaying an obvious philosophy that leaving the river cleaner than you found it is spiritually uplifting. Foodstuffs can be burned in the fire only–please DO NOT incinerate plastics or other nasty stuff. This can be packed out easier than you packed it in when it was full of something. DO NOT leave anything in the fire pit at all.

ABOUT FIRES: Fire pit rocks should remain on bedrock or mineral soil and away from trees or forest duff. This tinder can burn, unseen, for days and spring up several feet somewhere else. Keep your fires small and conserve wood. Don't use grates or grills that sit too high off the ground. Attend your fire at all times and make sure it's completely out before you leave camp.

Keeping campsites clean is up to you

14

Firewood can be picked up along the shore away from the campsite. Abandoned beaver houses are a great source of poplar and birch hardwood, especially in a land where most dry firewood is either dead spruce or pine. The use of stoves is recommended for summer use or when there are fire hazards or restrictions that make open fires illegal – even for cooking or warmth. You should always pack a saw and use an axe only for splitting – after a three-day rain the only way to get dry wood is by splitting it.

LATRINES: We lower ourselves to the debased creatures we are when it comes to taking a dump in the woods. We simply can't do it right. We need someone to take our hand and walk us down the proverbial garden path to show us how it is done with distinction.

Animals crap in the woods and you wouldn't know it. When humans answer the call they make sure everyone can see it! Trees are decorated with garlands of used toilet paper, trails and tent sites start to resemble cattle pens and there are more plastic tampon applicators scattered about then spent cartridges after a day at the firing range. And have you ever noticed the quantity of underwear that is left behind at campsites? Did people just forget to put it back on or is this some kind of ritual?

What is so difficult about doing it right? It's as if we've reverted back to babyhood before we were toilet trained. Some people are afraid to go more than a meter past their tent,

especially at night when some slithering beast will snatch them up at the most vulnerable moment. Fear compels us to do contrary things. There is obviously some deep psychosis or primordial turbulence in our brain-wave patterns during this biological function to make it impossible for us to scrape a tiny hole in the ground and bury our stool. We have no qualms about scooping-up after "Sparky" takes a dump in the park so

Humility...offered in the spirit of reverence to that which we seek out in nature, will help to preserve the integrity of our wild places

why is it so hard for us to carry out this basic function? We have become too accustomed to "flushing" ourselves down a toilet. We also believe that nature will look after this stuff for us – like it's going to dissolve right before our eyes or something.

Doing it Right! Latrines should be established far back of the tenting area or shore. Shallow holes should be scraped or

dug and filled in when finished. Grey or dish-water should also be dumped well back in the bush. Avoid using several-ply or coloured T.P. or try sphagnum moss for a change like the Indians once did.

OTHER CODES: Be a considerate camper, leave the campsite cleaner than you found it. Trees should not be defaced or cut or stripped of bark or denuded of branches for spruce bedding. In some of the more remote areas poles leaning up at campsites are for 5-pole pitch tents or kitchen tarps - DON'T cut them up for firewood!

It is also customary to leave a small stack of firewood behind for the next party. Latrines should not be established on small island campsites – a short paddle to mainland for such purposes is commendable. Let faster or more organized canoe parties pass you on a portage and don't leave your gear directly on the trail or canoes beached so others have difficulty getting by. Allow larger groups to occupy the bigger campsites, particularly if there are several small sites nearby. Respect the need for others to enjoy the quietude of the evening – leave your radios at home and keep the noise level to a bare minimum. Make sure to help those who require assistance.

Call the Canadian Recreational Canoeing Association to request your "Canoeist's Code" check list for responsible outdoor camping.

Canoes and Equipment

Todays adventurer has the optimum flexibility of being particular about the canoe he/she decides to paddle, and to make discriminating compromises (and there are always trade-offs), based on personal skills and preferences. When I first dipped my paddle in the water almost thirty years ago, the only choice was cedar/canvas, followed by fiberglass and the aluminum canoe, which was hailed as the premier whitewater craft. All you needed for quick repair was a rubber hammer and a tube of "liquid steel."

Cedar/canvas canoes are still used by traditional camps and the "prospector", to this day remains my all-time favourite for wilderness trips. Holes in the canvas were simply repaired using an old bandana and ambroid – a squeeze-tube of waterproof glue as the bonding agent. Broken gunwales and thwarts could be reinforced with cedar cut

from the bush and tin can lids, pushed between the ribs, shored-up punctured planking. Some of the old relics paddled by Camp Wabun in Temagami eventually had more tin parts than wood.

People have often asked my advice as to what canoe they should purchase, but it's a lot like trying to tell someone what clothes they should wear to a particular function. The canoe, I explain to them, should fit the purpose to which it will be condemned. If there was one craft that singularly excelled in all facets of canoeing, stands alone above all others, performs in all conditions superfluously...it hasn't been built yet.

The canoe is almost as important as a good attitude. I can assist people in choosing an appropriate canoe that will serve their particular purpose, but, without the right cerebral posture, no amount of hi-tech gear

or equipment will achieve perfect canoeing harmony. I collect canoes like people collect stamps. As a tour guide and outfitter I had 75 canoes to choose from. Since I am no longer in the "tourist" business I have whittled my selection down to half a dozen. There's one for photography, quiet and sleek; one for general tripping, stable and dependable; one for racing and one for whitewater and so on.

For general tripping, as one would do throughout the geography of this book, my favourite is the 17' Old Town Tripper. Its one of the heavier ABS canoes but it is the most versatile, and you can't beat the prospector lines for wilderness canoe trips...and it's virtually indestructible.

A broken paddle or wrapped canoe can utterly destroy an adventure and kill relationships...not to mention the loss of expensive equipment or injury. Regardless of what equipment you may select to take with you into the wilds, you must also know how to repair it if you have problems. Kevlar is light but seriously over-rated, and like the fiberglass canoe it can just as easily rip apart on a sharp ledge. Aluminum canoes are not only noisy and cold to paddle, but have that annoying tendency to stick to rocks, and lose their shape upon hard impact. Cedar/canvas canoes are a choice breed, but in low water it is abnormally cruel punishment to subject them to the burgeoning summer rock gardens of the shield rivers.

ABS canoes, while not pretty, are still the preferred choice of the serious whitewater or deep-remote wilderness canoeist. You don't have to do anything special with them except carry them. A pair of kevlar "skid-plates" should find their way on to each lower stem, bow and stern, as a sort of "bumper" system. This will more than double the life of your canoe.

Paddles should be revered as an extension of your own personality, like a paint brush or a pen – the creativity of the various strokes is limitless. I prefer wood to aluminum and ABS, however, the latter being more rugged I'll always carry one as a spare. Laminated paddles without reinforced kevlar tips should be avoided as they'll probably split first rock you kiss.

A paddle should fit comfortably in your hand, and if you're afraid of blistering, bicycle gloves with a gel-pad palm are ideal.

Other necessary equipment that should, or could, find its way into your hearts is a rescue throw-bag that can double as a track-line; additional flotation (commercial-type, inflatable), a quality life-jacket, not just a

Although ABS canoes have claimed highest ranking as "whitewater" craft, there are always trade-offs. The "best" canoe has not yet been designed.

P.F.D., but one with an added head support system. These are the basics – compromise anything but your own safety!

WATERPROOFING

Let's face it...river paddling is exciting, exhilarating, sometimes tenuous, dangerous and often stressful; but one thing we can all agree upon is that it is almost always WET! We are constantly in and out of the canoe; wading, lining, running, dumping and the stuff just gets wetter. But next to attitude, skill and canoe, the waterproofness of your personal gear is tantamount to the success or failure of your expedition. Without the proper precautions it is synonymous to living in a house without a roof on. The technique which you employ to keep your duffle dry is a matter of personal choice; again, like the canoe, if it works for you...fine, but for those who are prone to reversing the polarity of their canoes and getting their spaghetti wet - these tips are for you.

Poorman's Pack: You can portion your food and double pack it into plastic zip-lock bags

and insert them into hardier cloth "ditty" bags. Heavy cardboard boxes can be glazed with waterproof varnish and lined with heavy-duty garbage bags, or, liberate some waterproof restaurant food pails from your local greasy spoon or purchase the popular olive-barrel, now sold commercially by outfitters for about $10.00 each. Make sure you have a separate pack for your lunch and snacks – waterproofed as well.

Yuppy Gear: There is a whole industry devoted to supplying ingenious outdoor devices to a ready market of adventure seekers; and don't we like to show-off our own gadgets and trinkets at the airbase dock, the portage or campsite. But some of this stuff is actually useful, if not colourful. There is a variety of fold-seal or inflatable waterproof pouches that come in various shapes and sizes to accommodate anything from sleeping bag to kitchen sink.

Avoid the cheap waterproofed bags with the straps attached – the shoulder rig will yank off eventually if too heavily loaded. Most canoeists I've met don't respect their packs, or expect too much from them. My best advice is to buy quality and regardless of product, always pick up your pack by more than one shoulder harness if you want it to last.

Anything you carry with you that could be damaged or altered by becoming wet should be waterproofed. You could spend the family fortune on fancy gear but it is not a requirement for a successful trip – nothing can replace the wisdom born out of improvisation.

Below you will find the necessary list of repair tools for remedying minor damage to canoes or equipment:

Repair Kit: One roll 2" wide, grey duct-tape.

*A*dventure *Alternatives*

Although the best way to explore the very fibres of this watery network, without question, has to be by way of Canada's traditional method of travel – the canoe, this book may also prove to be a useful tool for the cyclist, hiker, winter camper or even the motor tourist. There are a number of provincial parks and conservation areas to explore, each with its own special features and character. There are also a number of attractions illustrated in this book that are easily accessed by non-four-wheel drive vehicle.

MOTOR CAMPING: (5-7 DAY VEHICLE TOUR).

Aside from the hospitality of the many small villages through Quebec and Ontario that offer quality services, the following is a partial listing of the more prominent special features that one could enjoy by vehicle:

Grande Chute on the Dumoine, Noire and Coulonge Rivers, La Verendrye Provincial Park, Alongquin Provincial Park (Achray and Barron River Canyon), Des Joachims dam and airbase, Driftwood Provincial Park, Samuel de Champlain Provincial Park, Talon

Chutes, Otto Holden Damn Devil Rock , Lady Evelyn-Smoothwater Provincial Park (day canoeing/cycling), Cobalt self-guided mine tour, Finlayson Point Provincial Park and Temagami Island old-growth pine tour. Here is a suggested route outline:

Ottawa, north on 105 to 117 through La Verendrye Park to Rouyn/Noranda; 391 to 101 to 65. Option to visit New Liskeard, Cobalt, west of 65 to Elk Lake and Lady Evelyn-Smoothwater Park and return; or, continue south on 101 to Ville Marie and Temiskaming to 63 and 533 to Mattawa with a dog-leg to Talon Chutes and Champlain Park. Continue southeast on 17 along the Ottawa Valley to Pembroke with the option to take the east Algonquin Park entrance to the Barron River. From Pembroke, cross Ile des Allumettes on 148 through Waltham and Fort Coulonge and return to Ottawa.

BACKPACKING/HIKING: Ontario and Quebec seriously lack quality hiking trails. There are pathetically few trail systems throughout the valley and not one that couldn't be easily completed in half a day's walk. Most existing trails are part of provincial park or conservation area attractions and geared to the pleasures of the transient motor-camper. The trails generally access some vantage or scenic point and have interpretive literature available to help guide you through. The trails serve as a temporary diversion from whatever else you may be doing such as canoeing or vehicle-camping.

MOUNTAIN BIKING: I have done quite a bit of consulting work with this relatively new outdoor sport and through my own past outfitting business offered Canada's first "fly-in and pedal-out" wilderness cycle tours. Although bicycles can be attached easily to the floats of bush-planes, you can save the extra tie-down charge or external-load fee, by simply removing the wheels of your bike and packing it inside the plane with the rest of your pannier packs.

I've mentioned a few places to mountain bike already but the possibilities are up to your own creative imagination. There are numerous fly-in and pedal-out trips that one could easily put together, for instance; a 3-4 day pedal out from Lac St. Patrice on the Noire River route, directly back to the airbase at Des Joachims via back-country/non-paved roads; Anvil Lake on the east boundary of the Lady Evelyn-Smoothwater Park is another excellent choice for a 3-4 day pedal out to Longpoint airbase. You could even plan a cross-park tour on the provinces most expensive ($10 million) Red Squirrel road extension that was closed by native and environmental blockades in 1989...really, for any of these trips all you have to do is scan the topo maps for a road connected lake, large enough to accommodate a float-plane (minimum 1.5 km. long). Be prepared though to wade to shore if the plane cannot beach!

FISHING: Surprisingly, the fishing is still generally good along all of the watershed river routes–specifically where motor-anglers have difficulty in getting access. Few canoeists angle and this has somehow established the remote river as the Icon of sportsfishing

...hence all the illegally constructed roads built by some local fish and game interest groups who have depleted stocks elsewhere.

I'm not about to divulge any secrets, believing that the fish deserve a sporting chance these days. I support only "catch and release" angling practices, and admire the conservation consciousness of the fly-fishing fraternity that I have had the pleasure to trip with in the past. If this is your sport, just make sure that you have the appropriate angling licences in both Ontario and Quebec before you throw your line into the water.

Compact kits or break-down rods are best suited for canoe tripping and don't forget a pair of needle-nose pliers/cutters in case someone gets stuck with a hook. Should this happen, here is what you have to do: First cleanse the finger and hook with an anti-bacterial solution, push the hook through so the point breaks the skin, cut the shaft of the hook then pull it out by the barb end. Make sure the wound is cleansed daily. Another suggestion for canoe trippers – don't leave your lures attached to your rod while running whitewater...if you dump, the lure is surely going to skewer someone during the rescue process! Please practice responsible angling habits and clean your fish away from camp-sites.

Nature Observation – A few camera tips

You round a meander on the river and suddenly confront a huge bull moose, up to his shoulders in the shallows feeding on water-lily tubers. The light's perfect–beads of water glistening off velvetized antlers, rich chocolate-brown coat gleaming in effervescent response to water and sun, jowels bulging with aquatic plants...you've prayed for this moment to happen. Still unseen, the canoe glides to within a few meters, and then... where's my camera! You reach down in suffused panic, snap your pelican case open, snatch up your thousand dollar Nikon only to find that you left the wide-angle lens on and there's only one picture left on the roll! By now the moose has wandered off, at his own leisure, and by the time you get set up you just managed to get another ass-end shot for your non-album wildlife collection.

This happens to me more often than I would normally admit. I almost always leave my

Nature photography is not just the art of taking pictures...it is the depth of perception and the fundamental understanding of nature itself

camera out of the case and prepped for quick response, but it's not always being prepared for confrontation that ensures success. Being knowledgeable about wildlife traits and habitat are essential ingredients, as are the methods of approach, and even the way in

which you paddle your canoe.

Most animals are active in the early morning or evening–the heat of the day often makes them lethargic and at which time they will be lost deep within the depths of the forest shade. Black flies in June will drive moose out into the water to feed in the weed beds, and black bear are often seen beachcombing for washed up carrion, usually along deep-set bays that act as collecting depots to the prevailing winds.

Travelling into the wind will not give you away - most animal species are near-sighted but have a keen sense of smell and hearing.

With proper paddle strokes, patience and perseverance and a knowledge of the environment and behavioural patterns of animals and birds, you should have some measure of success. Wilderness creatures, contrary to some urban beliefs, are not lined up along the shorelines waiting for their pictures to be taken; and in some areas, outside of popular parks such as Algonquin, wildlife still is as elusive as it should be.

Regardless of brand your camera should have a waterproofed home while running rapids or portaging. Hard cases are much better than inflatable sacks that puncture easily on hot days. Inflatable bags are acceptable but make sure you take along plenty of duct-tape for repairs. Always keep some desiccate pouches in your case too - these will help to reduce the amount of moisture inside the pouch itself. Make sure you have extra film and spare batteries - most small village stores will not have a good selection of camera batteries. A small tripod is handy for shots under 125 sec. or for time exposures. A polarizer is also practical and used to cut down the severe glare of the day's sun on sky and water, but remember..the best pictures are not planned; and, take advantage of the early morning light - it's magic may only last a few moments but the picture you take will last a lifetime.

Access and Air Charters

Over the years I have learned that there are certain things that you do not take for granted. Like, expecting your car to be safe and sound – parked along some remote logging road, or even at a maintained government access point for that matter. You are often safe enough if you park for less than five days and avoid the weekends, or, for a few bucks leave your vehicle with someone living near your desired access jumping-off location. And never assume that you can just leave your vehicle without letting someone know – such as the police. Whenever possible, you should arrange to leave your vehicle at the airbase if flying and arrange a pick-up shuttle through an outfitter, or someone local – they'd probably jump at the chance to earn a few extra dollars.

For air charters it is imperative that you make bookings well in advance and that you have all your gear and canoes at the docks at least one-half hour before your scheduled flight. Air access is entirely subject to the weather and delays may cause a back-up of fishing, hunting and canoeing parties. Slow-downs can be prevented by having your gear properly packed and ready with all track lines and loose paraphernalia (throw bags, bailers, fishing rods, etc.) removed from the canoes. Floatplanes are restricted to one tie-down or canoe load per trip, two passengers and gear. If flying in a "beaver", there are no weight restrictions; however, both Cessna 180 and 185's usually limit gear weight to 175 pounds (excluding passengers and canoe). Most airways running with Cessna's also limit the length of canoes to under 18 feet. Flight costs vary and are charged by the calculated air mile there and return. It is wise to arrange destination drop points in advance. Airbase staff often give better water-level status information than government forestry branch offices too, chiefly because of the feedback from their canoeing clients. They can also let you know if a river is particularly busy and when to avoid peak periods.

Bradley Air Service, Des Joachims, P.Q.

Safety and Emergencies

Canoeing could kill you...just as easy as driving drunk without a seat belt fastened on will. Before we even embark on any wilderness adventure we have to seriously gauge our energy capacity, general health,

Wrapped cedar/canvas on the Dumoine

preparedness and over-all stamina and skill level of the group. Plan out emergency evacuation procedures with every member of the party and make sure that each participant knows how to get out. Each person should also carry a sharp knife, waterproofed matches and know exactly where the navigation maps are. Someone in the party should have lifesaving skills such as CPR and it wouldn't hurt to practice inter-group knowledge of such skills as a pre-trip or en route part of the itinerary.

Someone should be informed of your trip plans and always allow enough time for inclement weather – once you press yourself or the group to get out then you encourage problems. Stop when you get tired and make sure that each person knows the symptoms of hypothermic reaction to cold air or water. Accidents happen more commonly due to fatigue, peer pressure or haste to accomplish some goal. Each member should make known to the group, any particular medical problem they may have and be able to deal with a situation if it arises. A quality first-aid kit is essential.

If a person has suffered a severe life-threatening injury, but can be moved, this should be done quickly to the nearest open area where a helicopter or plane can land safely. Three smokey fires on a prominent point, set in a triangular pattern will quickly hail a plane. You should also be familiar with points of access or roads along the expedition trail.

– Section III –
The Rivers

Nipissing hunter calling moose at Paresseux Falls, Mattawa River

LEGEND:

PORTAGES IN YARDS	P. 75 yds.
FALLS: Do not run anytime	
CHUTES or DIFFICULT RAPIDS REQUIRES CLOSE EXAMINATION	
RUNNABLE RAPIDS CAUTION STILL APPLIED	
DIFFICULT RAPID RED ASTERISK INDICATES INSET MAP	*R or *R
INTERMEDIATE RAPID BLACK ASTERISK INDICATES INSET MAP	*R or *R
KILOMETERS OUT TO OTTAWA RIVER	90
BUSH ROAD	- - - - - -
FLY-IN ACCESS	
INSET MAPS:	
RAPID CLASSIFICATION	CII
ROCKS EXPOSED UNDER NORMAL CONDITIONS	
DEEPWATER "V"	
LEDGE	L
EDDY	E
LARGE STANDING WAVES OR DEEPWATER HAYSTACKS	W
SOUSE HOLE or HYDRAULIC AERATED WATER CAUTION	S
SPOTTER SAFETY RECOMMENDATION	
DIRECTION of CANOE:	Primary Run	
	Secondary or Optional Run	
	Ferry	
CAMPSITES: SIZE BASED ON 4-MAN, SELF-SUPPORTING TENTS	
LARGE: 6 OR MORE TENT SITES	▲
MEDIUM: 3-5 TENT SITES	▲
SMALL: 1-2 TENT SITES	△
SITES WITH LETTER INDICATION: E-EXCELLENT M-MEDIOCRE P-POOR	TR: – TOPO. MAP REFERENCE

How to Use This Book for **Detailed River Descriptions**

RIVER CLASSIFICATIONS:

You can judge the difficulty of a river by the number of CII or greater rapids, the length and difficulty of portages, remoteness and practicality of rescue during an emergency. The chart on page 22 indicates general specifics of each river and you should be able to gauge the skill level required for safe paddling.

In my past experience as guide and outfitter, I have come to the realization that nobody likes to admit that they are novice; and although I don't consider myself to be an expert canoeist, I have had the opportunity to meet many hundreds of them over the years. I have also seen as many derelict canoes scattered along the rocks of each and every river in this book.

If you do not have the skills - you do not whitewater paddle. It's as simple as that. You either sign up for a clinic or join a guided expedition where you will learn the compulsory strokes; then, and only then, do you attempt to run a whitewater river. And for those who believe that whitewater rafting is a good primer for canoeing - guess again. The volume of water on a rafting run will flush you through to an eddy, eventually; if you screw up on a boulder-strewn CIII canoeing rapids you're likely to get sandwiched between a rock and a wrapped canoe, chewed-up and spit out at the bottom where you're buddies will have to pry your head out of your rear end.

Being able to READ whitewater is an acquired art. It takes years to develop. You can pick up the basic nomenclature from how-to books and video's, or you can don the latest L.L.Bean or Mountain Co-Op outdoor gear, but it won't bail you out of a bad play on a rapid. This is dangerous fun – riskier if you don't know what you're doing...and many people have died because they won't admit their weaknesses.

Choose a route that best suits your ability; travel in groups of at least two canoes (three's best because if you destroy one canoe completely you can triple up and still get out). Work co-operatively with your partner, be patient and know that any screw-ups are the fault of BOTH paddlers. The level of forgiving qualities on a run is judged by the gravity of error – one wrong decision could ruin your trip by damaging your equipment or hurting someone. And...we are not inviolable – we can make mistakes; even good paddlers are known to make bad judgement calls. Know your weaknesses and make them known to others in your party. Don't succumb to peer pressure – that's when things begin to go wrong!

WATER LEVELS:

Water levels play a dramatic role on any river excursion. Water flowing over a boulder in the spring may be left high and dry on a summer run. Some rivers possess that capricious characteristic of always having

Water levels play a major role in trip dynamics

enough water through the entire paddling season, while others may be run only when water levels are high in the spring.

The information in this book is based upon average to lower water level conditions that predominate through July to September when channels are well defined. Rapids are assessed, the same as general river-level conditions, in relation to the high-water mark, seen as a darkened line along the shore or any partly submerged rock. As in the case of all detailed descriptions found in this book, the assessment was charted from water levels that ran about one-third to one-half meter below the high-water mark.

LOW-WATER CONDITIONS:

Water levels lower than that described in this book may necessitate more lining, wading or portaging. Rock "gardens" may become rockier and ledges certainly "ledgier"...in essence, obstacles become more visible and channels better defined. It also maximizes the potential for getting "hung-up" if you don't employ good technique. Because volume is lower, you generally have more "adjusting" time to manoeuver but you also have to watch your ferry's and eddy turns more carefully because of surface rocks.

Low water levels can also allow more play-time along rapids too difficult to run during high-water flow. This is usually accomplished by part running and part lining or lifting over ledges, and makes a good alternative for those who hate to portage but have the more creative whitewater skills. Rapids along the Coulonge are excellent for this type of low-level fun.

HIGH WATER CONDITIONS:

Spring run-off may raise the level of a river by as much as four meters, particularly along the upper stretches. Just look at the bark bruises where the ice has skinned the shore trees, or the "floaters" that are left high in the overhanging branches. This was the prime time for running logs down the river but one of the worst times for canoeing.

If you happen to hit a river during this period then this book will do you absolutely no good. Most runs are unrecognizable and the dangers inherent with "early-bird" trips can make for some pretty hairy experiences - including "polar bear dips".

Spring trips should not be planned until at least the third week in May. You may even beat the hordes of black flies at this time if you're lucky. Specialized equipment is a must; you know, wet or dry suits, added flotation, front deck splash-covers, that sort of thing. Advantages to high-water levels are smoother ledges, submerged rock-gardens, high volume (great roller-coaster rides and surfing!), and certainly less traffic.

High-water trips can be dangerous for these reasons:

1. Cold water factor. Water temperatures below 50 deg(F), (10 Celsius), bumps the classification of rapids up to the next level because of the risk factor.
2. Larger volume and greater flow presents the risk of "submarining" and less time to manoeuver. Washing-out at the top of a long run means a lengthy, cold swim.
3. The approach to dangerous chutes or falls creates certain hazards and normally longer portages.

4. Less canoe or air traffic relates to less timely rescues during emergencies or evacuations.

DETAILED RAPID MAPS:

The objective of these maps is to:
1. Grade the difficulty of the run.
2. Describe the general conditions, hazards, etc.
3. Illustrate primary and secondary running channels.
4. Indicate the length of the run.

It is NOT to make the running of rapids any easier for the inexperienced paddler or neophyte. It is very important to note that channels may vary with water level and canoeists should use their own discretion based on the main key factors affecting the safe navigation of any fast-water situation. Many rapids round bends..."sweepers" or fallen trees, may present hazards that paddlers may not be aware of or prepared to deal with. In general, any fast-water that cannot be closely scrutinized from the top, should be scouted, particularly if the flow is greater than your ability to initiate remedial ferry's or eddy-turns to shore.

Any rapid with a red indication means caution. These are CII runs or greater, requiring technical skill at an intermediate level. This does not necessarily mean that the CI's present no risk– sweepers can often pose a problem even in swifts. Spring run-off, especially along meandering-type rivers, often undercut the banks and wash fresh timber into the flow every year. These floaters often come to rest at the most inappropriate places.

Rapid Classification

This classification of rapids conforms to the International River Grading System (IGRS), which includes a total of six classifications. Since Class or Grade III rapids are considered the maximum safe rating for open, stock recreational canoes, not modified for whitewater, only the first three grades are listed. Each class is defined, including "technical" ratings. This information will enable you to assess your own skills and experience and apply them to the routes described in this book.

CI: Definite deep water, clear channel with well-defined downstream V, small regular waves to 1/3 metre. Beginner's level.

CII: Definite main channel with optional secondary channels visible in high water. Rock gardens, ledges present with standing waves to 2/3 metre. Technical moves such as eddy turns and ferrying are required. Intermediate level paddler.

CIII: Maximum for open canoes – spray deck optional for rockered whitewater canoes but recommended for low-profile designs. Definite main channel with high volume, often narrow, steep-pitched V ending in an hydraulic/souse. Less reaction time. Boulder gardens, high ledges present with waves to one metre or more. Scouting and rescue spotters mandatory. Advanced level only.

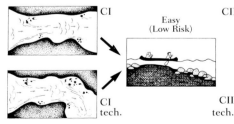

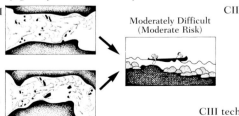

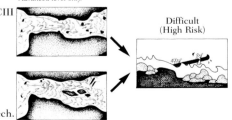

CI tech: As CI with greater volume or some minor technical maneuvers requiring basic skills. Advanced beginner's level.

CII tech: As above with greater volume and larger waves, rock gardens with indefinite main channel; may be clogged with sweepers, snags, logjams or larger boulders. Low-profile canoes may swamp. Experienced intermediate level paddler.

CIII tech or CIV: As above with greater volume, questionable main channels often split; tight passages and steep drops with serious aerated holes present. Specialized whitewater equipment/ canoes required. Playboats with flotation or decked canoes only. Scouting and safety teams required. Expert level only.

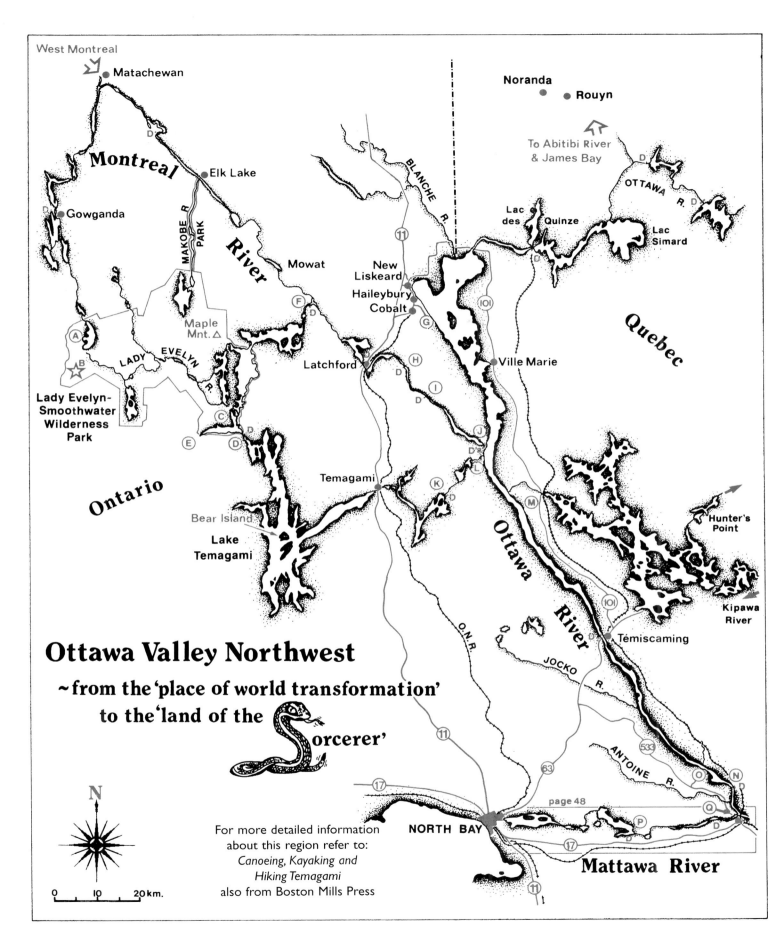

Ottawa Valley Northwest

~ from the 'place of world transformation' to the 'land of the Sorcerer'

For more detailed information about this region refer to:
Canoeing, Kayaking and Hiking Temagami
also from Boston Mills Press

N

0   10   20 km.

ABOUT THE MAP...

The rivers and lakes illustrated on the map form the upper watershed network of the Ottawa valley. Even Lake Temagami at one time drained through a small northern outlet into Diamond Lake. Today, it's effluent flow follows a singular drainage route south to Lake Nipissing along the Temagami River–another popular whitewater route. The map also shows the pattern of existing dams throughout the watershed.

A. "Shonj-a-waw-ga-ming", Smoothwater Lake and "place of world transformation". (See "Hunting Territories" Map on page 9). Site of an ancient native community and the headwaters of the Montreal River.

B. "Ish-pud-i-na", or Ispatina Ridge, highest point in Ontario at 2,275 ft. above sea level. Source of many Anishnabai legends. Snake Portage, located just south of Smoothwater Lake is the place where Nenebuc shot the great snake and turned it into a rocky ridge.

C. "Non-wa-kam-ing", or Diamond Lake and site of Fort Destruction–a short-lived fur trading post that was set up by Bear Islanders to counter rival trade in the late 1800's. The site was occupied by the Teme Augama Anishnabai up until 1942 when A.J. Murphy built a dam at the Diamond Lake outflow, flooding them out permanently. Murphy, an agent for J.R. Booth, had cutting limits around Diamond and told the natives that they had no right to occupy the land.

D. Sharp Rock Portage: the original north outlet of Lake Temagami before a burm-type dam was constructed by logging ventures in the mid 1900's.

E. Wendabun Stewardship Authority: native co-operative land management area with the Ontario Government. Site of environmental and native road blockades to save one of North America's last remaining old-growth stands of white and red pine. (*Ontario Premier Bob Rae was arrested here in 1989)

F. Mowat Landing: or the "Rennebester Settlement". Mowat was in charge of Fort Matachewan but eventually left the post and settled over a traditional native community

site known as, "land of Mattawapikan". Mowat took it upon himself to move in and settle because the natives were not considered to have any rights. Mowat continued his trading activities with the Montreal factors

T he Spirit of the Ottawa River, from the highlands of La Verendrye to the shores of Lake Temiskaming, has been silenced by dams and exploitive development — it's as Canadian a tradition as maple sugar pie. The river is changed forever. It seems fitting then that this adventure should begin at a place of clear water and roadless wilderness ... such a place does exist high up in Temagami's uplands — the headwaters of the Montreal River.

at Fort Temiskaming, or the English at James Bay from Fort Albany.

This is also the site of the Mattawapika dam located at the confluence of the Montreal and Lady Evelyn Rivers. Built in 1925, the dam flooded the majority of prehistoric native heritage sites on Lady Evelyn Lake, once known as the "haunt of the moose". It was first constructed to raise the level of the river so logs could be hauled out, and then refurbished later and maintained as a reservoir holding-dam that could feed the new power station at the Lower Notch on the Montreal River.

G. Devil Rock: a 320 foot vertical precipice overlooking Lake Temiskaming, and the site of many Algonkian legends. Hiking and ski trails make it accessible year-round to the public from the South Lorraine road at North Cobalt. (*See right-up "Devil Rock to Mattawa").

H. Hound Chute: One of the two small power stations built in the mid 1900's that would service the booming silver mines at Cobalt.

I. Ragged Chutes: Site of the Compressed Air Plant, believed to be the last of its kind in the world. Using water falling down a 351 foot shaft, it sends compressed air through an extensive network of pipes that cover the Cobalt mining area. One feature of the plant was the "blow-off" of mixed air and water that once shot a column of water high over the Montreal River.

J. Lower Notch Hydro Dam: built in 1970, it flooded the lower Montreal river as far up as Ragged Chutes. The drop to the Ottawa valley from here is over 200 feet.

K. Holding dam that was constructed in the mid 1900's when the Matabitchuan was used for driving timber.

L. Another holding dam that effectively flooded beautiful Fourbass Lake and site of the unique log flume with a vertical height of 200 feet. A small power station was built at the bottom of the pitch-off. This is also the site of the traditional portage route to Temagami used prior to the building of the railroad in 1903. The junction of the Matabitchuan and Montreal rivers was once a well-established native gathering area.

M. Indian Portage: a gruelling two mile, uphill carry, pond-hopping to Lake Temiskaming through the village of Laniel. This was the key access to Kipawa and Dumoine country or beyond, still used frequently by Temagami resident canoe camps since 1910.

N. Otto Holden Hydro-Electric Power Station. (See "Mattawa River" detailed map for more information)

O. Authors homestead site at Snake Creek from 1976 to 1984.

P. Talon Chutes Dam & Portage. (See "Mattawa River" detailed map).

Q. Hurdman Power Dam. (See "Mattawa River" detailed map).

Montreal River

INFORMATION TO KNOW:

Classification: Novice

Total Distance: 246 km. (Smoothwater Lk. to Ottawa R.)

Vertical Drop: 665 ft. (includes 200′ drop at Lower Notch)

Days Required: 10 to 12

Number of Campsites: 1 per 5 km. (Total: 52)

Number of Runnable Rapids: 21 (80% CI)
Distance: 6.5 km. or 3% total overall.

Swifts: 2 km.

Total Distance Fast-Water: 8.5 km. (4% of total distance)

PORTAGES:

Novice: 20 portages (10,485m.)

Advanced Novice: 14 portages (5,115m.) 50% reduction

Attributes: Incredible diverse topography beginning in the heart of the Temagami "Rock-Knob-Uplands", skirting the Temiskaming Clay Belt to the north and the typical "shield" country to the south. An enjoyable river for canoeists with basic skills or for those who need a break from the fast rivers. A good precambrian mix of lake and river travel.

Negative Factors: The Montreal may be considered too docile or tame for hard-core paddlers. The number of control or power dams have altered the "wild" nature of the Montreal below Matachewan and the clarity and purity of the river water is questionable along this stretch.

Whitewater Characteristics: Most rapids are shallow and may require wading, lifting through or lining as opposed to running –especially after mid-July. During highwater conditions, channels are deep and easily located. Novices can portage around all of the rapids and still enjoy the sanctity of the river environment.

CHOICE TRIPS:

Sunnywater to Longpoint Lake: (Dist. 132 km., 7-8 days)
Reference Material: "Temagami Canoe Routes", Routes 16,17,18 & 19.

A Smoothwater Lake – headwaters of the Montreal

Lower Notch Hydro Dam

This trip requires a float-plane drop into Sunnywater Lake from Longpoint Airways, the base from where you will eventually return via Sydney Creek. Sunnywater Lake is famous for its water clarity (up to 85 feet) and the fact that just south of the lake are the "Aurora Trout" ponds–the only fish of its kind found in the world (*protected specie). Smoothwater beach, native history, wildlife along the Montreal, the gentle rocky slopes north of Gowganda cloaked in jackpine, excellent campsites, scenery...all attractive features on this route. Sydney Creek, more of a garland of pretty lakes, offers easy access back to your start point.

Anishnabai legend relates the story of how the world was transformed here. The transparent waters and demonstrative landscape of Smoothwater Lake has been a "shangri-la" for both native and recreational paddlers ever since Nenebuc slew the giant lynx. During the Iroquois wars of the 1940's, local natives found security within the almost impenetrable fortress of hills that suspend the lake; while Temagami canoeists, since the late 1890s, made Smoothwater their projected goal on the arduous trek up the trout-streams or Lady Evelyn river, and then headed off after a rest day to the Sturgeon or Montreal where they would complete their respective loops back in central Lake Temagami.

To sit on the white-sand beach on the east shore and watch a summer storm engulf the southwest mountains, highest ridge in Ontario, is a spiritual happening. The Matachewan anishnabai would call the occuring rainbow at the storms end, "ani-miki-unujeabi", or thunder's legging string. This is a sacred place and you shouldn't go here unless you tread lightly and humble yourself in the face of mother earth.

The Montreal River has long been established as part of the native "nastawgan" travel routes. When a trade post was set up at the mouth of the river in 1679, a two-century long quest for furs was initiated between the French and the resident Anishnabai, and the Montreal, of course, was to become an important link to the resources of the interior.

In the 1830s, as timber supplies dried up along the lower Ottawa valley, the company men moved their operations further up the valley and began cutting trees along the shores of Lake Temiskaming in 1837. It wasn't until J.R. Booth purchased limits west of Latchford in the 1870s that the Montreal, like all of the other valley rivers, fell to the axe and logs began floating down-river to Lake Temiskaming.

Local chronicals claim that a hammer thrown at a fox by a logger, employed to lay rails for the new T & NO railway in 1903, inadvertently unearthed a vein of silver that sparked one of the biggest mineral boom's in Canadian history. Silver claims were quickly staked from Cobalt to Gowganda by 1908. Just a year before the New Liskeard Speaker reported about the rush;

"About 25 canoes go upriver daily from Latchford..."

This method of travel wasn't abandoned but a series of steam-powered boats, situated above each set of rapids west of Latchford, made the going much easier for miners and developers. Beginning at the railroad depot in Latchford, the steamships carried mining supplies up and down from Pork Rapids, to Mountain Chutes and on the Elk Lake City (first known as Bear Creek Village after the Makobe River).

Travel along the river was precarious because of the continued log drives and it wasn't long before a railroad was built to Elk Lake in 1913. The town itself burgeoned from a city of tents to a population of almost 10,000, half of which were transient fortune seekers. The town also had an odd habit of burning down every so often.

With the railway and improved roads came development; and with the clearing of the land came a scourge of terrible wildfires that scorched the landscape across the Montreal valley. In 1930, Booth made his final timber

drive down the river and then sold his rights to E.B. Eddy. A.J. Murphy, a notorious agent

Mountain Chutes...before 1975 few canoeists wore approved safety jackets (P.F.D.'s)

for Booth, continued his own operations around Lady Evelyn Lake. Logs were driven down both the Makobe and Lady Evelyn River until the 1940's.

My most memorable trip down the Montreal was in August of 1970. That was the year they built the Lower Notch hydro-dam. It's as vivid as the day I was there–below Ragged Chutes, the Montreal had been denuded of all trees for as far as you could see. Tent camps had been set up and men, in little groups,

were working furiously feeding huge fires that consumed the brush piles. The logs had been scavenged already by local timber companies and we had happened on to the clean-up work crews. The trees were cut back to accommodate the new lake and men were poaching deer as they wandered accidentally into the open ground.

Five kilometers from the Ottawa River the Montreal was "fenced-off" and huge signs warned us that the river had been diverted into sucking caverns. We portaged along a new road and managed to hail a ride from a dam worker as far as Lake Temiskaming. I also remember this trip when I was 19 years old and full of beans–I had lost my only pair of shoes and socks in the Ragged Chutes rapids and had to portage the rest of the trip in my bare feet!

I re-visited the lower Montreal seven years later. A horrid transformation had taken place; the water was mirky and the steep banks along the entire river were collapsing...and I thought of the pretty meandering river that once was...now 200 feet below my canoe.

$\mathcal{M}$akobe River, Waterway Park

INFORMATION TO KNOW:

Classification: Intermediate
Total Distance: 40 km.
Vertical Drop: 300 ft. 7.5'/km.
Days Required: 2-3
Number of Campsites: 1 per 2.5 km. (Total: 16)
Number of Runnable Rapids: 34 (65% CI)
Distance: Total 7.5 km. or 19% of total river distance.
Swifts: 2.5 km.
Total Distance Fast-Water: 10 km. (25% of total running distance)

PORTAGES:

Novice Intermediate: 17 portages (6,595 m.)
Creative Intermediate: 8 portages (1,955 m.)

Attributes: Scenery, seclusion and excitement all rolled in to a long weekend expedition. Inexpensive flight to the headwaters from Longpoint Airways. High potential for wildlife viewing. Steepest elevation drop per

kilometer of all watershed rivers and the longest total distance of runnable fast-water related to overall river distance.

Negative Factors: There is only one...that the river isn't a bit longer! The Makobe should be run in May, soon after break-up making wet or dry suits part of mandatory equipment.

Whitewater Characteristics: Unless spring rain keeps the level up, the river quickly becomes a veritable garden of rocks. It has a small drainage basin so even a torrential overnight downpour could effectively raise the water level enough to clear most center-channel rocks. The Makobe is a small, but surprisingly volatile shield river. There's not much room to make mistakes, but then the runs are pretty straightforward and channels are deep if caught during high flow; otherwise, the potential for rock-bashing is extremely good. Not a lot of opportunity to ferry or eddy-out once committed on one of the steep-pitched runs. I used to run a group trip down the Makobe during the third weekend in May, every year, and each time

we were portaging through a foot of snow still...no black flies, the occasional snow flurry, but great whitewater fun.

CHOICE TRIPS:

1. Makobe Lake to Elk Lake (Montreal River)

Trip Aids: "Temagami Canoe Routes", refer to route # 12.

This is a dynamite 2 to 3-day trip, accessed by floatplane from Longpoint airways (705)624-2418. Vehicle parking and lodging is available at Longpoint which is located 25 km. west of Elk Lake on highway # 560. You can arrange shuttle pick-up from Elk Lake at the lodge, or make arrangements to be picked up by the floatplane at the M.N.R. dock at Elk Lake to avoid the shuttle back to the airbase. There is a good possibility that you'll see moose on this trip, especially cows with newborn young so take your cameras!

2. Florence Lake or Gamble Lake to Elk Lake

Trip Aids: "Temagami Canoe Routes", refer to routes # 2 & 12.

This one week trip, again should be done in late May or early June. This route takes in some dramatic scenery, beautiful and diverse as you descend a particularly exciting portion of the Lady Evelyn River, work your way up the Gray's river (easy), and then reach the height of the Makobe headwaters for the final drop down to the Montreal River at Elk Lake. Access to Florence can be arranged either through Longpoint Airways or Lakeland Airways in Temagami (705) 569-3455, or, you can self-shuttle your party in to Gamble Lake or the Lady Evelyn River bridge.

General Notes

I've lost count of the number of times I've gone down the Makobe and each time has been as exciting as the first trip. The Anishnabai call this waterway "bear going in to the water." The river and the source lake at one time were an important hunting ground for the Temagami band. You can actually paddle this route in as little as one day, but I prefer to explore the more secluded spots and play in the rapids over a three-day period.

Alexander Lake is very pretty, particularly from the vantage point of the campsite on the northwest break past the narrows. The rapids at the north end offer good play and those can be easily run again and again. Fishing for northern pike is also a plus on the Alexander.

You'll notice as the Makobe River hits the Montreal there are steep sided dirt banks. During prohibition "blind pigs" or bootleggers, hid in "burrows" along the Makobe, and they would sell their illegal hooch to the local crowd from these carved out dens. It was said that if you stood on the bridge, you could see wafts of smoke emanating from the steep banks along the Makobe.

Looking upriver from Fat Man's Falls

Lady Evelyn River

INFORMATION TO KNOW:

Classification: Advanced Novice

Practical Distance: Gamble Lk.to Mowat Lnd.(North Branch/South Channel) 80 km. Florence Lk. to Mowat (South Branch/South Channel)100 km.

Vertical Drop: 375 feet

Days Required: 6 - 8

Number of Campsites: 106

Number of Runnable Rapids: 20 (85% CI)

Distance: Total 4 km.

Swifts: 2 km.

Total Distance Fast-Water: 6 km.

PORTAGES:

Novice: 20 portages (4,865 m.)

Advanced Novice: 8 portages (1,675 m.) 66% reduction

*Calculations include South Channel run because of runnable whitewater.

Attributes: High number of available established campsites and the ability to reduce the number of portages en route make it attrac-tive. Probably one of the most diverse and incredibly beautiful accessible river canoe trips in Canada. Seven waterfalls and several chutes are classic attractions, along with the side trip to Maple Mountain.

Negative Factors: Portages are extremely steep and rough at the waterfalls. Relatively high traffic along the north channel (Center Falls/ "Golden Staircase") during summer months. Rocks become very slippery when raining.

Whitewater Characteristics: Rapids are generally shallow and rocky by early July. White-waterists should run the river in May or June for best results. The river is narrow so once you are committed there isn't much room for lateral corrections. In the summer most rapids can at least be partly run or partly lined. You can avoid a lot of portages around the chutes in the summer by lifting or wading through.

LADY EVELYN RIVER

I couldn't very well leave out my all-time favourite river–the "trout streams", that gem of a cascading waterway that has been my home for a good part of my life. I'm not about

Fly-fishing at Bridal Veil Falls

27

to detail the wonders of the Lady Evelyn and I purposely omitted it from the expedition tally from the perspective of the Ottawa valley theme. I've travelled the Lady Evelyn on over 75 separate trips, both up and downstream; as a guide it was a popular excursion for my nature observation tours, and I have to admit...I never tired of its capricious nature.

It is not a river to paddle simply because it exists, or it's a park - it's a pathway to knowledge and self-discovery. The gallant Lady is an aristocrat who embellishes all that is meritable about the natural intricacies of a river. She is an educator... a benevolent spirit who has no qualms about sharing her secrets unselfishly, to those willing to nurture their patience and curiosity.

Too often, paddlers concentrate only on the hardships of the trout-streams, a river made infamous by its collection of precarious and sometimes precipitous portage trails, bouldery rapids and slippery rocks. The Lady Evelyn epitomizes a land ravished by nature herself, through time, and recently...by man.

Anti-environmental sentiment has run rampant within local logging communities since the incorporation of the Lady Evelyn-Smoothwater Wilderness Park in 1984. Logging, and later sport hunting was restricted, and in 1994 the access road and bridge will be removed so even anglers will have to portage in like everyone else.

Lady Evelyn River...easy, except for the portages

Disgruntled local sportspeople have often made threats that they would burn down the wilderness park stating that, ..."if they can't use it then nobody else will either!" A lame threat—I don't think so...I know these people. In June of 1992, during a strong northwest wind, local sportsmen ignited a fire on the south shore of McGiffen Lake. Anglers have often cut and cleared all-terrain-vehicle paths to once inaccessible lakes by way of recent logging clear-cuts...this was no exception.

The fire quickly fanned out and was soon out of control. I was on the river at the time and because of the intensity, canoeists were being evacuated. There were 150 fire-fighters and several government water-bombers working the wildfire but it took several days to contain. It ravished over 25 square kilometers of Lady Evelyn landscape and a 4 kilometer stretch of the river.

Fire is a natural element in the course of ecological balance, yet, incendiary pleasure to quell some relentless grudge is reminiscent of prehistoric logic gone awry. Because of the controversial access problem, particularly illegal-access, the Ontario government fuzzified the actual cause of the fire. The Ontario government has continually allowed uncontrolled vehicle access to the wilderness park since its inception.

Below Fat-Man Chutes

Devil Rock to Mattawa

THE STORY OF DEVIL ROCK

A long time ago, a small band of Teme Augama Anishnabai were netting fish in the deep waters below the cliffs of "Devil Rock" on the west shore of Lake Temiskaming. When they returned to their nets they discovered that someone had been stealing their fish. They continued to watch their nets and soon saw three "may-may-quay-shi-wok" or spirit people come out astride of an old log for a canoe and using sticks for paddles.

The Indians pursued them, and the fairies being shy, covered their faces behind their long hair. Finally the Indians caught one. Then the Indian said, "Look behind!" When the fairy turned quickly they caught a glimpse at how ugly he was. The Indians took a knife from this fairy and the rest disappeared, riding their log canoe through the rock wall to the inside. They could be heard crying from within the rock where they lived. The Indians, now feeling sorry for the fairy, threw the knife at the rock and it went through to the inside and the owner got back his knife.

The may-may-quay-shi-wok are very old creatures who go beyond the power of God, and who dwell amongst the ledges and cliffs, especially where you would find rock-paintings made from their blood. They are completely covered in hair, paddle stone canoes, and are generally feared by the Algonquin because they have the power to create illusion.

Lake Temiskaming...a corruption of the Algonquin term Teme Augama, or "deep lake", was referred to as Oba-dji-wan-on Sag-a-hi-gan or "narrow-current lake", as it constricted between very steep hills past Ville Marie. It was a gathering place for natives and for whites because if its medial location to the several trade and travel routes that branched off in all directions.

I have paddled this stretch of the Ottawa on two occasions, both taking place in the early 70's when they were still booming timber down the river. We could actually paddle faster, at a regular pace, than the tug could haul its boom. It's a dangerous piece of water and canoeists have traditionally crossed-over the lake from the Matabitchuan to reach the Indian portage and Kipawa on the far side.

St. John's School from Claremont, Ontario, held the philosophy that encouraged "confrontation with difficulty and danger". That's fine if you really know what you're doing. However, in June of 1978, on the first day out for a group of St. John's paddlers, this belief led to deliberate risks and foolishness that culminated in the deaths of 13 young boys. Their canoes swamped in the cold water as they fought to cross the lake during heavy winds...the spirit of Devil Rock, once again claiming more luckless victims.

These are not predictable waters. The temperament of the Ottawa is characterized by its ability to funnel high winds through its steep-hilled chambers, transforming still-water to that of a seething, tempestuous, white-capped monster in a matter of moments. To be caught in the middle of the river here could very well mean a quick demise in the frigid waters–even in July.

I also quickly learned that the level of the river fluctuates daily above the La Cave dam at Mattawa. This realization reared itself while camped below Temiskaming

Devil Rock – a place of magic

The Ottawa River from the Author's Snake Creek homestead

29

village. I woke up to find my pots, grill and assorted equipment that I had left by the shore, under three feet of water! My canoe, although tethered, was floating out in the bay, bobbing in the morning riffles almost in a mock tribute to my stupidity.

The river here, from Temiskaming to Mattawa is almost pristine, untouched and undeveloped...and very beautiful, surrounded by steep hills that rise several hundred feet to the skies on both sides. I remember thinking aloud, wouldn't it be wonderful to live up in these hills, build a cabin with a little garden, look out across the majesty of the valley every day.

Little did I know then that this would actually happen seven years later.

SNAKE CREEK: PATH-FINDER TO HOMESTEADER

I met Roxy Smith at Camp Wabun on Lake Temagami in 1975. The camps often hired Mattawa guides and cooks because of their willingness to work hard for cheap pay. For most it was like summer holiday to be able to go to Lake Temagami and work for the Americans.

That was the summer when Roxy told me about the 400 acres of land that his family owned at Snake Creek, a non-existent community located 20 kilometers north of Mattawa and just happened to be the exact place that I lusted over a few years back while paddling the Ottawa and looking up into the hills. Snake Creek once blossomed as a small village at the turn of the century, anticipating the building of the Temiskaming railway to take place on the Ontario side of the Ottawa. There was a school, three churches and several scattered subsistence homesteads, but, when the rail line was constructed on the Quebec side, the settlement disappeared–except for the Smith family, Irish immigrants whose farm now controlled the only "cross-over" river landing. The actual Snake Creek was a small river that pitched off a high waterfalls into the Ottawa River on the Quebec side, directly across from the Smith farm. Once the rail line was built following the creek inland, a logging depot did flourish for several decades and the only access by road and barge was through Roxy's farm.

My wife and I did build a cabin; first on leased land high up in the hills where we could look out over the valley. Most of the lumber had to be hauled the two

High ridges and rock faces were believed to possess immortal souls – natives were obliged to make "tobacco offerings" to appease the spirit that dwelled within.

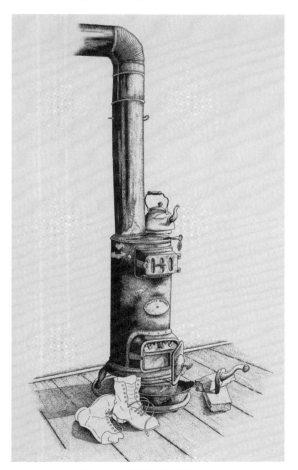

Homestead "Quebec" Heater.

kilometers up to the top plateau by toboggan in the winter. A few years later we purchased 30 acres from the family on lower land that we could drive to. Here we built a larger cabin, sank a sand-point well, and rigged up our own power generating system, and ...oh yes, we had a garden of sorts but we spent most of the time trying to keep the coons and moose out of it than it was worth.

We also engaged in the occasional armed confrontation with local sportsmen and poachers who looked upon us as outsiders and strange because we didn't live in town. The same bunch would also pester Roxy's brother who looked after the old farm down the road, steal out of his garden or have drinking parties in the backs of their pick-up trucks, taunting the 80 year-old pioneer without remorse. I figured that if you buckled under the least bit then this wild gang would have your number and we were never going to have any peace. It was the only time in my life where a 30:30 Winchester and a 100 lb. German Sheppard became the instruments of my own solice in the wilderness.

It was a hard life, but they were wonderful years with many adventures, and a great learning experience. Roxy told me of how his father would walk out into the La Cave rapids, long before they built the dam, and snag 75 lb. sturgeon as they swam by; and how they'd build the "ice-bridge" across the Ottawa River to the Quebec side so they could drive their teams of horses over to haul timber for the company, and how two-inches of steel-ice would be enough to support a whole team. And when they built the Holden Dam in 1953, how three men fell into the cement works unnoticed, and were encased in the thick stone sarcophagus to this day.

Each day was a different chapter ... audacious communion with nature–if there wasn't a bear clambering up the back steps there would be a skunk or porcupine under the house, or mice and squirrels in the attic, and the black flies! We called them quarter-pounders and they made sure that you were part of the food chain. I also had the opportunity to explore two smaller rivers that flow into the Ottawa as well - the Jocko and the Antoine, two beautiful ribbons of active current wending their way through the hills.

Mattawa River

If your ambition is to lose a quick 5 to 10 pounds in just one day then may I suggest partaking in the annual North Bay to Mattawa canoe race. Organized by the North Bay/Mattawa Conservation Authority for the past twenty years, the course originally ran from Ville Marie south to Mattawa, and then on to North Bay. With the development of sleek-profiled racing shells, the heavy waves of the Ottawa was just too much for the lightweight boats. The number of swampings prompted the Authority to change the race to its present course along the Mattawa River only.

The river is 64 kilometers long, has four mandatory portages and eight CI to CII rapids thrown in for variety. Early voyageurs once remarked that this section of the trade route, from Montreal to Lake of the Woods, was the most arduous, having to line their heavily laden canot de maitre through the shallow rapids along the Mattawa.

The distance of the race, for a traditional paddler of my vintage, could be considered just an average travelling day. As an outfitter, it was hard to get any of my clients to accept an easy 20 kilometer jaunt on open water–by today's standards. And really, that's a good thing...people taking more time to enjoy the ammenities of nature. It eludes me though why, each year, for the past ten years, I have made this annual speed-trek down this jewel of the past. Insanity! It's not about winning, or even being competitive, because it is so difficult to race against the much faster, sleeker designs. I suppose it has something to do with the alluring challenge...to see if you've still got it...a gentler macho alternative to big-game hunting maybe.

I don't know how, but I've even won a few times; probably because the other racers felt sorry for these guys dressed in army fatigues and suspenders, plodding along in this relic cedar/canvas, water-logged "prospector", patched with ambroid and bandana with tin can lids shoved in between the ribs to cover the broken planks; I swear we psyched everyone out, they just let us win for best presentation and costume.

But the "hut-strokers" always had problems at the portages and the rapids; they'd be forever getting tangled in their intravenous gatorade tubes and they'd end up two-manning at the carry's or cracking up on a rock in the middle of a run. The chorus of "hut-hut-huts", as they zig-zagged down Talon Lake, sounded like the evening chant of spring-peepers in a woodlot swamp.

Yes, it is somewhat of a tradition with me...where else along life's meandering pathways can you actually test your skill at pissing while running with a canoe over your head? Or peeling an orange with one hand without breaking pace? Or submitting your body to unnatural physical torment for eight straight hours just so you can wake up the next morning in excruciating pain?

"Porte de l'Enfer", hell's gate; a native ochre-mine said to be inhabited by an evil demon

But if you really want to enjoy the attributes of this great river you have to spend at least three days in a canoe, and just amble down at your own leisure. It's an accessible waterway and there are several points in which to start or end a quality long weekend adventure.

The segment from Pimisi Lake and Talon Chutes, downriver as far as Samuel de Champlain Provincial Park, is the only semi-remote portion of the river and very enjoyable as a one or two day jaunt. If you are travelling alone, then you have the option of a self-shuttle - leave bicycles at Champlain Park and drive to the private campsite at Pimisi where you can park for a nominal fee. It's no more than an hour and a half pedal along the highway to retrieve your vehicle. There is a wide variety of things to do along the river and Champlain Park offers some excellent hiking alternatives and a voyageur museum.

ABOUT THE MAP: The entire Mattawa River Valley lay nestled in the Laurentian corridor between the city of North Bay to the west, and the village of Mattawa to the east. The upper map depicts the Mattawa in its entirety to the point where it junctions the Ottawa River. Details of the "whitewater-section" of the river are illustrated at the bottom. Each letter designation found on the map is explained below:

A. MANITOU ISLANDS: Site of significant Native legends and folklore.

B. SAGE COMPLEX: Underground Strategic Air/Ground Warning command centre. Part of the "early-warning" system manned co-operatively by the Canadian and U.S. armed forces. It monitors air space activity over North America. In the 1960's, North Bay's Bomarc Missile Base, located on hwy#11 north at the present site of Canadore College Helicopter Base, was also a prime U.S.S.R. target during the arms race.

C. TYYSKA SITE: In 1973 archaelogists under Dr. Tyyska examined ancient religious ruins that predated "Stonehenge" by 2,000 years. This aboriginal shrine consists of various stone platforms and stairways representing stages in the human spiritual journey. It also includes petroforms, petroglyphs and serpent mounds. This site is not public.

D. "THE STEPPING STONES": A shoal traversing the narrows at the end of Trout Lake.

E. "PORTAGE de la TORTUE": (Historic trail only-no portage).

F. RIVER ROUTE: Series of short portages;flow controlled by a dam at the north end of Turtle Lake. Drop of about 25 vertical feet to Talon Lake. Optional secondary route.

G. "PORTAGE de la MAUVAIS MUSIQUE": 200m. An easy trail from the Turtle Lake creek to Robichaud (Pine)Lake.

H. "PORTAGE PIN de MUSIQUE": 456m. An easy drop down to Talon Lake.

I. "PORTAGE de TALON": 330m. Holding dam controlling level of river below. Old log flume once used during timber drives (no longer visible). The tiny island below chutes was once called the "watchdog" by natives and voyageurs. Offerings of tobacco were left for the residing spirits. A rocky portage with some steep sections.

J. FAULTLINE: Nipissing natives often worshipped outstanding rock features along the river. Here, both sides of the river are walled-in by 30m. cliffs. Very impressive!

K. RAPID 1: "Decharge des Perches"-portage 157m. CI, shallow, start right of center channel between old dam cribs. Follow deep channel on left side, centering off then a hard right to finish at bottom. Be prepared to step out!

L. RAPID 2: Portage 225m. CI, shallow, easy beginning with drop through deep tongue, keep far-right for best channel...watch for

Mattawa River

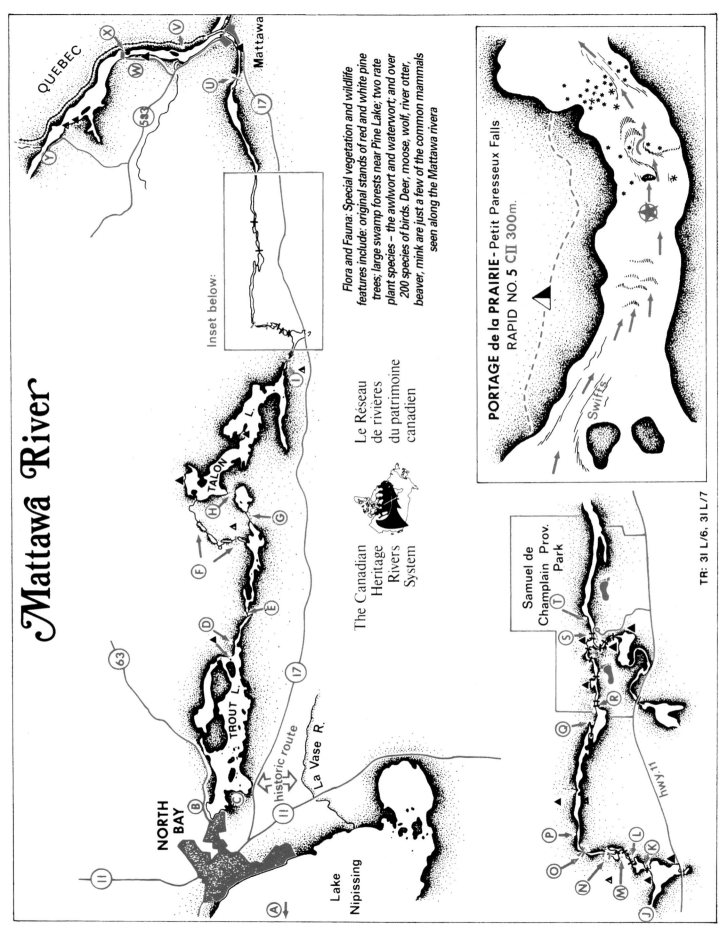

Inset below:

Flora and Fauna: Special vegetation and wildlife features include: original stands of red and white pine trees; large swamp forests near Pine Lake; two rate plant species – the awlwort and waterwort; and over 200 species of birds. Deer, moose, wolf, river otter, beaver, mink are just a few of the common mammals seen along the Mattawa rivera

Le Réseau
de rivières
du patrimoine
canadien

The Canadian
Heritage
Rivers
System

PORTAGE de la PRAIRIE - Petit Paresseux Falls
RAPID NO. 5 CII 300m.

Swifts

QUEBEC

Mattawa

Samuel de
Champlain Prov.
Park

NORTH
BAY

Lake
Nipissing

historic route

La Vase R.

TALON L.

TROUT L.

TR: 31 L/6, 31 L/7

main flow at bottom and thread through rocks or get out!

M. *"PORTAGE de la CAVE"*:100m. by-passes rapid#3 & 4. RAPID#3: Cltech.50m. double drop ...precise line-up for downstream tongue (approach cautiously or scout). Rocks are jagged! Drop through, holding left of bottom waves to avoid kissing concealed rock.*If rapid #1 & 2 are easily run then you should be able to squeeze through here with caution. RAPID #4: Cl.30m. A shallow but easy grind into pond (just past portage).

The Mattawa River from Samuel de Champlain provincial park's 9 km "Etienne Trail"

N. *"PORTAGE de la PRAIRIE"*: 287m. See Inset for detail. RAPID#5: CII:300m. NOTE: Kiss this rock or you won't line up for the drop through the hole...you'll end up over the ledge. Backwater left, drop through pulling hard right to avoid waves and rock; follow through main lick at bottom shallows. Best run on the river and campsite to match!

O. *PARASSEUX FALLS*: "Portage des Parasseux": 402m. DO NOT RUN! Natives believed the falls to be inhabited by spirits.

P. *"LA PORTE DE L'ENFER" (HELLS GATE)*: Speculated to be a native "ochre" mine.

"In the side of a hill on the north side of the river, there is a curious cave, concerning which marvellous tales are related by the voyageurs." (Alexander Henry, Aug. 1761).

Voyageurs maintained that the cave was inhabited by a fierce, flesh-eating demon; its' blood composed of red-ochre which was

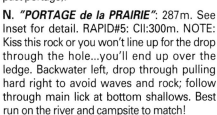

collected by the Indians and used for ceremonial purposes.

Q.. *"LES EPINGLES"*: Portage unnecessary, swifts only through rocky shallows. Keep left of center for 25m.

R. *"PORTAGE des ROCHES"*: Portage 150m. PORTAGE #6: Cltech:175m. Very rocky with confusing channels when low-water conditions prevail. Keep generally right of center all the way down main (right) channel ...veer right at bottom.

S. *"PORTAGE CAMPION"*: Portage 184m. "Samuel de Champlain Provincial Park". RAPID 7: Cltech:200m. Several center channel rocks to dodge when low, thread through but hold central play all the way but veer right at end swifts to avoid shallows. *High water play: ...hike up to Moore Lake in the park (Amable du Fond River), and run rapids from here back to the Mattawa River and Campion

rapids. A blast during spring run and a fast CII for over a kilometer!

Champlain Park: It's well worth a stop-over. Excellent hiking trails and the Voyageur Heritage Centre. Learn more about the geology and history of the valley.

T. *"PORTAGE de la ROSE"*: (Historic trail only-no portage). It is interesting to note that these particular rapids were flooded when the Hurdman Dam was built to supply the town of Mattawa with hydro-electric power.

U. *"PORTAGE de PLEIN CHANT"*: (Hurdman Dam), Portage 270m. along trail and road.

V. *"MOUNT ANTOINE"*: Rises several hundred feet above the river and at one time supported a nest of bald eagles.

W. *"MOUNT ANTOINE SKI HILL"*: One of Ontario's most spectacular.

X. *"LA CAVE DAM"*: (Otto Holden): Built in 1952 producing 205,200 kilowats of power. The dam is 762m. long, 40m. high and has created a 48km. lake, drowning the La Cave rapids.

Y. *"SNAKE CREEK, ONTARIO"*: Homesite of the author from 1976 to 1984. Once a bustling community at the turn of the century, anticipating the construction of the Temiskaming railroad on the Ontario side of the Ottawa. Settlers disbanded after rail line was built on the Quebec side.

$\mathcal{M}$attawa to Pembroke

If you were to take a window seat at the Valois diner in Mattawa, overlooking the Ottawa River and the hills of Quebec, you might just be witness to a pack of wolves running a deer into the water. It happens quite a bit, apparently...I've even seen it myself and in the winter it really is tragic and you sit there helpless quaffing back their famous home-made raspberry pie and ice-cream wondering about the cruelty of the natural order of things.

What stands out most vividly about this part of the Ottawa, besides home-made pie, is the seemingly endless distance between points of land. You'd paddle half a day focussed on

the same spear of trees, questioning whether you were actually making headway, or if some imperceptible force had taken hold of your craft in animated suspension.

The river is inordinately wide, the hills are precipitous and with surprisingly little development, particularly on the Quebec side. There were always places to camp...a beach, a grassy clearing that may have served as an old logging depot or homestead, or even underneath a cottage which our sorry group of vagabond paddlers took advantage of on one occasion, while racing a rather nasty storm down the river at night.

The most peculiar animal confrontation happened while I was cruising down the middle of the river on a calm day and noticed a slight disturbance and a tell-tale "V" trail in the water ahead. This was a kilometer from shore–what would be out swimming this far I wondered? I surged ahead to investigate and it turned out to be a marathon red squirrel high-tailing it to Quebec. I veered the canoe over and sure enough, he took advantage of the situation and climbed aboard and took his position on top of the packs while I paddled him the rest of the way over. As soon as the canoe hit the shore he let out a barrage of chatters, hopped down and sprang at the first pine tree he came to. I guess the pines are greener on this side. I can only think that he must have fallen from some overhanging branch and into the river below, became disoriented, and then began the English-channel crossing of the Ottawa.

The only other bizarre experience was the rounding of a point on the Ontario side near Chalk River, and coming upon this bubbling cauldron of water that seemed like it could engulf a house. Thinking it was some wonderful, natural underwater geyser or some such entity, we were miserably disappointed when we learned that it was some blow-off from the nuclear power station.

In 1950, when Ontario Hydro built the Des Joachims dam, it flooded both the "Rocher Capitaine Rapids" at Bisset Creek and "des rapides des grelots" (bed of river covered in round boulders), later known as "Rapides des Deux Rivieres & Trou Rapides" for the "pothole" formations at the present site of Deux Rivieres. At Bisset Creek there was a 797 pace portage while "Devils Portage" at Deux Rivieres, on the south side, was used by travellers up until the creation of Holden Lake.

Also drowned was the early fur-trade fort at the mouth of the Dumoine and naturally, the rapids at Des Joachims - once a difficult half-mile portage that was located just above the present day airbase, over "high rugged mountains", as claimed by Nicolas Garry in 1821. Sir William Logan of the Geological Survey Branch in 1847, gave the drop in the river at Des Joachims as 23'3" - a respectable vertical plunge for any rapid. The name and its origin is disputed between that of a brother of the wife of Chevalier de Troyes (Joachims de L'estang?), or was it after Saint-Joachim (father of the virgin Mary?), however, on early maps drawn by the cartographer Franquelin, the portages bear the name of the former.

Rapides des Joachims, better known as D'Swisha or just Swisha, was once a booming lumber-town in the late 1800s...the village was a dock site for the Pembroke steamer and boasted of timber slides and booming facilities to serve lumber company interests. On the Dumoine, nearby, the headquarters of the logging operations was at Rowanton where you can still see the tall, ruined chimney.

Many of the valley men, an ethnic mix of French, Metis, Irish, Scots, German and Native, made an exodus to the shanty camps to cut timber each fall. Des Joachims hotels were the first place the rivermen came to spend their paycheques. Paymasters seldom paid all the men at the same time because the local village watering holes would get plugged up all at once.

John King, an early lumberman on the Ottawa remarks,
"Oh, the rivermen! When the camps would break up in the spring the first hotel they'd come to they'd be into it and settle a lot of battles right there. You know it wasn't scientific. They'd go at each other and battle. They were strong. They'd kick, kick hard like horses, you know, any way to get a man down. Then they'd get their name up to being the best man along the river."

Below Deep River the Ottawa takes on an almost surreal composure; abrupt monolithic rock faces rise out of the depths, shrouded in ethereal morning mists and coddled by lazy currents. It's a wonderful visage that can only be enjoyed from the perch of boat or canoe.

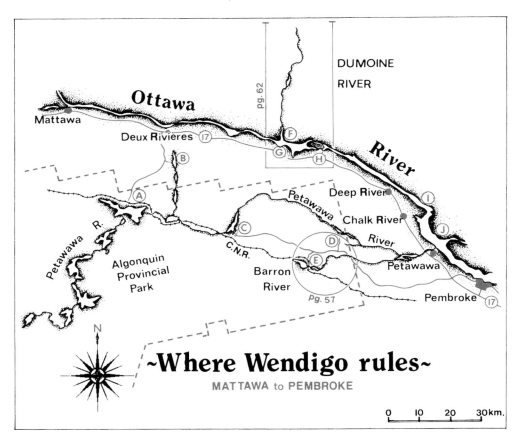

~Where Wendigo rules~

MATTAWA to PEMBROKE

0   10   20   30km.

ABOUT THE MAP:
A. Brent Station Access (Petawawa River) – Start point
B. Wendigo Lake Access (Petawawa River) – Start point
C. Lake Travers Access (Petawawa River) – Start point

D. McManus Lake Access (Petawawa River) – Start point
E. Achray (Barron River) – Start point
F. Site of Historic Fort Dumoine
G. Driftwood Provincial Park/Pine Valley (Dumoine River) – End point

H. Rapides des Joachims (D'Swisha) & Rolphton – airbase
I. Oiseau Rock – Scenic attraction
J. Historic Fort William

$\mathcal{P}$etawawa River

"...the river being, as far as the level country, almost a constant succession of rapids, which cannot be ascended in less than 7 days, by a light canoe in the dry season, and is hardly ever attempted at any other time"

(Alexander Sherriff, Royal Engineers, 1820s)

After the U.S. invasion of Canada and the War of 1812, a protectionist paranoia pervaded political thought for almost three decades. Should the United States have effectively closed off the Great Lakes, an alternate northern route to Georgian Bay could keep Upper Canada's machinery plugged in. In terms of geographical setting the choices were scant; physical obstructions and periods of low flow hampered positive feedback from Royal Engineers who scrutinized the possibility of a "lift-lock" system along the Petawawa River. In 1826, Lieutenant Henry Briscoe reported:

"...(the river) is nearly one entire rapid, its banks are very high and rocky, in many places 60 and 100 feet perpendicular: in the last 20 miles it forms several small lakes. We left it by a portage of 1 mile (portage road through the village of Petawawa) to avoid the rapids and falls with which it is impeded at its junction with the Ottawas."

A decade later, still searching for an improbable lock-route across the province, William Hawkins, Deputy Provincial surveyor, explored the river and further noted:

"...its timber is red (red pine), its soil is red (red clay and sand), its rock is red, and its waters are red, deriving their colour from the soils and rocks over which they pass," he continues, " averaging each lock at 10 feet, it would require 79 locks to connect the waters of Lake Huron and the Ottawa by this route."

Although the introduction of railways in the mid 1800s replaced much of the water-related travel, the idea of a northern lock system still surfaces from time to time. Even today there is much talk about opening the French and Mattawa routes to recreational boat traffic, which in my mind, would seriously degrade two historically valuable waterways even further than they already are.

The Petawawa, for some inane reason, has attracted military interests for three hundred years. It began in 1686 innocently enough with a French military expedition headed north on a quest to capture English fur-trade posts on Hudson's Bay. The "Kici-si-bi Anishnabai" or "big-river-people", Algonkin natives who were camped at the mouth of

"Wendigo", an evil, cannabilistic demon was said to have roamed the winter woods in search of luckless victims.

the Petawawa, beat drums and waved a white flag in an attempt to entice the soldiers to shore so they could trade with them.

Today, the huge Canadian Forces Base Reserve restricts traffic on the lower Petawawa as far as the Algonquin Park east boundary at McManus Lake. I suppose the CFB were concerned that canoeists may unwontedly become targets at the nearby firing range or be trampled by bushwhacking tanks.

The "Pee-ta-waw-wee" or "a noise heard far away", probably acquired its cognomen by those paddling the Ottawa River from whence the sound of rapids could be heard some distance away.

Natives considered the source of the Petawawa to depart from Wendigo Lake and along what is now called the North River that flows south into Radiant Lake–not the present recognized source waters that hail from the interior highlands of Algonquin Park.

I have always found it interesting to note that the multifarious Algonkian native bands each had their own personalized settings for commonly shared mythical demons, demi-

gods, and bush sprites. Along the Dumoine and Coulonge rivers Wendigo hailed from Lake Dumoine environs; the Petawawa and Barron river anishnabai enjoyed the presence of this evil manitou who's home ground erupted from the bowels of, what else... Wendigo Lake.

"The most dreaded of all the supernatural beings that are evil or hostile to man is the Wendigo, a personfication of the starvation and craving for flesh that so often befell the Ojibwa in the later months of the winter. The Wendigo is a human transformed by cannibalism into a monstrous giant with supernatural powers. A sorcerer through witchcraft may prevent a hunter from killing any game, and reduce his family to such straits that one member, crazed by hunger, kills and eats a brother or sister. Then the appetite for human flesh becomes insatiable. The cannibals' body swells to the size of a pine tree and becomes hard like stone, impenetrable to arrow or bullet and insensible to cold. Naked save for a loincloth, the monster roves the countryside seeking more victims to devour. Its breathing is audible for miles; and its shouting weakens the limbs of the Indian it pursues. It haunts the country only in winter, when it attacks its victims during snow storms or unusually cold weather; with the first melting of the snow it retreats to the north."

(Jenness, 1935)

Logging interests severely altered the Petawawa landscape and to some considerable degree, changed the character of the river itself. The mid to late 1800s saw the decimation of the great pine stands, to which the subsequent accumulation of stumps and debris left behind, contributed to a number of wildfires that scorched the Petawawa/Barron region through 1868 to 1876.

To facilitate easy passage of cut timber during spring log drives, the actual physical presence of rapids and falls were disturbed by the construction of 2,743 ft. of slides, 11,140 ft. of booms, 3,208 ft. of retaining dams and 30 piers. That's about 6.5 kilometres of unnatural man-made rigadoo that, I suppose, could be endeared to the romance of the era.

The environment suffered, not to mention the innumerable deaths, many of them runaway children who found work along the rivers as "green hands", often succumbing to a horrible, cold, fate...crushed beneath tons of jammed logs and quickly forgotten. The last river drive on the Petawawa was in 1945 and employed 150 men.

I made a slight departure from my normal approach at detailing a river for the singular reason of fraternal respect for the "Friends of Algonquin Park"–the organization responsible for supplying public information presently working on its own Petawawa guide–I simply did not want to undermine their generous work. I will, however, force upon you a few of my own adventures and cerebral wanderings that may make a trip down the Petawawa a trifle more intriguing, if not totally abstract.

The Petawawa River drains an area of 1,600 sq. miles, slightly less than the Coulonge at 1,820 sq, miles. It originates 155 km. west of its Ottawa River mouth at the west end of Algonquin Park and descends 1,050 vertical feet before terminating at Allumette Lake. That's a drop of 6.5 feet per kilometre...not bad considering the number of lake interruptions along the way.

Although passive in nature for the most part, the Petawawa is an intimidating intermediate classed waterway requiring precise skills, good judgement and humility–particularly during high-water runs.

I remember my first trip on the Petawawa; it was 1968 and we were paddling, no...wading and lining our canoes upstream! Our sorry-group of woebegone trippers had been out a month, the Mattawa and Ottawa rivers now behind us. We were trying to work our way to Canoe Lake in the Park for a pick-up by way of the Petawawa.

With the help of a tattered 1946 Department of National Defence topo map we managed to wend our way up the miles of rapids. Wading and lining seemed the only options as portages hadn't been used for some time and it was more work "bush-pushing" than staying with the river. At Rollway Rapids we came across a freshly erected cairn and marker for Blair Fraser. On May twelfth, just two months earlier, this well-known and respected political journalist drowned while attempting to make a spring run. Known also for his daredevil-try and vigour, he is best known for his love of wild places; he writes:

" It is no coincidence that our national emblem is not a rising sun, a star, a hammer, a sickle, or a dragon, but a beaver and a maple leaf. Nor is it coincidence that there are more paintings of wilderness lakes, spruce bogs, and pine trees on Canadian livingroom walls than in any other nation on earth. We may scoff, we may deny, but the wilderness mystique is still a strong element of Canadian ethos."

(1974: quoted in the House of Commons after his death)

We sat there on the rocks, contemplating, wondering what must have gone wrong. Nobody wore PFDs in those days. My eyes followed the current, over ledges, around boulders and through the haystacks; thoughts reaching the black pool below in an eddy that bequeathed no secrets that day. I looked at my own water-logged, kapok-stuffed life preserver and wedged it back under my seat.

Just west of Lake Travers there were no portages cleared so we were forced to follow the railroad tracks. All I remember is someone shouting, "Traaaain cuhhhh-mingggg ..." and having less than five seconds to dump the canoe and press my body up against the wall of the narrow rock-cut. No warning...no sound, it just appeared out of nowhere. We could have been far worse off. Only minutes before we had crossed over the rail bridge that spanned the Petawawa river–a boiling rush of water 40 metres below. I ran...there was no place to go if a train did come. We were lucky.

There wasn't much traffic on the river back then; we saw no other canoe party in ten days. Years later, as interest in river paddling blossomed, portages were constructed so that canoeists no longer had to play Russian

Roulette with the rail traffic. That same day I almost stepped on a Massassauga rattler. It was sunning itself by the shore rocks... strange, it made little impression on me then...I was just glad to be alive!

We ran out of food at Cedar Lake and were windbound for two days. The winds finally died and we made a fevered attempt at crossing the lake that night. We crashed on the beach at Brent Station; no tents, we just spread out our sleeping bags on the sand. I remember that place well; that was the night the bear walked over the end of my bed. We couldn't get rid of him, he just kept coming back. He managed to root through our food packs with cool indifference. It didn't matter - we had no food left anyway.The river had that used but abandoned aura about it...like a vintage car that's been tucked away in a barn for twenty-five years. All the same, it imbued that magical presence of a Tom Thomson painting–strokes of bold colour yet with innocent simplicity.

PETAWAWA PADDLE AND PEDAL TOUR (3-4 days)

If you are equipped to car jockey more than one vehicle then you have several options open as to where you can start your expedition–Kiosk, Brent, Wendigo Lake or Lake Travers. All river trips have to terminate at McManus Lake access point (#21) because of the military play area downstream. It's also recommended that travel permits be picked up at the Sand Lake gate (east entrance to Algonquin Park) on your way in.

For those with only one vehicle, and you're planning a long-weekend jaunt, you may want to bring along a couple of mountain bikes. You can leave them near the McManus Lake access point, locked and concealed, but first make sure the tires are pumped, gear and chain is lubed and your water bottle is filled. It's a dusty, 56.3 kilometre ride back to Lake Travers over hilly terrain but the road is good and you should be able to average 14 kilometres per hour for a four to five hour trek back to your vehicle.

From Lake Travers to McManus the Petawawa is 52

The Petawawa...early runs are not for the timid

kilometres in length and takes an average of three days to paddle at a moderate pace. Four days gives you a good buffer. This is my favourite leg of the river, probably because it reminds me so much of the Temagami area.

Although well travelled today there are now ample campsites and good portages circumventing dangerous water - the likes of Crooked or Rollway rapids. The 100 to 150 metre cliffs at and below the Natch rapids are

worthy of inspection as they are home to rare ferns (look but don't touch!). It's also the site of a Tom Thomson painting.

The upper stretch is strikingly rugged, demonstrating geological artistry at its optimum performance; rugged stoneworks, escarpments topped by spires of misty spruce and pine and lonely campsites inhabited by the "Me-megwe-si", ugly creatures covered in hair that live along the high ledges.

The lower river changes towards Whitson Lake and you will encounter a variety of forest types, such as the silver maple, that are more indigenous of more southern climes.

Be cautious on the Petawawa; play it safe... many lives have been lost because the foolhardy or ill-equipped always place themselves above the power of the river. Be humble, be wise and examine all runs carefully.

$\mathcal{F}$our Days on the Barron River

HIKE, BIKE & PADDLE TOUR

Of all the trips through Algonquin Park with which I've made acquaintance, since the mid 1960's, this particular gem has to be one of my favourites. I call it the "hike, bike and paddle tour."It's the kind of thing you do when you've got four days and you don't want to break into a sweat - a couch potato trip where you can find a nice campsite and sack out for a day.

When I first visited this area there was no road to Achray...it was a rail depot; and, nobody that I knew had ever paddled the Barron - I doubt that there were even any portages cleared twenty years ago. I believe what may have put the Barron on the map was the tragedy involving three young boys who were mauled to death by a black bear back in the late 70's.

The Barron is a tributary of the Petawawa and has an amiable character that is quite approachable by any level canoeist. Both the Petawawa and Barron river basins are part of the Fossmill Drainage Pattern...a trough that emptied meltwaters from retreating glaciers from Lake Algonquin (a glacial-historic term for the much enlarged Lake Huron). Glacial waters flowed through the Barron canyon southeast to the Champlain Sea which covered most of the lower Ottawa Valley 12,000 years ago.

The Barron canyon, considered to be the most spectacular of all Algonquin Park features, began as a fault, or fissure in the

earth's crust millions of years ago and eroded by wind, rain and ice to its present state.

The river, once called "pittoiwas", was named after Augustus Barron in 1890, a member of the House of Commons. Like its parent river, the Barron too formed part of the log drive network and modifications were made to ease valuable timber through the narrow chutes and rapids. Some 2,134 feet of

Giant Snapper...below High Falls

log slides and 388 feet of dams were established along the river, some of these 'works' are still visible today.

Just west of the Sand Lake gate (east entrance), the road crosses the Barron at Squirrel Rapids. There is a well-used landing and parking lot adjacent to the river here–a good place to "bush" your mountain bikes or leave a second vehicle. It's 27 kilometres along the access road to Achray, a still active rail yard and site of one of the park's prettiest public campgrounds. Rock outcroppings

spaced by sandy beaches support a second growth of pine.

After intense logging ravished the land and wildfires scorched the general Barron River area, forest cover took some time to return because of the thin soils. Tom Thomsons painting of the lone "Jack Pine" is only one of several renderings of the "rebuilding" era - forests trying to make a comeback after a century of exploitation. Thomson toured the park from 1912 to 1917 his work often depicting scenes of regeneration, and destruction as the background hills in his Achray painting suggest. The stump from this tree can still be seen about a kilometre east of the campground.

Thomson's paintings often made representation of the active logging drives, which I am sure at the time, must have appeared to be quite adventurous and romantic. However, the full impact of the fires and excessive cutting has only recently been acknowledged by a more environmentally tuned-in public.

His motifs pronounced the pangs of a seared landscape, and although simply stylized through the use of wide brush strokes, it was quite blatant that background vistas illustrated hills denuded of growth. Looking south from Achray you do notice a kind of forest "mange". Charred stumps from fires a century ago, and of more recent burns, can still be seen along the river.

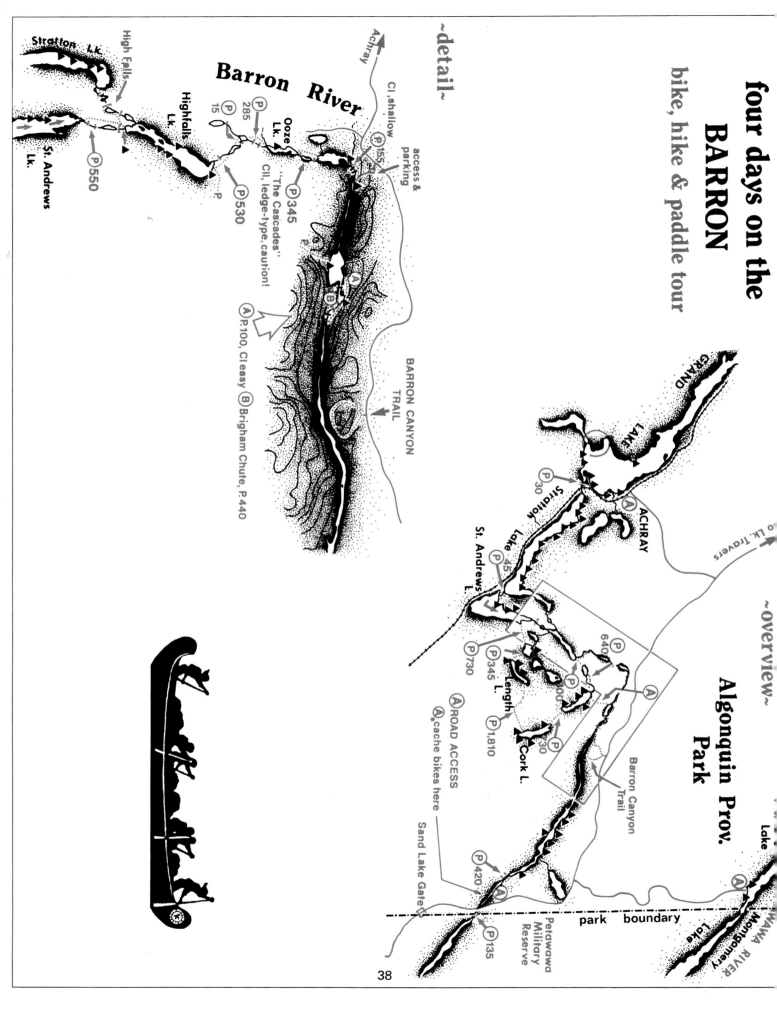

four days on the BARRON

bike, hike & paddle tour

~detail~

Barron River

Stratton Lk.

High Falls

Highfalls Lk.

St. Andrews Lk.

(P)550

(P)530

(P)345

(P) 15

(P) 285

Ooze Lk.

(P)155

Cl, shallow

Achray

Achray

access & parking

"The Cascades" CII, ledge-type, caution!

(A) P.100, Cleasy (B) Brigham Chute, P.440

BARRON CANYON TRAIL

~overview~

Algonquin Prov. Park

GRAND LAKE

(A) ACHRAY

(P)30

Stratton Lake

St. Andrews L.

(P)45

(P)730

(P)345

(P)1,810

Length L.

Cork L.

(P)640

(P)30

Barron Canyon Trail

(A) ROAD ACCESS

(A) *cache bikes here

Sand Lake Gate

(P)420

(A)

(P)135

Petawawa Military Reserve

to Lk. Travers

park boundary

PETAWAWA RIVER

Montgomery Lake

Lake

Although dressed in subtle qualities, for me the river still had that typical Ontario park "tended" feel to it, as if the government were creating a facade to mask on-going timber extractions, forest experiments and mock war-games. Even the wildlife seemed to act out of character.

For example...as I sat by the shore one evening, at a campsite on Stratton Lake, perched comfortably against a rock still warm from the afternoon sun, working on my second mug of toxic bush coffee (laced with even harsher Canadian whiskey), I caught site of a white-tail deer swimming towards the campsite about 100 metres out.

The lake was a few hundred metres across and the deer, once recognizing that the site was already taken, veered off and headed directly down the lake. It veered again, back to this shore, hesitated, turned again and swam back to the far shore, remained in the water, spun around, crossed the lake once more but didn't get out; instead it swam back again to the far shore, hesitated...

By this time I was losing interest in this marathon ungulate and went back to my dreams...and hot java. I had never seen a swimming animal do that before; usually, once headed in a specific direction a moose or bear will maintain course until it reaches land. I suppose the nature of the land, if changed, may have some influence on the personality of the wildlife...who knows?

Aside from having the province's most adept swimming animals, the Barron is truly an enjoyable paddle with superlative campsites with a typical rock and pine anatomy. I prefer to stay with the river, explore High Falls, run some of the liquid stuff down normally un-runnable cascades, rather than take the pond-hop that by-passes most of the rapids. There's a few portages but none are difficult, and just enough sensible fast-water to put a spark in the engine.

The Canyon itself is...well, see it for yourself, it's quite something. When you've finished your paddle and you are on your way back to Achray on your bikes, make sure you stop at the Barron Canyon Trail. This 1.5 kilometre hiking loop follows the north rim of the 100 metre deep canyon. If you thought the view looking up at this monolith was inspiring visions, wait until you peer over the edge of this precipice.

The 27 kilometre bike ride back to Achray should take you less than two hours to complete. Again, make sure your bikes are prepped for the trip and don't forget water bottles - the ride could be hot and dusty.

For more information about the Petawawa and Barron Rivers you can contact:

The Friends of Algonquin Park
P.O. Box 248
Whitney, Ontario
K0J 2M0

Canadian Recreational Canoe
Association
1029 Hyde Park Rd. Suite 5
Hyde Park, Ontario Canada
N0M 1Z0

Barron River Canyon

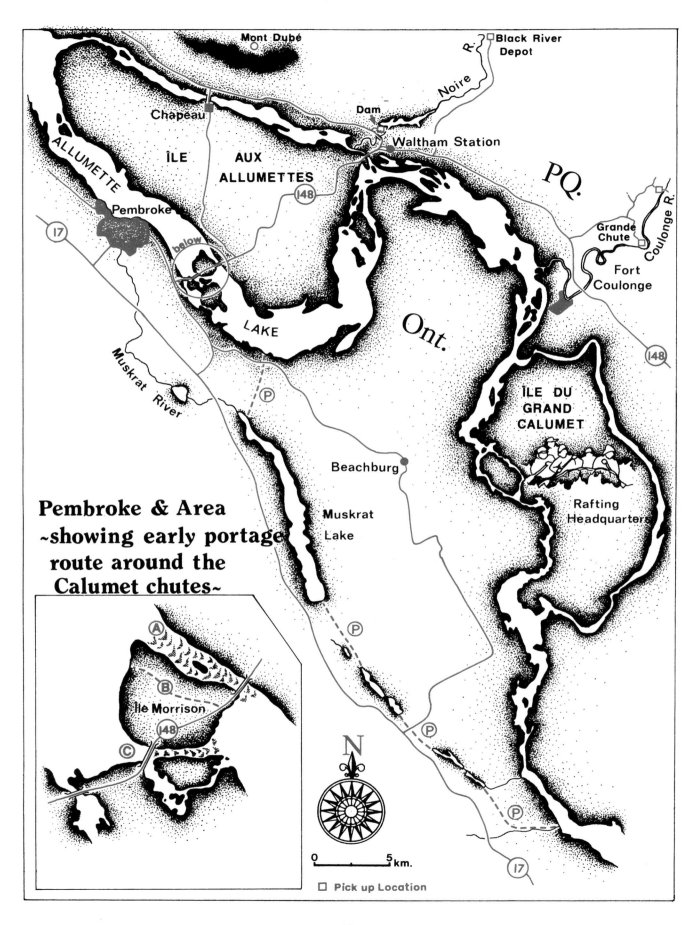

Black River Depot

Noire R.

Mont Dubé

Chapeau

ÎLE AUX ALLUMETTES

Dam

Waltham Station

P.Q.

148

Coulonge R.

Grande Chute

Fort Coulonge

148

17

Pembroke

ALLUMETTE

below

Ont.

Muskrat River

LAKE

ÎLE DU GRAND CALUMET

Rafting Headquarters

Beachburg

Muskrat Lake

Pembroke & Area ~showing early portage route around the Calumet chutes~

Ⓐ

Ⓑ

Île Morrison

148

Ⓒ

N

P

P

P

P

17

0   5 km.

☐ Pick up Location

Quebec's Triple Play

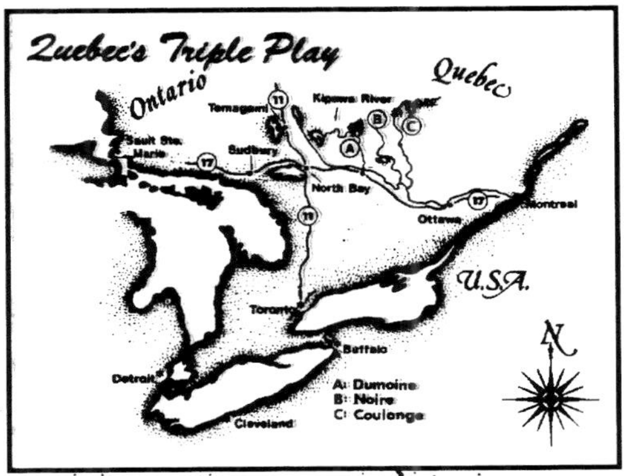

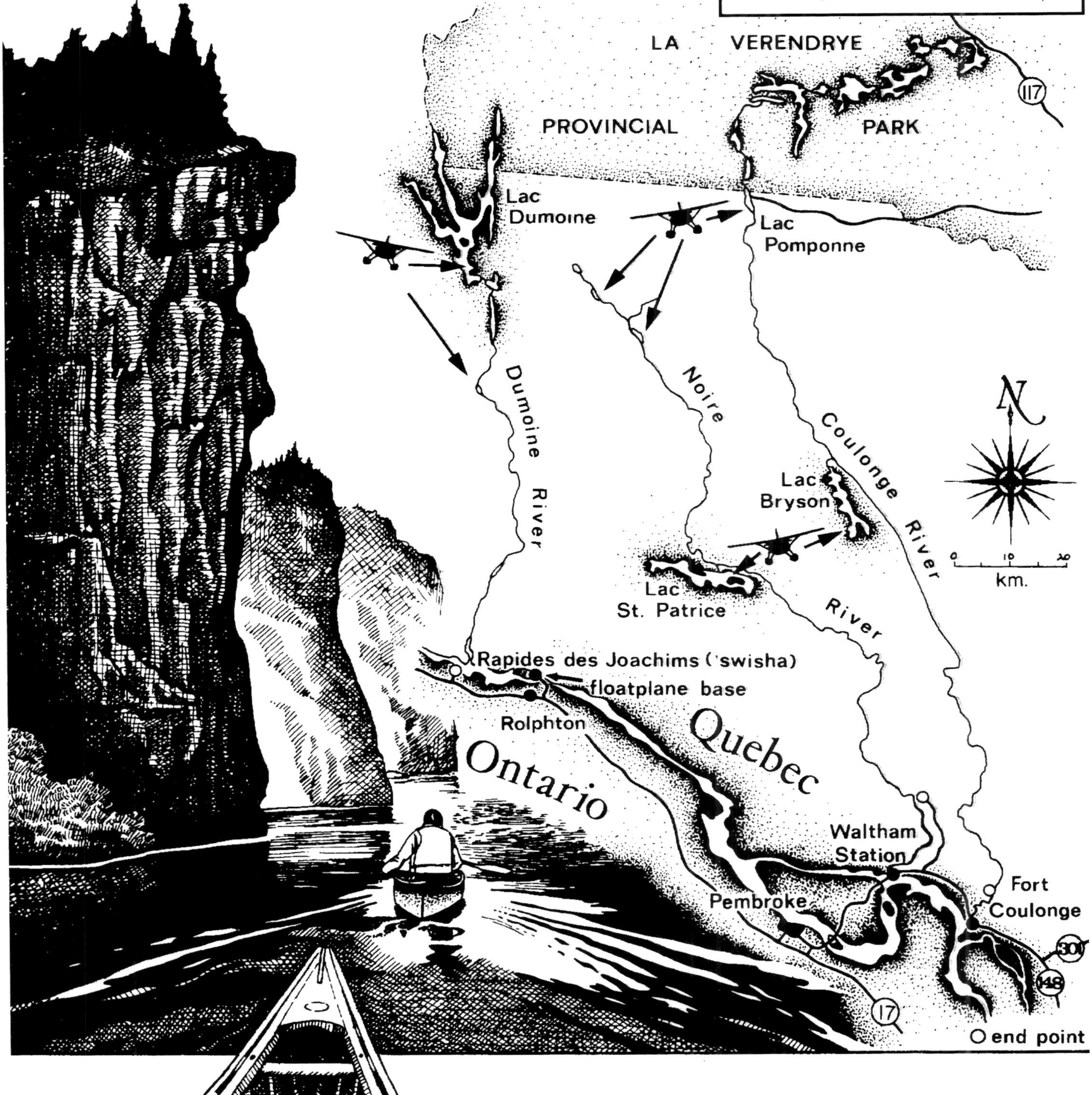

ELEVATION DROP CHART

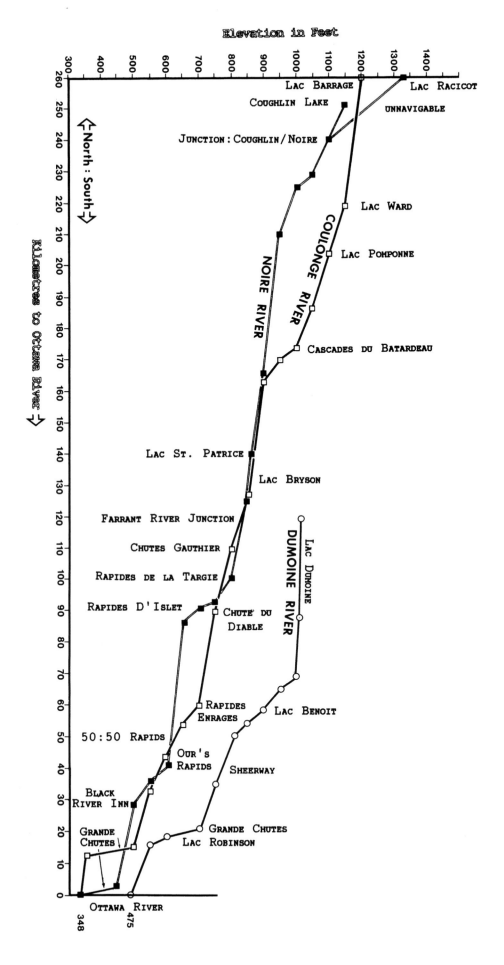

Elevation in Feet

Lac Barrage
Lac Racicot
Coughlin Lake
UNNAVIGABLE
Junction: Coughlin/Noire
Lac Ward
Lac Pomponne
COULONGE RIVER
NOIRE RIVER
Cascades du Batardeau
Lac St. Patrice
Lac Bryson
Farrant River Junction
Lac Dumoine
Chutes Gauthier
DUMOINE RIVER
Rapides de la Targie
Rapides D'Islet
Chute du Diable
Rapides Enrages
Lac Benoit
50:50 Rapids
Our's Rapids
Sheerway
Black River Inn
Grande Chutes
Grande Chutes
Lac Robinson
Ottawa River
348
475

← North : South →

Kilometres to Ottawa River →

AN ELEVATION DROP CHART is invaluable as a planning tool for assessing the difficulty of a whitewater river. The steeper the pitch, the more rapids, chutes and falls you will likely encounter. These grid drops will also indicate the more difficult rapids, the most portages and the longest travel days during your expedition. The amount of flatwater breaks can also be determined–this is an important factor to consider should you prefer a more leisure pace.

42

Rivière Dumoine

" ...but of course this is all in a days work for a guide.
Instantly dependable and above all honest and reliable, and to be able to
take care of any emergency, and to be able to paddle one hundred miles
should the occasion demand. This business of guiding calls for
real men, men and strong men only!"

**–From the Dumoine River Dairy of Michael J. Buckshott "Up Towards
the Height of Land with Camp Wabun for Boys" – Temagami, Ontario**

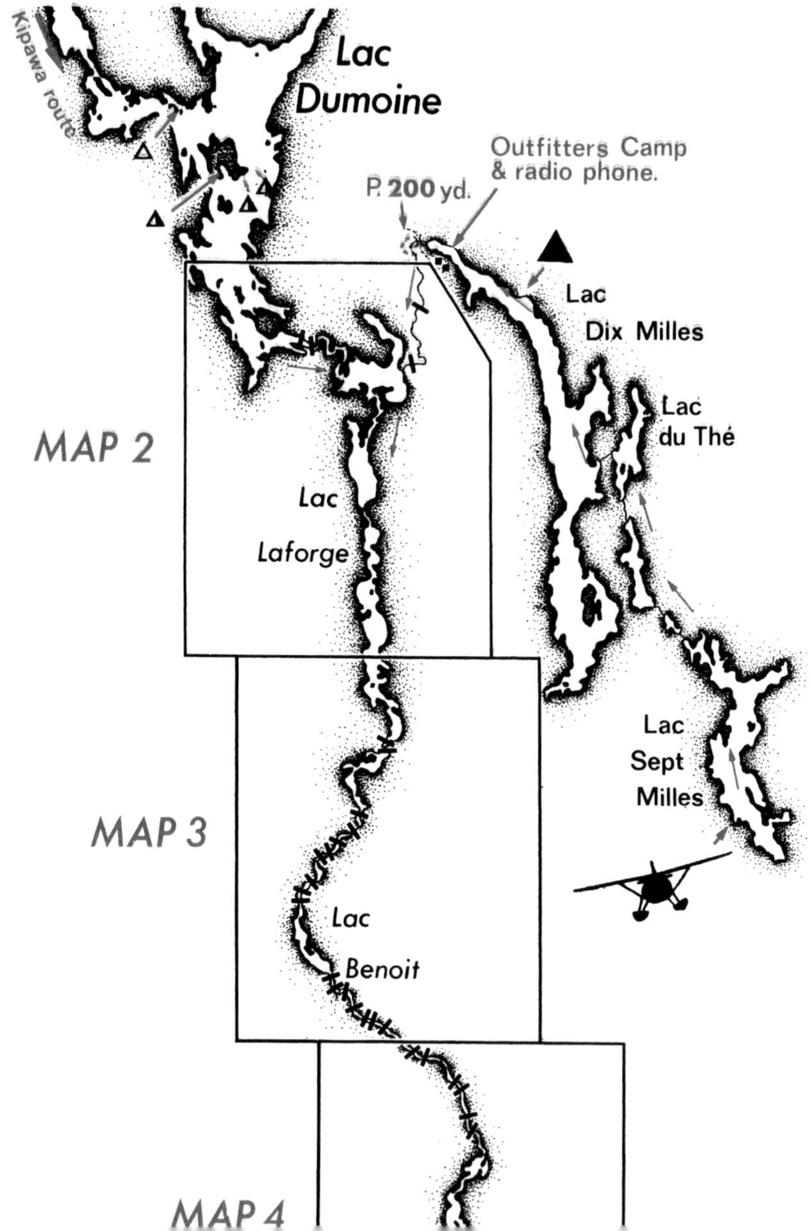

Rivière Dumoine
Map 1

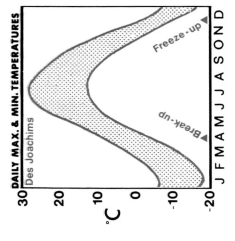

DAILY MAX. & MIN. TEMPERATURES

Des Joachims

Freeze-up ▶

◀ Break-up

°C 30 20 10 0 -10 -20

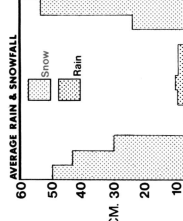

AVERAGE RAIN & SNOWFALL

▢ Snow ▢ Rain

J F M A M J J A S O N D

CM. 60 50 40 30 20 10

HOW TO USE THIS GUIDE:

The river is divided into 6 sections or roughly 6 days of travel time. Allowance is made for 1 rest day. Some river segments may require more travel time, for example; sections of the river taking the most to the least paddling time are as follows:

Map 3, 6, 4, 5, 2 and 7.

Fly-in starting points are:

14 day trips: Hunter's Point/Kipawa Route (access from Kipawa Airways)

8-9 day trips: Lac Sept Milles (access from Des Joachims)

7-8 day trips: Lac Dix Milles (as above)

7-8 day trips: Lower Lac Dumoine (as above – 1992 cost: $270.)

5-6 day trips: Lac Manitou (Des Joachims base)

4-5 day trips: Lac Laforge (as above – 1992 cost: $238.)

3-4 day trips: Lac Benoit (Des Joachims base)

Provisions for pick-up shuttles should be arranged prior to your flight in. Vehicles may be left at the air base in Des Joachims (D'Swisha), or Pine Valley Campground located directly across from the mouth of the Dumoine. Make sure that you check in at the camp before leaving your vehicle. Never assume that you can just leave your vehicle without notice. There are camping and showers available at the park and there is a nominal fee for these services.

Each map section as indicated, details river information according to the 1:50,000 topographic series charts and makes reference to specific maps relating to each river portion. Detailed or "inset" maps illustrate the more difficult or confusing rapids, portages and other key points.

For those paddling back to the airbase, allow an extra day's travel time from the Dumoine mouth to Des Joachims. Note the details shown below concerning the portage around the dam. A very pleasant paddle if the wind co-operates.

Lac Dumoine

Outfitters Camp & radio phone.

P. 200 yd.

▲ Lac Dix Milles

Lac du Thé

Lac Sept Milles

Lac Laforge

Lac Benoit

Kipawa route

MAP 2

MAP 3

MAP 4

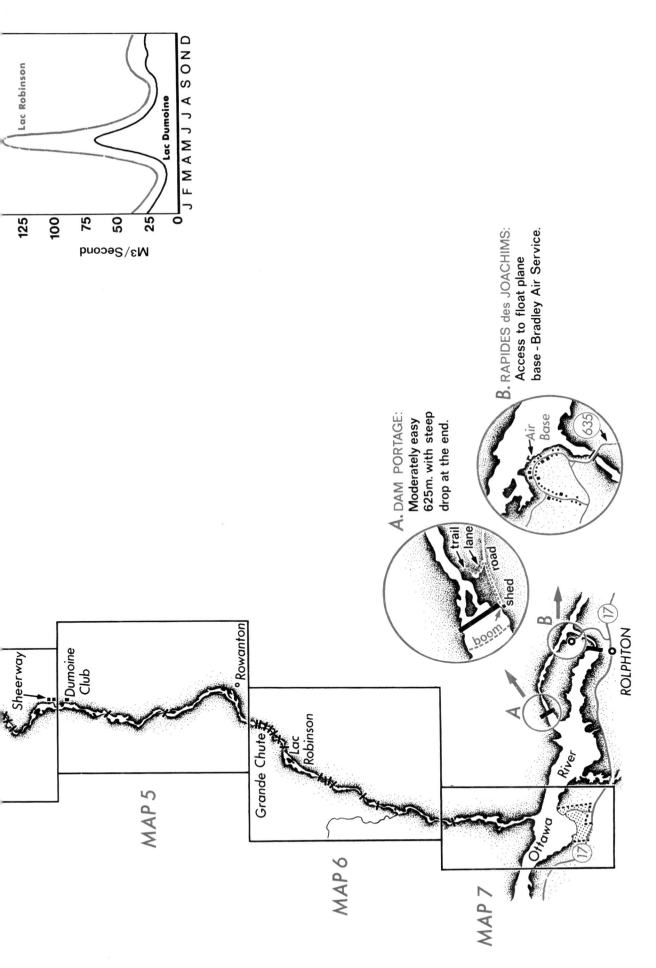

M3/Second

125 100 75 50 25 0

J F M A M J J A S O N D

Lac Robinson

Lac Dumoine

A. DAM PORTAGE:
Moderately easy
625m. with steep
drop at the end.

trail
lane
road
shed
boom

B. RAPIDES des JOACHIMS:
Access to float plane
base - Bradley Air Service.

Air
Base

635

Sheerway

Dumoine
Club

Rowanton

MAP 5

Grande Chute

Lac
Robinson

MAP 6

A

B

17

ROLPHTON

Ottawa
River

17

MAP 7

45

INFORMATION TO KNOW:

Classification: Intermediate

Total Distance: 90 km. (from Lac Dumoine south)

Vertical Drop: 500 ft. or 5.5'/km.

Days Required: 6-7

Number of Campsites: 1 per 2km. (Total: 46)

Number of Runnable Rapids: 39 (50% CI's)

Distance: Total-9km. or 10% of running distance.

Swifts: 7.5 km.

Total Distance Fast-Water: 16.5 km. or 18% of running distance.

PORTAGES:

Novice Intermediate: 13 portages (5,050 m.)

Creative Intermediate: 11 portages (2,795 m.) 55% reduction.

Attributes: Compared with the Noire and the Coulonge, the Dumoine has the most CII or greater rapids classification – an indication of overall vertical pitch when you look at the elevation drop chart on page 42. It also has the most campsites per kilometer which is an important factor for this Icon of whitewater rivers because of the summer traffic flow. Other positive factors include; highest scenic value, best over-all flow throughout the season and the most reasonable float-plane costs.

Negative Factors: High traffic flow (up to 50 parties per week during peak season, *this may change now having the Noire and Coulonge as options). The Dumoine also has the longest distance portages, some patchy sections of still water and the sometimes formidable Ottawa River crossing – all of which could be a deterrent from paddling the Dumoine.

Whitewater Characteristics: The Dumoine has earned its reputation through its well-advertised, boulder or rock-garden style rapids...challenging, steep drops with plenty of action. Longish CII's which are hard to scout, require additional caution, good ferrying skills and a dash of sporting blood.

Highwater Notes: CI's become voluminous CII's, rapids offer more options or channels, straighter and much smoother runs with less ferrying. Greater caution must be employed while running rapids above the many chutes or falls. This translates into longer portages.

Lowwater Notes: Bouldery rapids with definite but sometimes difficult main channels. More lining necessary and longish C II's become precarious as you try hard not to get hung up.

By the end of the century, lumbering was well established on the Dumoine and every spring the rapids were full of logs making their way

Riding the hump below Little Steel Falls

Autumn at Bald Rock

down to the Ottawa. Most of the lumbermen didn't know how to swim and death by drowning was common.

One year, for example, a boat upset at the bottom of Big Steel Rapids and the company paymaster died. He was buried at the bottom of the rapids and, as was customary, his boots were nailed to a tree above him. So many good boots were nailed to trees along the rivers that those who needed a new pair often traded in their own.

Settlement on the river had not kept pace with the growth of lumbering and coloni-zation had proceeded slowly in the Dumoine wilderness. Backwoods farmers, scratching at the few pockets of hillside soil, were able to produce the hay, oats and pork that the

timber industry needed. As road access from the outside improved, supplies for the timber camps were imported from further afield and one after the other, the farms along the Dumoine were abandoned.

Most of the farms that once stood on the banks of the Dumoine have long since dis-appeared into the bush. However, one farmstead survives though it is no longer worked – at Sheerway. It was owned at the turn of the century by one Adelard Sauve, whose wife was known in the region as an active trapper. Some years later, Charlie and Margaret Johnson bought the farm. Charlie acted as the "unofficial caretaker" of the upper end of the Dumoine Rod & Gun Club, esta-blished in 1918, and their fine old log house was for many years a refuge for sportsmen.

Charlie Johnson was killed in 1952 when his plane crashed into the mountain just north of the lodge. The club bought the house and land around it for $5,000., installed lights, plumbing and a gas refrigerator and made it the centre of their hunting and fishing activities.

Farming is a thing of the past on the Dumoine; trapping continues sporadically on a small scale; logging is still a major activity but canoeing seems to have taken premise over the last few years. Canoeing on the Dumoine is not a recreational newcomer. Since the early 1900s, boy's canoe camps such as Keewaydin and Wabun, based out of Lake Temagami, shared the Dumoine watershed with the loggers and other user groups.

DUMOINE RIVER DIARY

Lac Dumoine:

I remember my first trip down the Dumoine... I was paddling solo in a 16' kevlar prospector while my two friends paddled a newly constructed cedar/canvas. We had started at Hunter's Point, a week ago, generally heading north-east with the wind behind us. Now, as we turned south just above Ile Quabie, the wind was in our faces, relentless and unforgiving.

We were wind bound for a day...that wasn't so awful, and it was good karma to let tired muscles rejuvenate and write in my trip diary. Looking south from our small beach campsite you could view the abrupt track of hills that marked the edge of the Laurentian plateau

and the 100 km. descent to the Ottawa River. The deciduous growth that composed the low visage of Baie de Kipawa was now replaced by a welcomed landscape of craggy pine-covered slopes.

For its size, Lac Dumoine did not possess an abundance of established campsites; however, mine (and probably everyone else's) favourite campsite, has to be the one located before the first set of rapids on a longish point decked with second-growth pine–a great spot for an instruction/rest day stop-over. Just don't count on this site being vacant–there is one site that's not too bad just around the corner in the deep bay past the point.

The sound of the first set of rapids will ignite the adrenalin and initiate the long descent to the Ottawa River. It's a good primer, or practice rapid, then an easy carry around a small falls over a sandy trail to a large beaching area below–a fine spot for a trail lunch.

On the River:

The exhilaration of the first rapids was nurtured well into the meanders; we knew there would be no more fast water until tomorrow so we let the feeling permeate our chatter for several miles. The meanders, with its' secret ponds, is a good place to spot feeding moose and great blue herons. The sand banks were cloaked with yellow birch, spruces and white pine, certainly a landscape more indicative of a passive, somewhat tropical-type watercourse and not of a precambrian adventure route. The entrance

to Lac Brulart, a rather nondescript water body, was guarded by a steep esker, a remnant of the great ice age that shaped the Dumoine River valley.

Lac Laforge:

An interesting segmented lake with high hills and pine swathed points. Lac Laforge is a popular starting point for long weekend sprints and casual one week holidays. What better place to spend a flog day than "Alligator Point", a mallet-shaped peninsula complete with pine-canopied campsite and sand beach cove. There were unlimited, level tent sites carpeted with pine browse, much like many of the campsites in the Temagami region. On the beach just down from the campsite were the rusting skeletons of two "alligators" (a kind of amphibious logging "skidder") that were employed during the early river-drive days. Further along the shore was an old homestead clearing with cabins still intact.

The lake has many sand beaches that would serve as lunch or swimming stop locations or even as an emergency campsite. The island site across from Alligator Point was another good camping location.

I spent some time just laying in the warm sand and the sun covered me like a cozy blanket and I was lost in the music of the wind through the pines. It would be easy to spend many days right here...but there were more adventures ahead.

Dumoine Campsite...a blend of sand, rock & pine

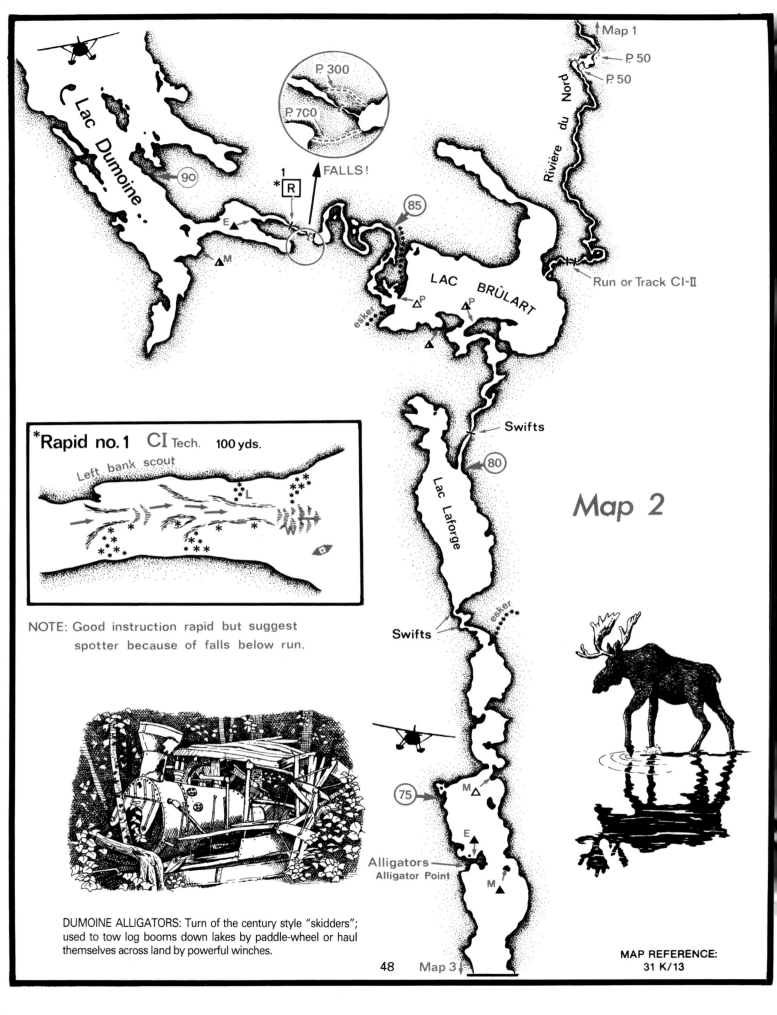

Map 1

P. 50
P. 50

Rivière du Nord

P. 300
P. 7C0

FALLS!

90

Lac Dumoine

*1 R

E

M

85

Run or Track CI-II

esker

LAC BRÛLART

P

P

Swifts

80

Lac Laforge

Map 2

*Rapid no. 1 CI Tech. 100 yds.

Left bank scout

L

W

NOTE: Good instruction rapid but suggest
spotter because of falls below run.

Swifts

esker

75

M

E

Alligators
Alligator Point

M

DUMOINE ALLIGATORS: Turn of the century style "skidders";
used to tow log booms down lakes by paddle-wheel or haul
themselves across land by powerful winches.

48   Map 3

MAP REFERENCE:
31 K/13

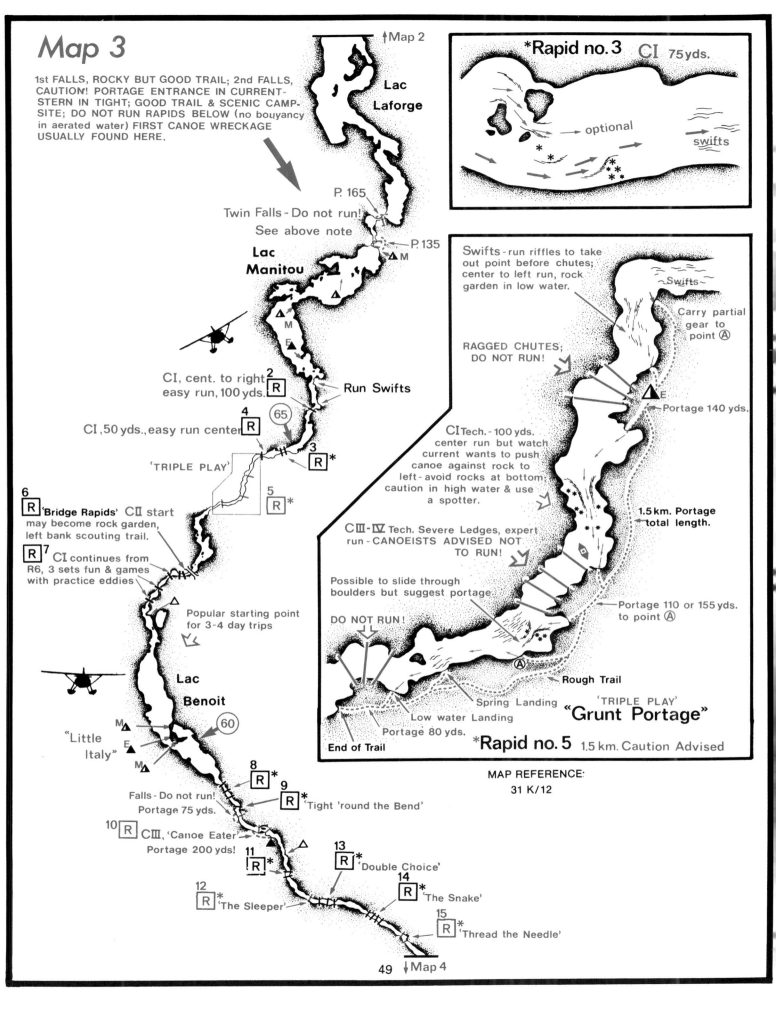

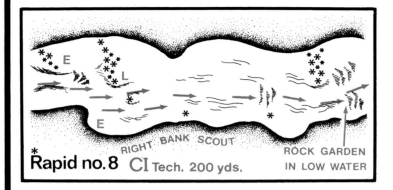

Rapid no. 8 CI Tech. 200 yds.

E L E

RIGHT BANK SCOUT

ROCK GARDEN IN LOW WATER

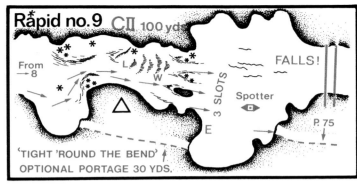

Rapid no. 9 CII 100 yds.

From 8

L W E

3 SLOTS

FALLS!

Spotter

P. 75

'TIGHT 'ROUND THE BEND'
OPTIONAL PORTAGE 30 YDS.

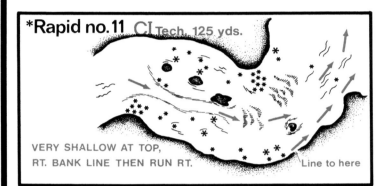

Rapid no. 11 CI Tech. 125 yds.

VERY SHALLOW AT TOP,
RT. BANK LINE THEN RUN RT.

Line to here

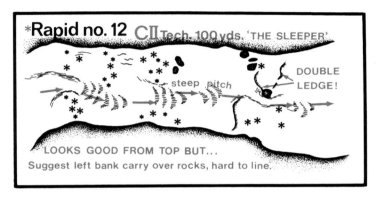

Rapid no. 12 CII Tech. 100 yds. 'THE SLEEPER'

steep pitch

DOUBLE LEDGE!

'LOOKS GOOD FROM TOP BUT...
Suggest left bank carry over rocks, hard to line.

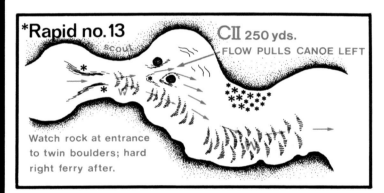

Rapid no. 13 CII 250 yds.

scout

W

FLOW PULLS CANOE LEFT

Watch rock at entrance
to twin boulders; hard
right ferry after.

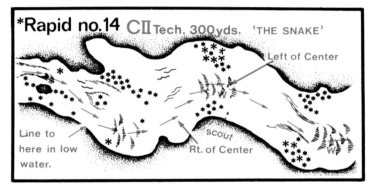

Rapid no. 14 CII Tech. 300 yds. 'THE SNAKE'

W

Left of Center

Line to
here in low
water.

scout

Rt. of Center

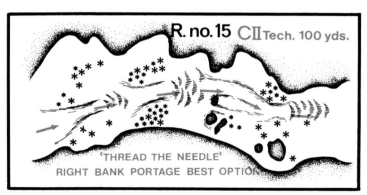

R. no. 15 CII Tech. 100 yds.

'THREAD THE NEEDLE'
RIGHT BANK PORTAGE BEST OPTION

THE LONGEST DAY

A dawn breakfast and hot black coffee generated the paddling machines and prepped us for a long day of portaging, scouting and river running. The portages at Twin Falls allowed us time to stretch tightened morning limbs; it also gave us the opportunity to examine the first carcass of a canoe below the second chute.

The run, tempting to some perhaps, clearly involved steep pitches and aerated water that renders any craft floatless. Possibly a fitting end to a department store canoe.

The "Grunt Portage" isn't as bad as you might perceive, just 'triple play' it. A 1 1/2 km trail can be whittled down to three short portages and a total of 350 yards but you still have to play your cards right! Portaging and scouting still absorbed a good deal of the day; the long run at "Bridge Rapids" sent us hurling into Lac Benoit in time to set up our next camp. The rapids below Lac Benoit, a series of CII's accounts for many lost canoes. The next section of river, as far as rapid #19, takes a lot of concentration. If it is getting late in the day then I would recommend camping on Benoit where there are several good sites. The next section of river, as far as rapid # 19. takes a lot of concentration.

If it is getting late in the day then I would recommend camping on Benoit where there are several good sites.

There is a good campsite below "Canoe Eater" but remember that it's a fair hike to the next one.

"Canoe Eater" is actually one of my personal favourite solo runs but I never let any of my clients attempt it—you'll always spot one or two broken canoe hulls on the rocks here.

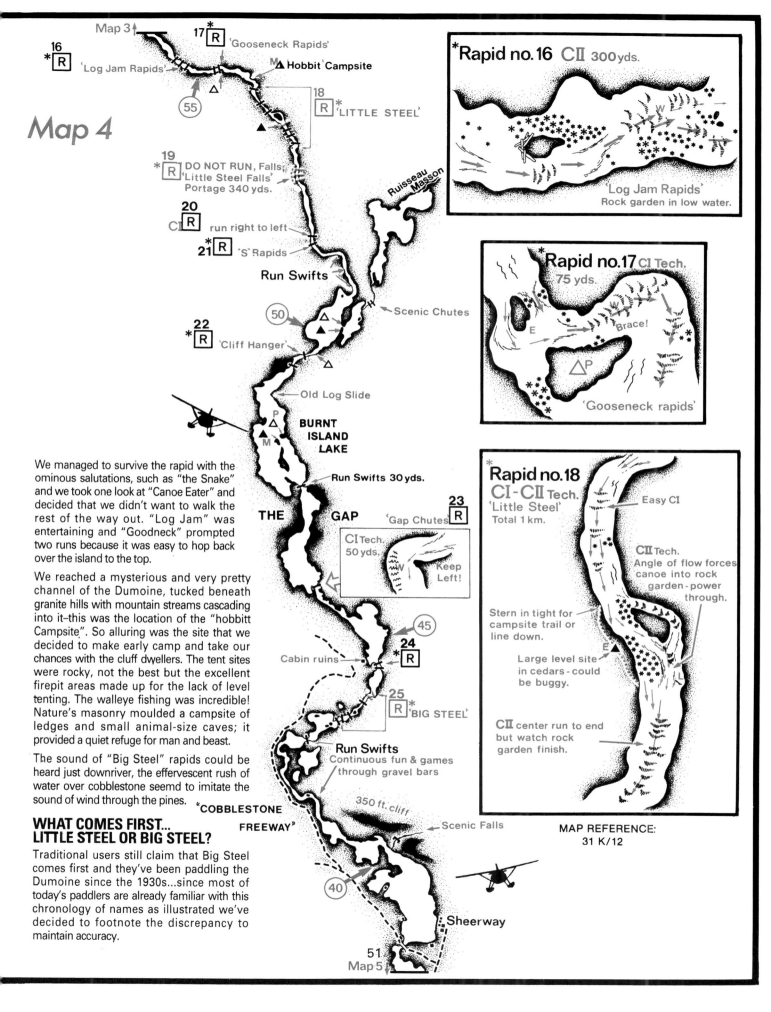

Map 3 ↑

*16 [R]
'Log Jam Rapids'

17 * [R]
'Gooseneck Rapids'
M ▲ Hobbit Campsite

(55)

18 [R] * 'LITTLE STEEL'

Map 4

Ruisseau Masson

19 * [R] DO NOT RUN, Falls;
'Little Steel Falls'
Portage 340 yds.

20 [R] run right to left
CI

21 [R] 'S' Rapids

Run Swifts

Scenic Chutes

(50)

22 * [R]
'Cliff Hanger'

Old Log Slide

P △
▲ M
BURNT
ISLAND
LAKE

Run Swifts 30 yds.

23 [R]
'Gap Chutes'

THE   GAP

(45)

24 * [R]

Cabin ruins

25 [R] * 'BIG STEEL'

Run Swifts
Continuous fun & games
through gravel bars

"COBBLESTONE
FREEWAY"

350 ft. cliff

Scenic Falls

(40)

Sheerway

51
Map 5 ↓

We managed to survive the rapid with the ominous salutations, such as "the Snake" and we took one look at "Canoe Eater" and decided that we didn't want to walk the rest of the way out. "Log Jam" was entertaining and "Goodneck" prompted two runs because it was easy to hop back over the island to the top.

We reached a mysterious and very pretty channel of the Dumoine, tucked beneath granite hills with mountain streams cascading into it–this was the location of the "hobbitt Campsite". So alluring was the site that we decided to make early camp and take our chances with the cluff dwellers. The tent sites were rocky, not the best but the excellent firepit areas made up for the lack of level tenting. The walleye fishing was incredible! Nature's masonry moulded a campsite of ledges and small animal-size caves; it provided a quiet refuge for man and beast.

The sound of "Big Steel" rapids could be heard just downriver, the effervescent rush of water over cobblestone seemd to imitate the sound of wind through the pines.

WHAT COMES FIRST...
LITTLE STEEL OR BIG STEEL?

Traditional users still claim that Big Steel comes first and they've been paddling the Dumoine since the 1930s...since most of today's paddlers are already familiar with this chronology of names as illustrated we've decided to footnote the discrepancy to maintain accuracy.

*Rapid no. 16 CII 300 yds.
'Log Jam Rapids'
Rock garden in low water.

*Rapid no. 17 CI Tech.
75 yds.
E   W   Brace!
△ P
'Gooseneck rapids'

CI Tech.
50 yds.
W   Keep Left!

*Rapid no. 18
CI-CII Tech.
'Little Steel'
Total 1 km.

Easy CI

CII Tech.
Angle of flow forces
canoe into rock
garden - power
through.

Stern in tight for
campsite trail or
line down.

E   L

Large level site
in cedars - could
be buggy.

CII center run to end
but watch rock
garden finish.

MAP REFERENCE:
31 K/12

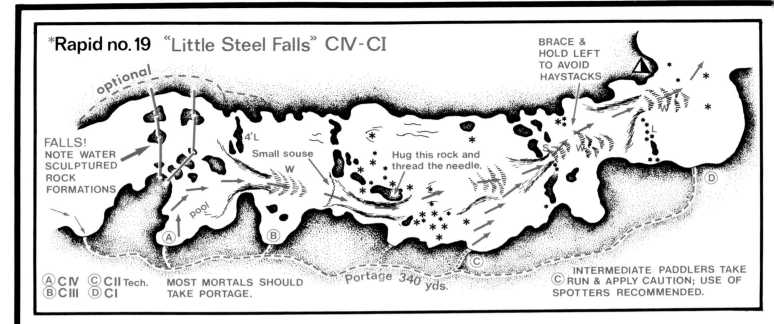

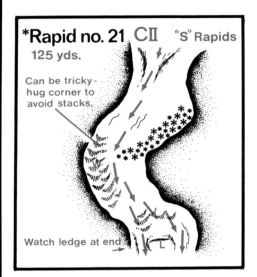

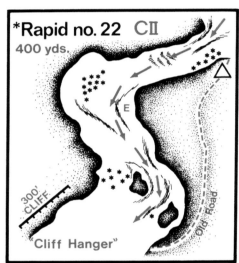

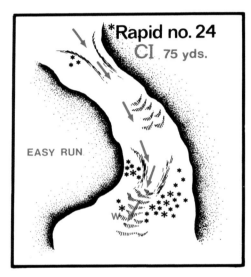

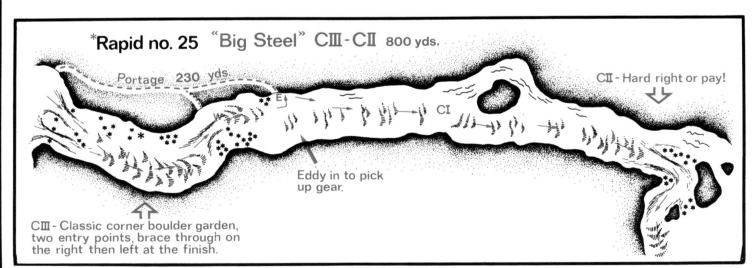

TAKE YOUR TIME AND ENJOY

If you've managed to make it this far then you've come half way. Remember, it's still a long way out; if you find that you're behind schedule–DON'T PUSH IT!

Most accidents are by-products from bad judgement due to fatigue. Pace yourself according to energy level and your weakest paddler. You should have allowed yourself at least one extra day for delays, bad weather or for the sake of sheer enjoyment.

Map 5

Map 4↑

Margaret Spry Shelter

E

Dumoine Club

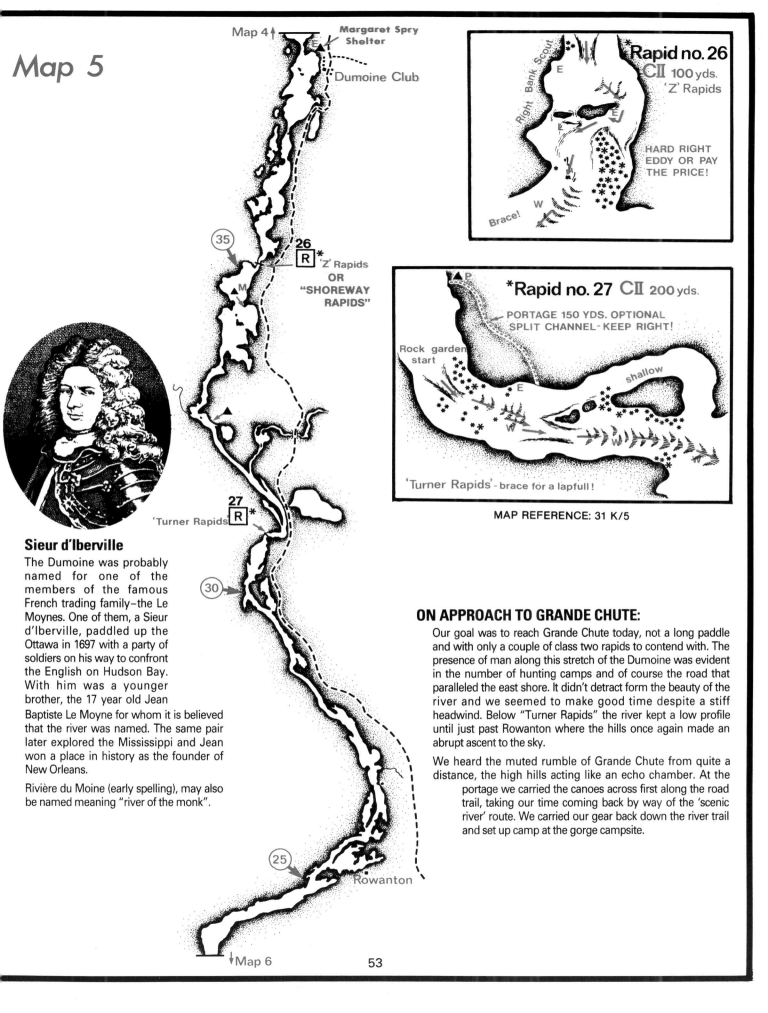

35

26
R * 'Z' Rapids
OR
"SHOREWAY
RAPIDS"

M

27
R *
'Turner Rapids'

30

25

Rowanton

↓Map 6

Rapid no. 26
CII 100 yds.
'Z' Rapids

Right Bank Scout

E

E

Z

Z

W

Brace!

HARD RIGHT
EDDY OR PAY
THE PRICE!

*Rapid no. 27 CII 200 yds.

P

PORTAGE 150 YDS. OPTIONAL
SPLIT CHANNEL - KEEP RIGHT!

Rock garden
start

E

shallow

W

W

'Turner Rapids' - brace for a lapfull!

MAP REFERENCE: 31 K/5

Sieur d'Iberville

The Dumoine was probably named for one of the members of the famous French trading family–the Le Moynes. One of them, a Sieur d'Iberville, paddled up the Ottawa in 1697 with a party of soldiers on his way to confront the English on Hudson Bay. With him was a younger brother, the 17 year old Jean Baptiste Le Moyne for whom it is believed that the river was named. The same pair later explored the Mississippi and Jean won a place in history as the founder of New Orleans.

Rivière du Moine (early spelling), may also be named meaning "river of the monk".

ON APPROACH TO GRANDE CHUTE:

Our goal was to reach Grande Chute today, not a long paddle and with only a couple of class two rapids to contend with. The presence of man along this stretch of the Dumoine was evident in the number of hunting camps and of course the road that paralleled the east shore. It didn't detract form the beauty of the river and we seemed to make good time despite a stiff headwind. Below "Turner Rapids" the river kept a low profile until just past Rowanton where the hills once again made an abrupt ascent to the sky.

We heard the muted rumble of Grande Chute from quite a distance, the high hills acting like an echo chamber. At the portage we carried the canoes across first along the road trail, taking our time coming back by way of the 'scenic river' route. We carried our gear back down the river trail and set up camp at the gorge campsite.

Map 6

MURDER ON THE DUMOINE!

At the ZEC station depot at Grande Chute, the couple operating the base kept a subsistence farm on the island above the falls, which included a small garden, a hen coop and even three goats . On my last trip through I didn't notice any goats – that's because a timber wolf swam the channel and killed the animals.

The young farmer kept a patient vigil, rifle nearby, waiting for a chat or buy a couple of chocolate bars. (1988)

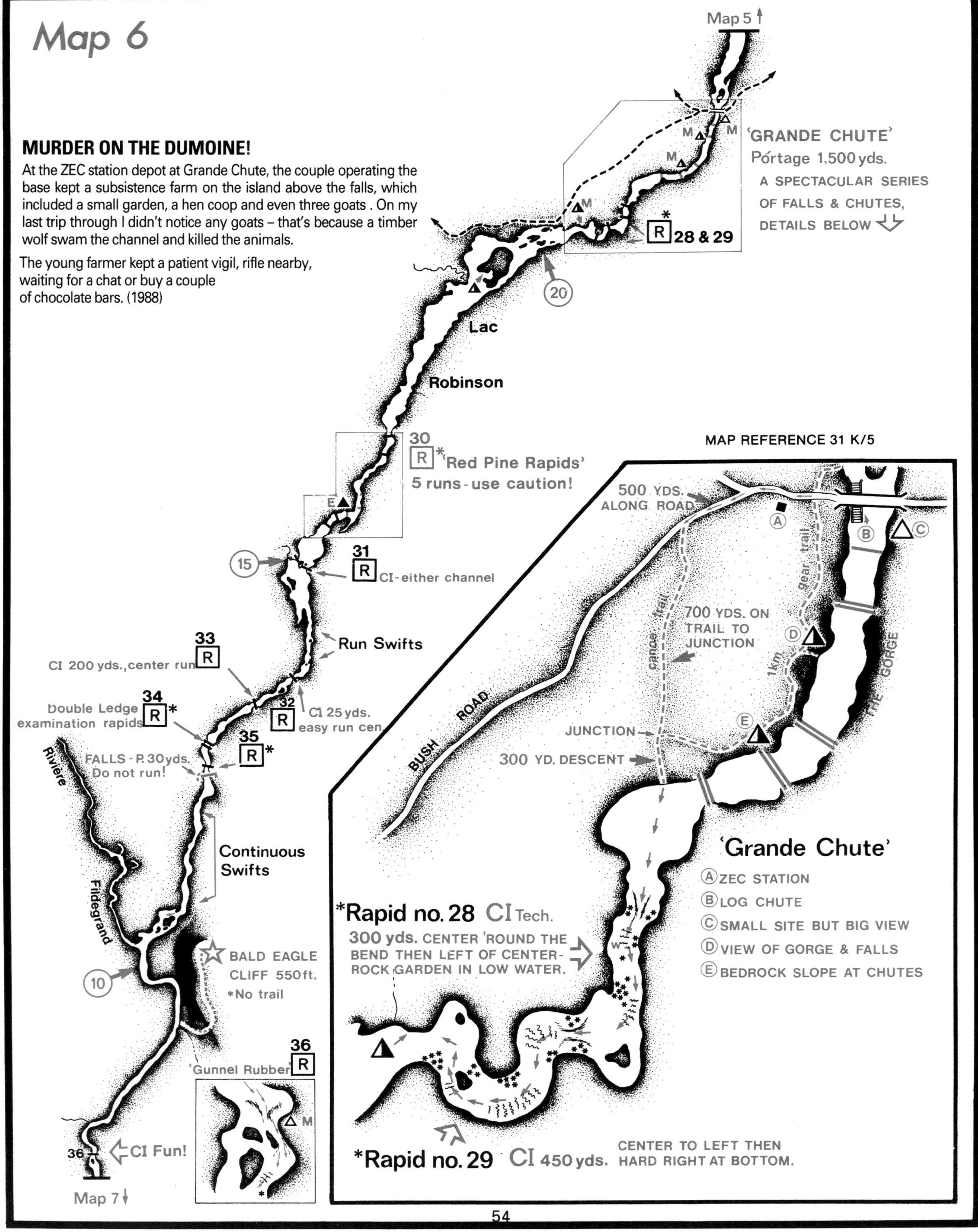

Map 5 ↑

M

M

M

M

△ M

'GRANDE CHUTE'
Pórtage 1,500 yds.

A SPECTACULAR SERIES
OF FALLS & CHUTES,
DETAILS BELOW ↓

R **28 & 29**

(20)

Lac

Robinson

30
R * 'Red Pine Rapids'
5 runs - use caution!

E △

(15) →

31
R CI - either channel

→ Run Swifts

33
R
CI 200 yds., center run

34
R *
Double Ledge
examination rapids

32
R
CI 25 yds.
easy run cen.

35
R *
FALLS - P. 30 yds.
Do not run!

Continuous
Swifts

Rivière

Fildegrand

(10) →

☆ BALD EAGLE
CLIFF 550 ft.
*No trail

36
R
Gunnel Rubber

36 ← CI Fun!

△ M

Map 7 ↓

MAP REFERENCE 31 K/5

500 YDS.
ALONG ROAD →

Ⓐ

gear trail

Ⓑ

△ Ⓒ

canoe trail

700 YDS. ON
TRAIL TO
JUNCTION →

Ⓓ △

1 km

THE GORGE

JUNCTION →

Ⓔ △

300 YD. DESCENT →

'Grande Chute'

Ⓐ ZEC STATION
Ⓑ LOG CHUTE
Ⓒ SMALL SITE BUT BIG VIEW
Ⓓ VIEW OF GORGE & FALLS
Ⓔ BEDROCK SLOPE AT CHUTES

BUSH ROAD

***Rapid no. 28** CI Tech.
300 yds. CENTER 'ROUND THE
BEND THEN LEFT OF CENTER-
ROCK GARDEN IN LOW WATER.

△

***Rapid no. 29** CI 450 yds.
CENTER TO LEFT THEN
HARD RIGHT AT BOTTOM.

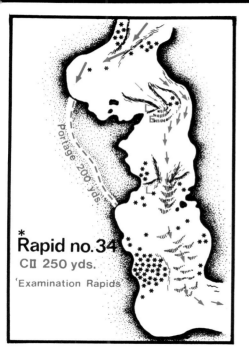

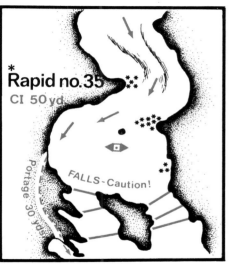

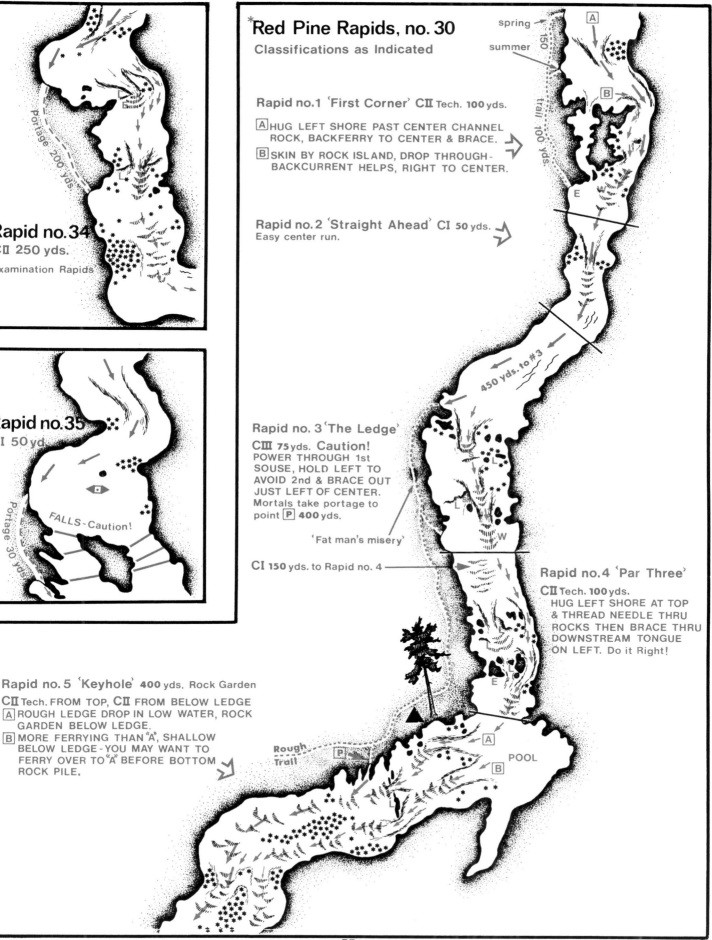

*Red Pine Rapids, no. 30

Classifications as Indicated

Rapid no.1 'First Corner' CII Tech. **100** yds.

A HUG LEFT SHORE PAST CENTER CHANNEL ROCK, BACKFERRY TO CENTER & BRACE.

B SKIN BY ROCK ISLAND, DROP THROUGH— BACKCURRENT HELPS, RIGHT TO CENTER.

Rapid no. 2 'Straight Ahead' CI **50** yds.
Easy center run.

Rapid no. 3 'The Ledge'

CIII **75** yds. Caution!
POWER THROUGH 1st SOUSE, HOLD LEFT TO AVOID 2nd & BRACE OUT JUST LEFT OF CENTER. Mortals take portage to point P **400** yds.

'Fat man's misery'

CI **150** yds. to Rapid no. 4

Rapid no. 4 'Par Three'

CII Tech. **100** yds.
HUG LEFT SHORE AT TOP & THREAD NEEDLE THRU ROCKS THEN BRACE THRU DOWNSTREAM TONGUE ON LEFT. Do it Right!

Rapid no. 5 'Keyhole' **400** yds. Rock Garden

CII Tech. FROM TOP, CII FROM BELOW LEDGE
A ROUGH LEDGE DROP IN LOW WATER, ROCK GARDEN BELOW LEDGE.
B MORE FERRYING THAN "A", SHALLOW BELOW LEDGE - YOU MAY WANT TO FERRY OVER TO "A" BEFORE BOTTOM ROCK PILE.

Rough Trail

POOL

spring
summer
150
trail 100 yds.

450 yds. to #3

*Rapid no.34
CII 250 yds.

'Examination Rapids

*Rapid no.35
CI 50 yd.

FALLS-Caution!

Portage 200 yds.

Portage 30 yds

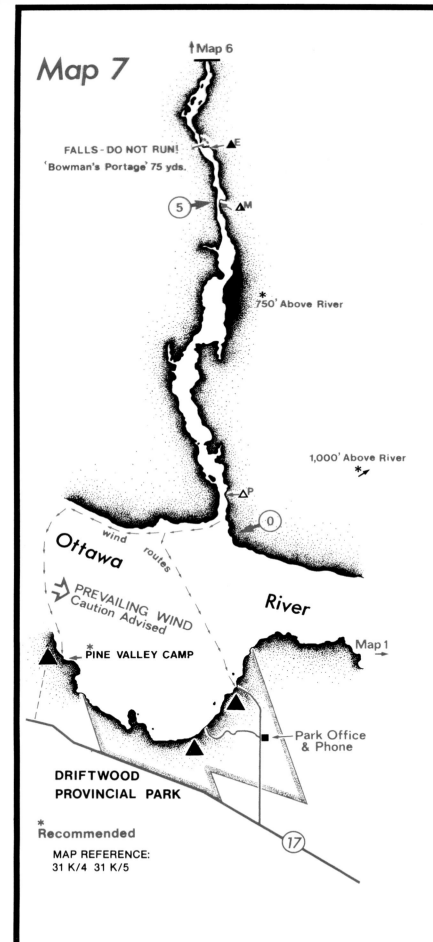

Map 7

↑Map 6

FALLS - DO NOT RUN!
'Bowman's Portage' 75 yds.

▲E

⑤→ ▲M

* **750' Above River**

* **1,000' Above River**
*↗

△P

⓪

Ottawa

wind routes

⇨ PREVAILING WIND
Caution Advised

River

Map 1 →

* **PINE VALLEY CAMP**

■→ Park Office
& Phone

**DRIFTWOOD
PROVINCIAL PARK**

* **Recommended**

MAP REFERENCE:
31 K/4 31 K/5

⑰

WINDING DOWN—The Last Leg:

From Grande Chute, through the Red Pine rapids and up to the junction of the Fildegrande took the better part of the day. We did allow ourselves three hours to climb Bald Eagle Cliff, a climax to our Dumoine trip. About 1.2 km past the river bend was a small creek, this was where we decided to start our climb.

The rock face was out of the question–a perfect rapelling cliff all the same. Even with tackling the low end of the cliff there were still enough precipitous ascents to make it interesting and challenging. There was no designated trail but progress was steady and unhindered right to the top. A magnificent view of the country we just paddled through certainly was worth the toil of the climb. That night we made camp at "Bowman's Portage" and celebrated our last evening on the Dumoine.

The following morning, after packing up, the wind began to blow steadily from the northwest; a bad sign as that would ultimately produce heavy rollers on the Ottawa. From the mouth of the Dumoine across to Driftwood Park there was 2 1/2 km of open water – a stretch where the wind had many miles to rally forces. Don't get fooled...it's generally calm going the first few hundred strokes until you get into the full force of the wind.

We pulled into shore before the crossing and rigged two canoes up 'catamaran-style' leaving about two feet between the boats to allow for wave surge.

The two poles were tightly secured behind both pairs of seats and we left a pot out for an emergency bailer, then headed out. By the time we reached the center of the Ottawa we were surfing 4-5 ft swells, paddling parallel to the waves during the lulls. It did help considerably hugging the Quebec shore then cutting out into the main flow so that we could use the wind to a better advantage. At times the ropes strained as we dipped and crested the growing waves; we took in water but not enough to be concerned about. I ruddered the craft while the other paddlers bore into the waves at timed strokes and we slid into the beach at Driftwood in no time at all. It would have been impossible to cross any other way.

Our adventure over, we pack up for the ride home and we're already planning our next trip down the Dumoine, or maybe the Noire, or Coulonge...

The Kipawa River

HUNTERS POINT TO LAC DUMOINE – 14 DAY EXPEDITION

For the more adventuresome paddler this 220 km route blends clearwater lake paddling with some exciting whitewater along the Kipawa River. Canoeists have the option to embark directly from the village of Kipawa (add 2 extra days) or avoid motorboats and big lake travel by flying directly to Hunter's Point by using Kipawa Air Charter Service.

Reminders of early timbering and settlement are clearly evident, not just in the ghost-town village of Hunters Point but also the old marine railways paralleling the portages up to Lac Pommeroy. The beautiful Laurentian landscape surrounding Lac Pommeroy makes it a popular first night camping spot. There are several excellent sites from which to select.

Prevailing winds often favour route direction from west to east, portages are not difficult and easy to locate. Scenery is diverse from steep sloped deciduous hills to low wetland marshes where wildlife is abundant. Canoe traffic is generally low throughout the season but there is some motorboat activity on the larger or more accessible lakes.

KIPAWA RIVER

Canoeists favouring the quick route to the Dumoine have the option of crossing Lac Watson instead of taking the downstream leg of the Kipawa River. This shaves two days off your trip. You do miss out on some good primer rapids and interesting countryside.

When entering the Kipawa River there is an easy chute between old bridge pilings and then a 5 km paddle down to the beginning of a series of class I and II rapids.

The lower part of the Kipawa to Rapides Elliot is quite scenic, hemmed in by a high bluff along the east bank. The upstream leg following Rivière du Pin Blanc requires some wading and lining but most of the swifts can be poled or paddled up without difficulty. Look for moose and wildfowl through the Ruissea Bog; keep your cameras handy and keep the 'gunnel-rubbers' quiet and you might get lucky.

The island campsite on Lac Divide (at the height between two watersheds) is a good place to pitch camp, break for lunch or swim. The creek outlet may be shallow but it is passable throughout the season with two short carries mandatory.

The upstream leg of the Kipawa necessitates some lining but again there is nothing difficult with which to contend except strong current in the early spring.

Baie de Kipawa (Lac Dumoine) keeps a low profile through an extensive bog area and it is evident that this is a popular spot for the fall hunter. There are a few campsites along the bog but some of the small cove beaches (gravel) can be used as makeshift campsites. As you paddle towards the heart of Lac Dumoine the scenery adopts the typical Laurentian highland appearance. It took a week to get this far, muscles are well primed, old paddling calluses are hardened and we're ready for the descent on the Dumoine.

A break for Bush Coffee

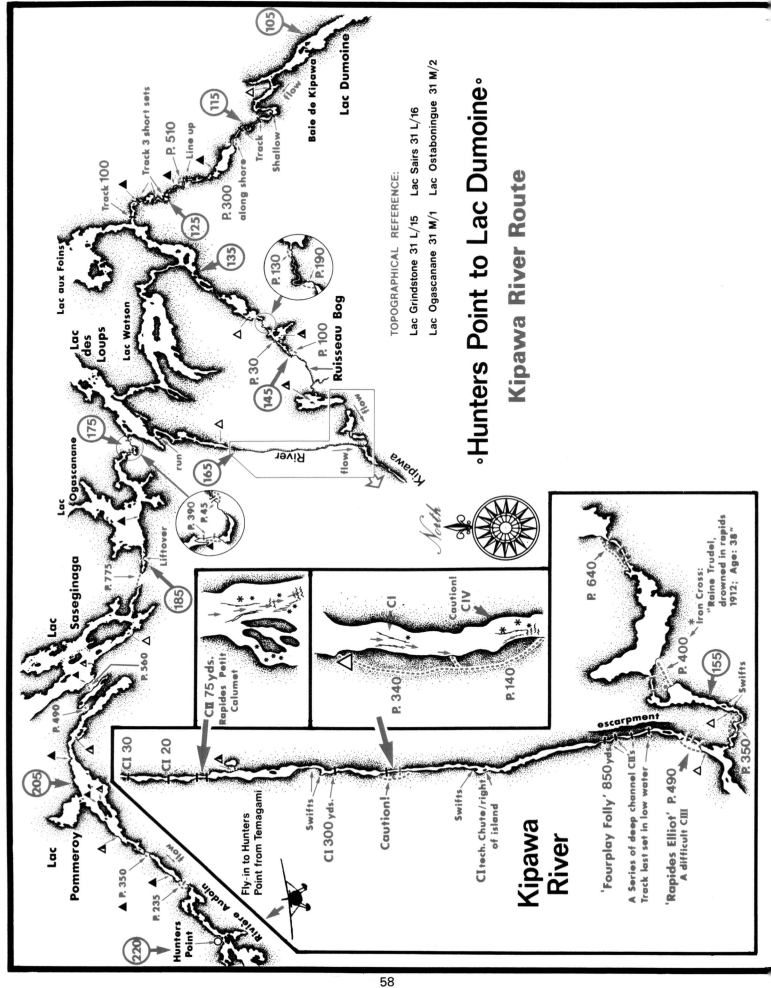

°Hunters Point to Lac Dumoine°

Kipawa River Route

Lac Dumoine

Baie de Kipawa

⊿ (105)

(115) Line up
P. 510
Track 3 short sets
Track 100
Track along shore
P. 300 Shallow
Track

TOPOGRAPHICAL REFERENCE:
Lac Grindstone 31 L/15   Lac Sairs 31 L/16
Lac Ogascanane 31 M/1   Lac Ostaboningue 31 M/2

Lac aux Foins

(125)

(135)

P. 130
P. 190

Lac des Loups

Lac Watson

P. 30
(145)
P. 100
Ruisseau Bog
⊿
⊿

Moll

⊿

Lac Ogascanane

(175)

run

(165)
River
flow
Kipawa

P. 390
P. 45
⊿

Lac Saseginaga

Liftover

P. 775

(185)

North

P. 640

Iron Cross:
*"Raine Trudel,
drowned in rapids
1912; Age: 38"

P. 400

CII 75 yds.
Rapides Petit
Calumet

CI

Caution!
CIV

P. 340

P. 140

(155)
Swifts

P. 560
⊿
⊿

P. 490

CI 30
CI 20
⊿

escarpment

P. 350

(205)

Swifts

CI 300 yds.

Caution!

Swifts

⊿

CI tech. Chute/right
of island

Kipawa River

'Fourplay Folly' 850yds.

A Series of deep channel CII's
Track last set in low water

'Rapides Elliot' P.490
A difficult CIII

Lac Pommeroy

⊿

P. 350
P. 235
⊿

Moll

Rivière Audoin

Fly-in to Hunters
Point from Temagami

(220) Hunters Point

Rivière Noire

*"A while on your patience I beg to intrude
I hired with Fitzgerald. He's agent for Booth
To go up on Black River so far away
To the old Caldwell farm to cut and make hay."*

**–Traditional Song, 2nd Verse,
"The Chapeau Boys"**

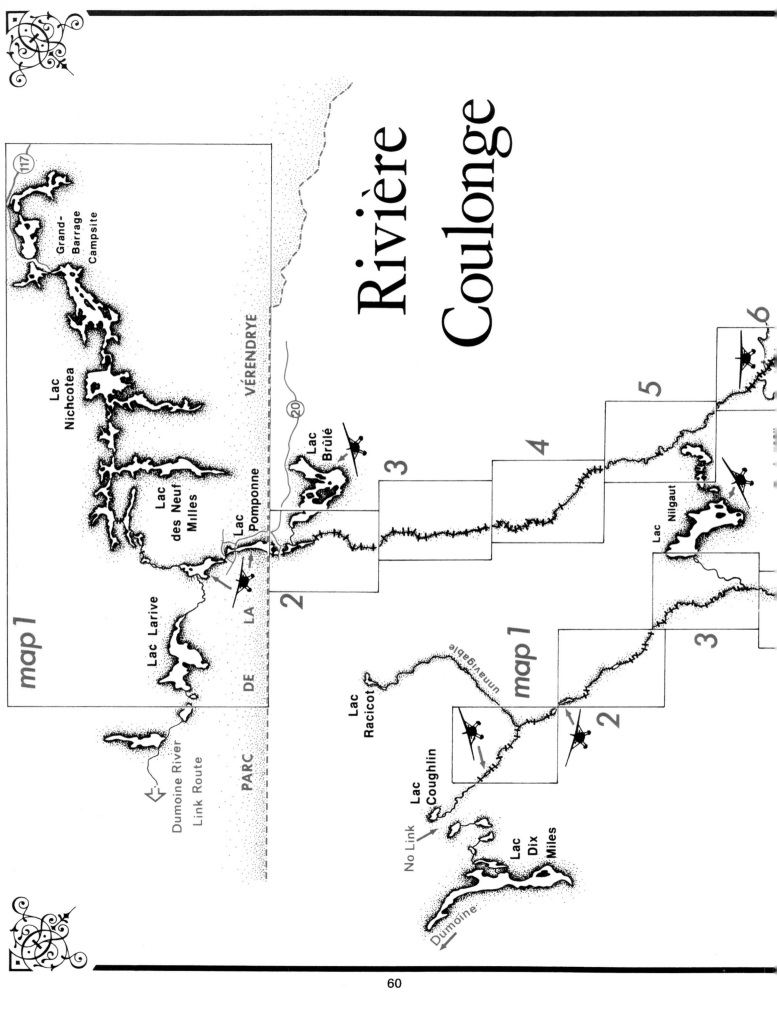

Rivière Coulonge

map 1

117

Grand-
Barrage
Campsite

Lac
Nichcotea

Lac
des Neuf
Milles

Lac
Pomponne

Lac Larive

VÉRENDRYE

PARC   DE   LA

20

Lac
Brûlé

1

2

3

4

5

6

Dumoine River
Link Route

map 1

Lac
Racicot

unnavigable

Lac
Coughlin

No Link

Lac
Dix
Miles

Dumoine

2

3

Lac
Nilgaut

Rivière Noire

HOW TO USE THIS MAP

The Noire and the Coulonge rivers have been divided into map segments much similar to the method employed for the Dumoine river description. Each map segment represents a particular section of the river, drawn from the 1:50,000 topographic series maps. It can also be interpreted in approximate days to complete your trip. Weather and flow charts for both the Noire and Coulonge are similar to the Dumoine (see page 46).

You can use this map to calculate which trip best suits your schedule, and as a guide to help organize appropriate flight and vehicle shuttles. Make sure that you allow at least one extra day per week's travel for possible delays incurred.

This map also indicates the link-up with the Dumoine River through Réserve Founique La Vérendrye, as it pertains to the access along the Coulonge headwater lakes. For more detail on this or to obtain canoe route maps, contact: Fédération Québecoise du canot-camping inc., 4545, av. Pierre-de-Coubertin, C.P. 1000, Succursale M, Montréal, P.Q. H1V 3R2.

Bryson

Lac Lynch

Lac Forant

Lac Raymond

Lac St.-Patrice

Lac Wright

Lac Jim

Quebec

Fort William

Chapeau

Waltham Station

Fort Coulonge

PEMBROKE

4 5 6 7 8 9 10 11 12 13

N

0 5 10 15 20 30 km.
0 10 20 20 mi.

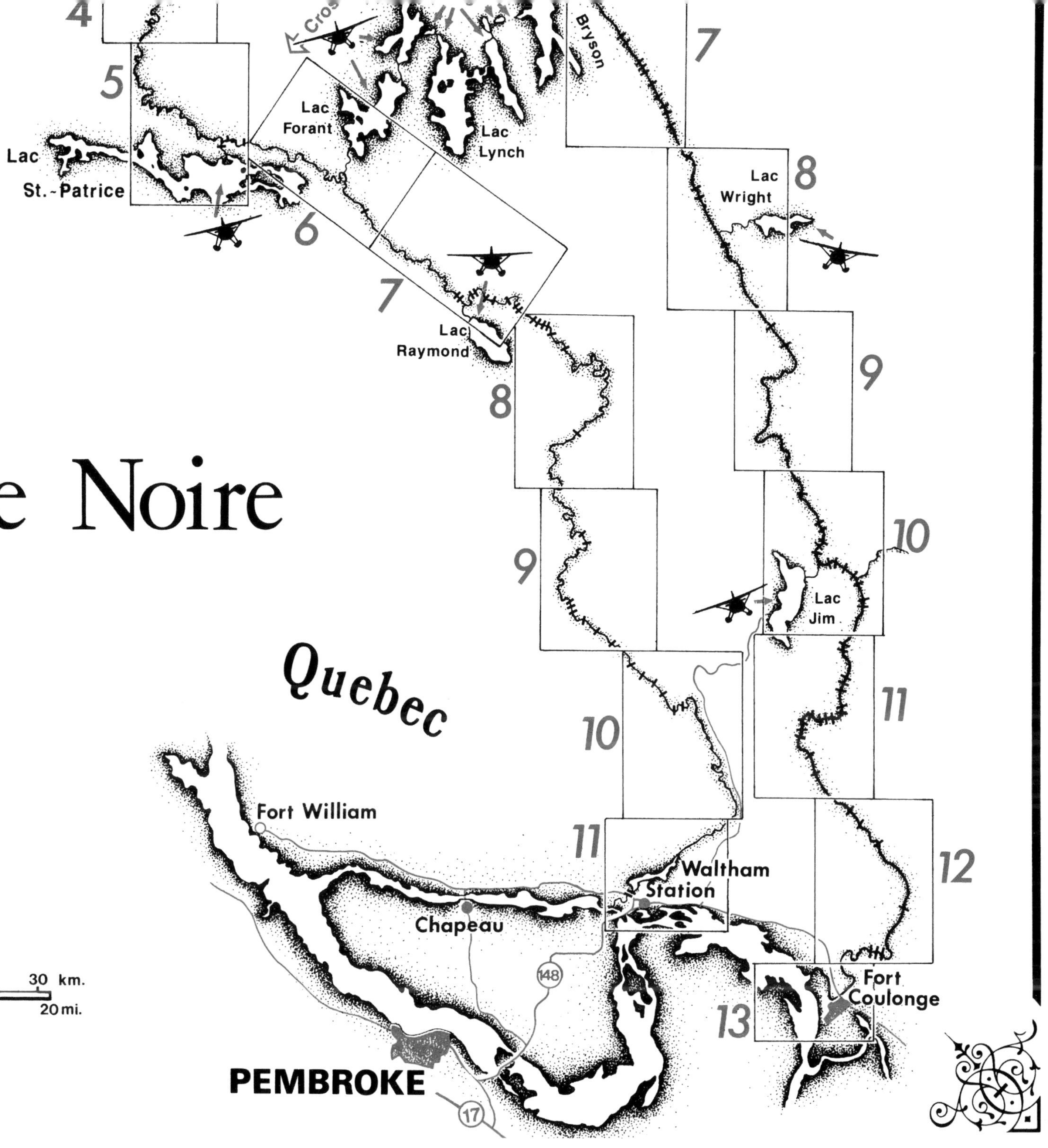

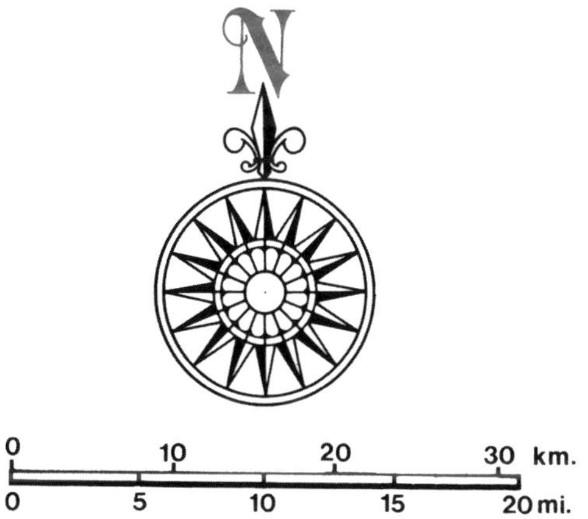

INFORMATION TO KNOW:

Classification: Upper: novice intermediate, Lower: Intermediate

Total Distance: 255 kilometers (from Coughlin Lake)

Practical Distance: 245 kilometers (Coughlin Ck. to Grande Chute)

Vertical Drop: 750 feet (including Grande Chute) 3.1'/km.

Days Required: 10 to 12

Number of Campsites: 1 per 5 km. (total: 43)*excludes many beach sites

Number of Runnable Rapids: 51 (60% CI's)

Distance: total 22 km. or 9.5% of total river distance.

Swifts: 5 kilometers

Total Distance Fast-Water: 27 km. (11.5% of total river distance)

PORTAGES:

Novice Intermediate: 12 portages (3,700 meters)

Creative Intermediate: 10 portages (1,625 meters) 55% reduction

Attributes: Compared with the Dumoine or Coulonge, the Noire has the highest total running length of rapids, the lowest distance of portages, the best opportunities to view wildlife, the lowest traffic, and offers the paddler the most seclusion value.

Negative Factors: Although picturesque, the Noire rates third of the three Quebec rivers and paddlers may find the upper river meanders monotonous. There is a lack of "traditional" open-water as typically found along shield-type rivers (pond-drop), and the Noire poses the greatest problems for emergency evacuation.

Whitewater Characteristics: Mostly shallow rapids along the northern stretch until Lac St. Patrice. During the summer, the lower river rapids are fast with tight turns and often bouldery. A good combination of ledge and straight wave runs with good volume throughout the season.

High-Water Notes: Of the three rivers, the Noire is the best during high-water flow for several reasons: smoother runs along the upper shallows translates into less lining and wading; less maneuvering on the bouldery CII's and smoother ledge drops, and the lowest risk at the approach of dangerous chutes.

Low-Water Notes: The river above St. Patrice may not be worth the amount of lining and wading if water levels are unusually low. Because of the Grande Chute dam at Waltham, levels below St.Patrice are maintained at a fairly constant level throughout the season. Lakes that feed into the Noire are dammed and water is released when the flow begins to diminish above the dam.

Access: Fly-In Charter Service:

Base: Bradley Air Service, Des Joachims (D'Swisha) P.Q.

Chief pilot: Ron Bowes, telephone (613)586-2374

Off-season: (613)839-3340 For location see Map 1, Rivière Dumoine

Destination Points: showing most popular lakes by price –

Coughlin Creek: 10-12 day trips

Dorion Crossing: 10-11 day trips

Lac St. Patrice: 6-7 day trips ($180. 1992)

Lac Farant: 5-6 day trips

Lac Raymond: 4-5 day trips

Note: Flight costs are based on total flight cost for two persons, gear and canoe, one-way only. You can make arrangements to leave your vehicle at the Black River Inn. Do not leave it unattended and don't take it for granted that the service is free. It's worth a few bucks to come back knowing that your vehicle is secure. You could also leave your car with one of the local residents beside the Waltham Power dam at Grande Chute, should you decide to paddle the additional 25 kilometers.

Dams like this one at St. Patrice maintain quality water levels throughout the canoeing season

There is no established service for leaving your vehicle; it is up to you to make your own arrangements.

Drive-In: There exists two roads that will take you to Lac St. Patrice. You may want to check with the authorities at the power station as to the status of the access road to Patrice, or the longer bush road to Coughlin Creek. Float-plane access is highly recommended for Noire river expeditions.

RIVIERE NOIRE DIARY

I looked at the marbled dash of the 1950 De Havilland Beaver, as always...concentrating on the levers and dials, trying to figure out what to do if I was ever in the precarious position of having to suddenly fly this thing. R.P.M.'s were just over 8,000, altitude 1,000, air-speed was 95 m.p.h., mixture lever forward, flaps on climb...yup, everything seemed to be in order.

Ron Bowes, chief pilot of Bradley Air Services' D'Swisha base for the past twenty-four years, sat at the controls. Ron had to be the calmest, coolest air jockey that I've ever had the opportunity to fly with...and I've flown a lot with various air services over northern Ontario and Quebec. Ron is the Perry Como of the airways; in fact I often worried that he'd fallen asleep he looked so relaxed.

The abrupt line of hills to the north marked the upper plateau of the Noire headwaters - an unnavigable tangle of continuous bouldery swifts and congested rapids. The Beaver swung northeast, up the Coughlin valley and Ron dropped Lissy and I down on a pond that seemed to be about as big as the average suburban backyard.

Upon our sudden arrival, a disgruntled bull moose who had been contentedly feeding on the lush, early-summer water lily tubers out in the creek shallows, made a quick retreat into the cover of the thick spruce at the end of the narrow lake. A trio of river otter bobbed their heads inquisitively as we unstrapped the 17' Old Town Tripper from the wing strut and began loading our canoe for the two week trip down the Noire.

It was obvious that few canoeists had ever been down this part of the Noire watershed - we would have seen some tell-tale sign like red or green canoe paint adorning the rocks in the shallow rapids. There was some evidence though, of early logging activities even along the Coughlin–huge spiked logs lay along the shores, probably serving as part of the "works" that were constructed to maintain spring flow and keep the logs moving.

Coughlin Creek, although notoriously hard work with a lot of wading, hauling and lifting through, was worth the effort if just for the fact that we enjoyed the added dimension of isolation.

We left the hills behind and began our slow descent through the maze of sand-banked meanders. There was an appreciable difference in water flow and the current picked up to about 5 k.p.h. Tamarac and jackpine predominated along the gallery of forest onlookers, and huge white-pine, somehow left behind during the heyday of the timber-drive, clung precariously to the edge of the eroding banks.

Wildlife personified! Everywhere, the sound of birds singing, chirping, fluttering and dive-bombing about. We saw Great Horned Owls, White-Throated Sparrows, Red-Winged Blackbirds, Evening Grosbeaks, Mergansers, Grebes, Nuthatch's, Blue and Gray Jays, Spotted Sandpipers, Yellow-Shafted Flickers,

map 1

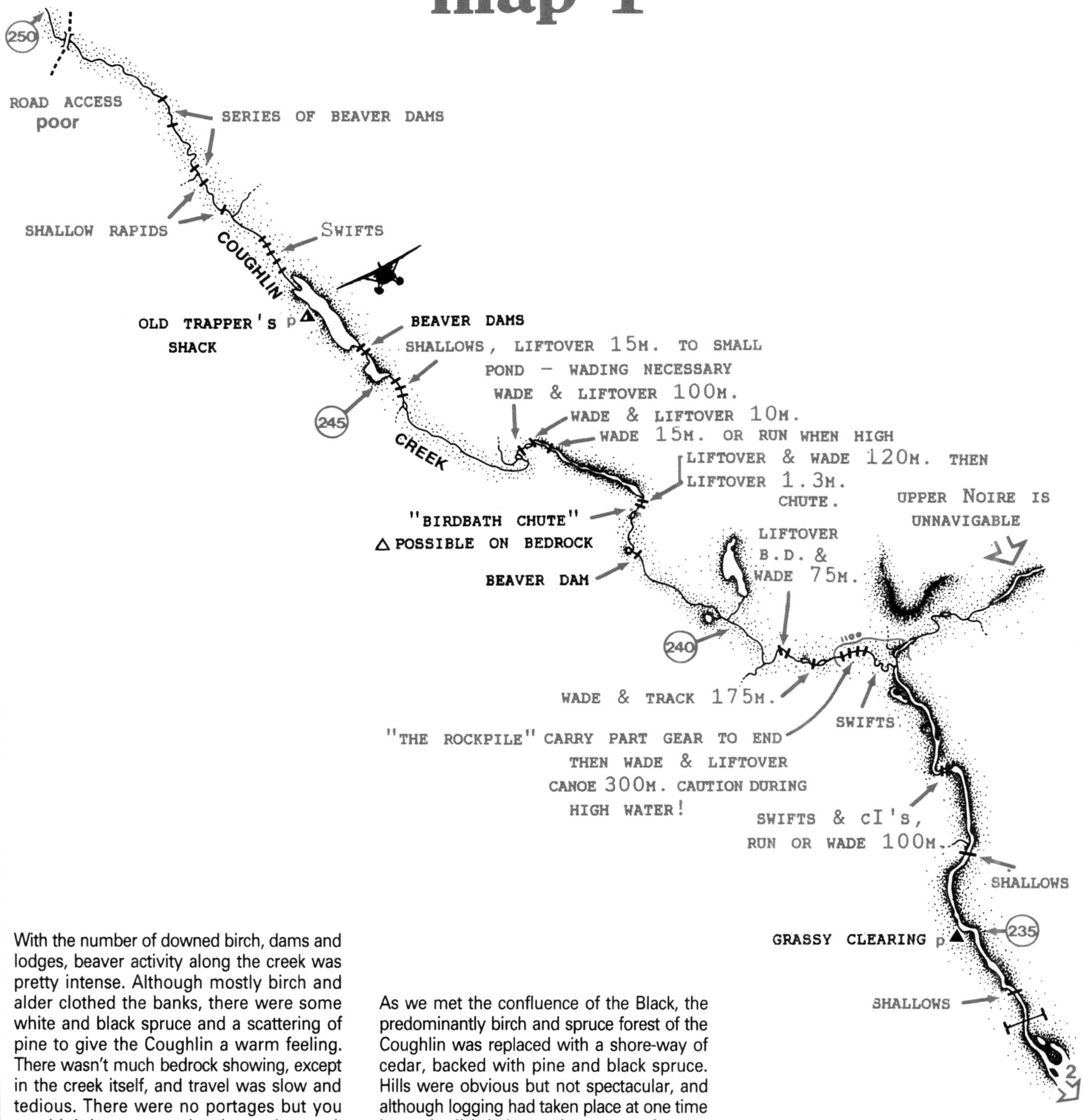

250 — ROAD ACCESS poor — SERIES OF BEAVER DAMS

SHALLOW RAPIDS — COUGHLIN — SWIFTS

OLD TRAPPER'S p△ SHACK

245

CREEK

BEAVER DAMS
SHALLOWS, LIFTOVER 15M. TO SMALL
POND — WADING NECESSARY
WADE & LIFTOVER 100M.
WADE & LIFTOVER 10M.
WADE 15M. OR RUN WHEN HIGH
LIFTOVER & WADE 120M. THEN
LIFTOVER 1.3M.
CHUTE.   UPPER NOIRE IS
                UNNAVIGABLE

"BIRDBATH CHUTE"
△ POSSIBLE ON BEDROCK

BEAVER DAM   LIFTOVER
                    B.D. &
                    WADE 75M.

240

WADE & TRACK 175M.

"THE ROCKPILE" CARRY PART GEAR TO END
        THEN WADE & LIFTOVER
   CANOE 300M. CAUTION DURING
           HIGH WATER!

SWIFTS

SWIFTS & cI's,
RUN OR WADE 100M.

SHALLOWS

GRASSY CLEARING p△ — 235

SHALLOWS

2

With the number of downed birch, dams and lodges, beaver activity along the creek was pretty intense. Although mostly birch and alder clothed the banks, there were some white and black spruce and a scattering of pine to give the Coughlin a warm feeling. There wasn't much bedrock showing, except in the creek itself, and travel was slow and tedious. There were no portages but you wouldn't have wanted to leave the creek anyway – it was just as easy to lift through as to carry around.

"Birdbath Chute", our first campsite, was pitched beside a bedrock shelf with a jacuzzi-type dunk hole, the top of which resembled an oversized birdbath. There was only enough room for one tent and it wasn't long until the black flies and constant drizzle forced us to seek shelter and tend to our bites.

As we met the confluence of the Black, the predominantly birch and spruce forest of the Coughlin was replaced with a shore-way of cedar, backed with pine and black spruce. Hills were obvious but not spectacular, and although logging had taken place at one time here, it didn't have that aura of over-exploitation and degradation.

The water of the Noire was tepid and very dark in colour, very shallow and almost still. River level was about one-third meter below the visible high-water mark and the trees along the shore which showed ice-damage from spring run-off, indicated an April flow that was at the level of my head if I was standing in the canoe.

Dorion Crossing, a two kilometer expansion in the river, would serve as the choice fly-in destination for any trip later than mid-June. From here down at least you could depend pretty much on enough water to float your canoe. A lot of rock-dodging for the next couple of days. **TR: 31K/13 31K/12**

map 2

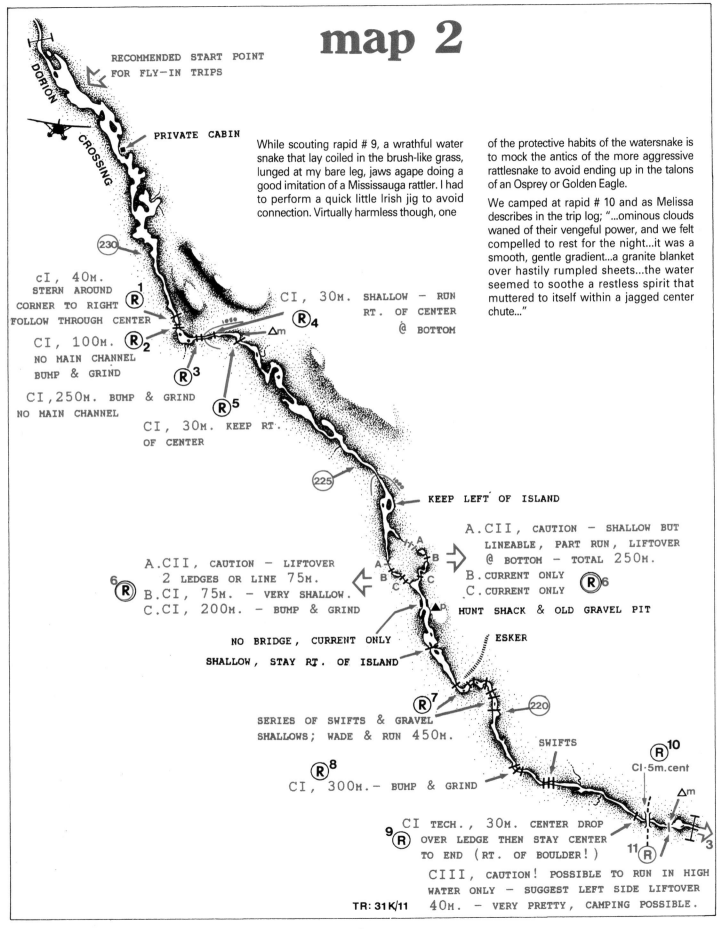

RECOMMENDED START POINT
FOR FLY-IN TRIPS

DORION CROSSING

PRIVATE CABIN

(230)

cI, 40M.
STERN AROUND
CORNER TO RIGHT
FOLLOW THROUGH CENTER

(R)1

CI, 100M.
NO MAIN CHANNEL
BUMP & GRIND

(R)2

(R)3

CI,250M. BUMP & GRIND
NO MAIN CHANNEL

(R)5

CI, 30M. KEEP RT.
OF CENTER

CI, 30M. SHALLOW — RUN
RT. OF CENTER
@ BOTTOM

(R)4

Δm

While scouting rapid # 9, a wrathful water snake that lay coiled in the brush-like grass, lunged at my bare leg, jaws agape doing a good imitation of a Mississauga rattler. I had to perform a quick little Irish jig to avoid connection. Virtually harmless though, one of the protective habits of the watersnake is to mock the antics of the more aggressive rattlesnake to avoid ending up in the talons of an Osprey or Golden Eagle.

We camped at rapid # 10 and as Melissa describes in the trip log; "...ominous clouds waned of their vengeful power, and we felt compelled to rest for the night...it was a smooth, gentle gradient...a granite blanket over hastily rumpled sheets...the water seemed to soothe a restless spirit that muttered to itself within a jagged center chute..."

(225)

KEEP LEFT OF ISLAND

A.CII, CAUTION — SHALLOW BUT
LINEABLE, PART RUN, LIFTOVER
@ BOTTOM — TOTAL 250M.
B. CURRENT ONLY
C. CURRENT ONLY

(R)6

A.CII, CAUTION — LIFTOVER
2 LEDGES OR LINE 75M.
B.CI, 75M. — VERY SHALLOW.
C.CI, 200M. — BUMP & GRIND

6 (R)

HUNT SHACK & OLD GRAVEL PIT

ESKER

NO BRIDGE, CURRENT ONLY

SHALLOW, STAY RT. OF ISLAND

(R)7

(220)

SERIES OF SWIFTS & GRAVEL
SHALLOWS; WADE & RUN 450M.

SWIFTS

(R)10
CI-5m.cent

(R)8

CI, 300M. — BUMP & GRIND

Δm

9 (R)

CI TECH., 30M. CENTER DROP
OVER LEDGE THEN STAY CENTER
TO END (RT. OF BOULDER!)

11 (R)

3

CIII, CAUTION! POSSIBLE TO RUN IN HIGH
WATER ONLY — SUGGEST LEFT SIDE LIFTOVER
40M. — VERY PRETTY, CAMPING POSSIBLE.

TR: 31K/11

and in the evening – Nighthawks and Whip-poor-wills.

Around every bend there was a fine, sandy beach that relayed a story of animal activity and daily business. There were always moose, otter, mink and fox tracks, and the drag-marks where beaver had come to cut fresh poplar or birch. They lived in the higher back-ponds and marshes off the river but came down to the Noire to liberate the lush growth behind the beaches, hauling it down to the water and across to the far bank and up the steep, well-polished trail to their secret havens.

The Upper Noire ... a diverse collection of meanders and shallow rapids

A common sight along the meanders were mud turtles; huge, prehistoric looking creatures with stegasaurus tails. Always the inquisitive one, Lissy immediately fell in love with Mr. "T" and we just had to go to shore to say hello. Amidst squeels of delight, the non-plussed hardshell was subjected to a barrage of gentle proddings and caresses, finally, having had a supplement of affection, it waddled listlessly into the root-beer river.

* * * * * * * *

Even before 1820, it was common practice for the men of the Ottawa Valley to leave their farms and families and hire on with the local logging company. From the 1860's to the 1920's, the largest timber limit belonged to the "lumber king", John Rudolphus (J.R.) Booth. He owned rights on the Dumoine, Coulonge and the Noire.

Most of the food and supplies for the men working high up on the river were portaged up to the bush camps by wagon.To save money on feed and transport costs, Booth bought or rented a farm up on his northern limits. The company horses, used to haul timber, would summer there and the farm would produce timothy that they could cut in August to feed the animals kept there. The "Old Caldwell Farm" dates back to 1875 on an old timber map that shows two of Booth's cutting licences.

An old gentleman from Chapeau recalls about the farm;

"It's a long piece up, around 65 or 70 miles by the road we used to go from Waltham, more or less following the river. It was built on a hill. There's not much clearance, you know, it was rough. If they cut hay, I don't know how they'd press it, or if they did press it. They'd keep horses there for the summer, but with all the flies, they didn't do well unless you brought them in and sprayed them."

The Caldwell farm probably afforded the men a diversion from the normal lumber-jack-fare of salt pork, beans and prunes by the presence of fresh cream, eggs and beef. The traditional grillade of the camps were fashioned from half fat, salted pork that had to be boiled several times before it became palatable and the men downed this with copious amounts of toxic "green tea".

LAC ST. PATRICE:

If you are fortunate you can find a meander campsite with an upper ledge in the pine and spruce. Myself, well...I'm not fond of sandy campsites in the rain and I'll pass several good prospects to find one where I can pitch the tent on a soft carpet of pine needles. Sand, which eventually permeates every crack and orifice imaginable, is forever being brushed off, dumped out of or crunched upon when you're eating. On sunny days it's nice; sand lacks that adhesive quality and I have to admit, there's nothing like soaking up the last of the sun's rays while stretched out on a warm beach.

We came upon the sole log jam of the trip. It was impenetrable so we had to carry around a newly constructed road and bridge – of course, a man-made obstruction that the river debris in the spring time could not get by. We started noticing

heavy stands of shagbark maple and yellow birch mixed with white, red and jackpine as we neared Lac St. Patrice. We decided that it was time to find an open lake where we could feel the summer wind, enjoy a rest day and explore a bit. It was an easy trek up the creek to Lac St. Patrice and we quickly made our way across to the nice island site about two kilometers from the dam.

We spent the afternoon cleaning up the campsite which had been recently trashed by fishermen, clearing tent sites and removing wind-falls that had been blown down over the bedrock tenting area.

Melissa had found an old fish-hook still attached to some line so she decided that the safest place for it was atop a tree, stuck into the trunk where no person or animal would get poked by it. That's when I heard the call for help. She had slipped and the hook lodged deep into her middle finger of her left hand and she was suspended halfway up this spruce tree by the time I got there and cut the line loose. This proved to be a predicament because I had left my hook-extractor behind in order to lighten the load for the trip, afterall, neither of us were fishing this trip so there really wasn't any use for it...wrong! Something about Murphy's Law at work here.

Needless to say, we couldn't get the hook out of her hand and she was too stubborn for a "walk-out" to get a ride into town from the access road saying that she wanted to stay with the river right to the end...what a Trooper! We still had at least five days to paddle and the best whitewater of the expedition.

It was getting dark by now and a grouchy storm was upon us. I shaved some cedar staves to form a sort of "finger-box" around Lissy's middle digit, bonded that together with duct-tape, stuffed it with T.P. and then wrapped the whole thing with a tensor bandage which gave it the appearance of a crude boxing glove.

The storm missed us but its ominous presence loomed about long after the sun had gone down.

Campsite at Lac St. Patrice

map 3

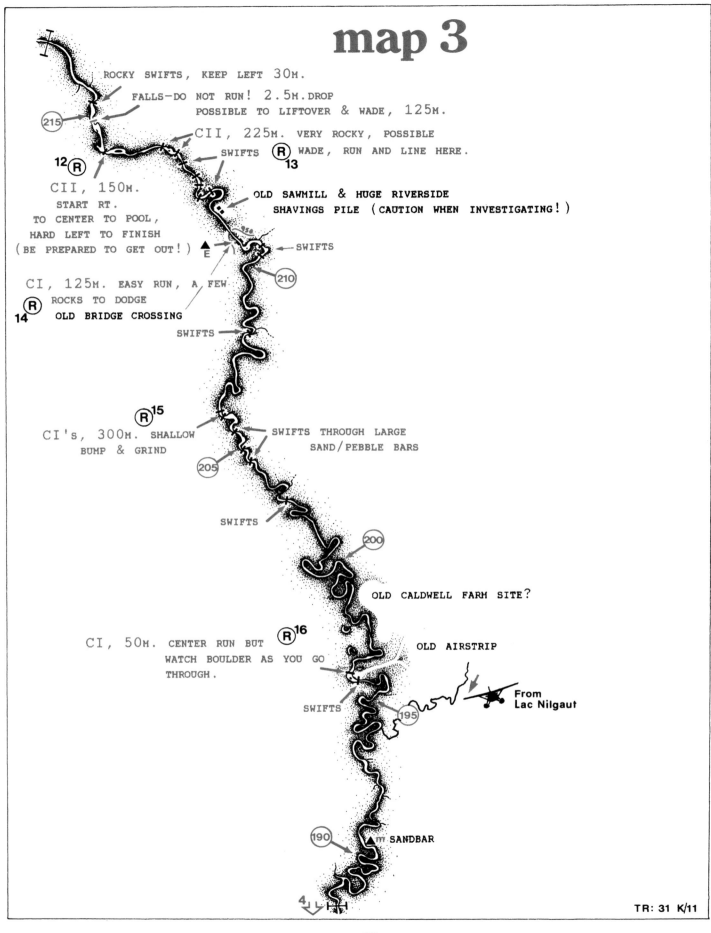

ROCKY SWIFTS, KEEP LEFT 30M.

FALLS—DO NOT RUN! 2.5M. DROP
POSSIBLE TO LIFTOVER & WADE, 125M.

(215)

CII, 225M. VERY ROCKY, POSSIBLE
SWIFTS (R) WADE, RUN AND LINE HERE.
13

12(R)

CII, 150M. OLD SAWMILL & HUGE RIVERSIDE
START RT. SHAVINGS PILE (CAUTION WHEN INVESTIGATING!)
TO CENTER TO POOL,
HARD LEFT TO FINISH
(BE PREPARED TO GET OUT!) ▲E ← SWIFTS

(210)

CI, 125M. EASY RUN, A FEW
(R) ROCKS TO DODGE
14 OLD BRIDGE CROSSING

SWIFTS

(R)15

CI'S, 300M. SHALLOW SWIFTS THROUGH LARGE
BUMP & GRIND SAND/PEBBLE BARS

(205)

SWIFTS

(200)

OLD CALDWELL FARM SITE?

(R)16

CI, 50M. CENTER RUN BUT OLD AIRSTRIP
WATCH BOULDER AS YOU GO
THROUGH.

From
Lac Nilgaut
SWIFTS (195)

(190) ▲m SANDBAR

4

TR: 31 K/11

map 4

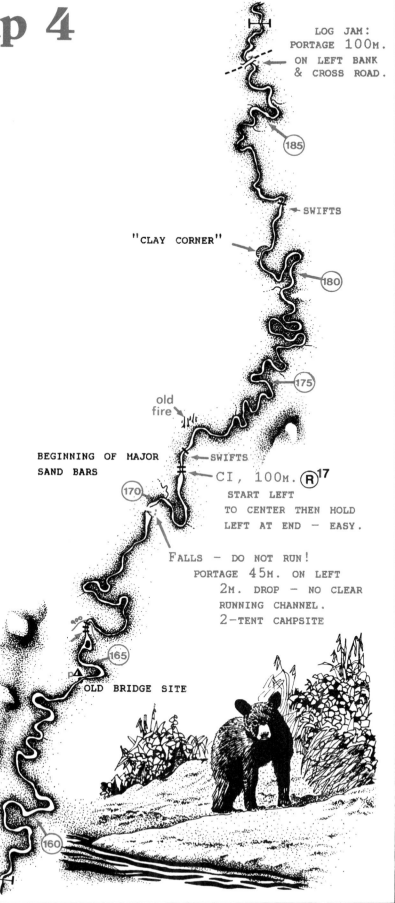

LOG JAM:
PORTAGE 100M.
ON LEFT BANK
& CROSS ROAD.

185

SWIFTS

"CLAY CORNER"

180

175

old fire

BEGINNING OF MAJOR
SAND BARS

SWIFTS

CI, 100M. (R)17

170

START LEFT
TO CENTER THEN HOLD
LEFT AT END — EASY.

FALLS — DO NOT RUN!
PORTAGE 45M. ON LEFT
2M. DROP — NO CLEAR
RUNNING CHANNEL.
2-TENT CAMPSITE

165

OLD BRIDGE SITE

160

Today we paddled 30 kilometers. It probably could have been walked in a straight line in under an hour. We took turns soloing and often just sat and let the current carry the canoe downstream. This broke the monotony of the constant cloned scenery of the meanders.

The river had a particular charm about it but it was hard to button-down just where that omnipresent aura was emanating from. It was somewhat like riding a fleuvial conveyor-belt in an airport luggage pick-up...round and round.

We saw three black bears. The first, a huge male, followed close behind by a smaller female (I figured it was a size-gender kind of distinction), who upon seeing us, crashed head first into a tree and then they both broke and ran for deep cover. The third bear, a much younger fellow, was busy excavating the side of a sand bank, probably trying to extricate a Kingfisher out of its nest.

We came to within a few meters of the cub, not beaching the canoe in case MA showed up, but we did manage to get a few good camera shots and save the life of the Kingfisher or whatever was hiding in the bank.

TR: 31 K/11, 31 K/6

map 5

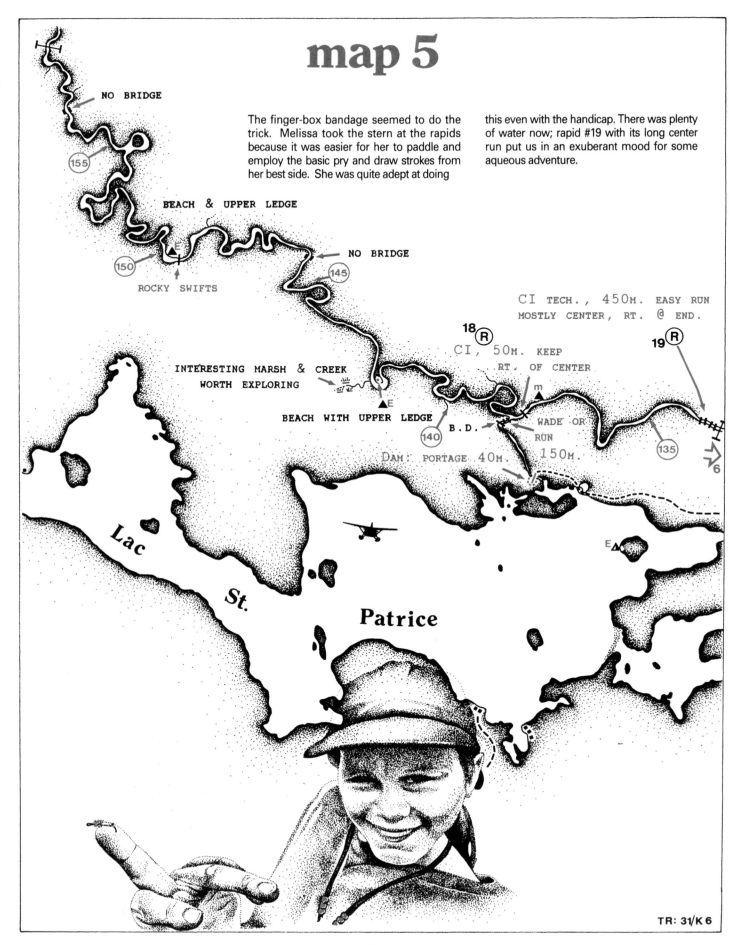

NO BRIDGE

(155)

BEACH & UPPER LEDGE

(150)

ROCKY SWIFTS

NO BRIDGE

(145)

The finger-box bandage seemed to do the trick. Melissa took the stern at the rapids because it was easier for her to paddle and employ the basic pry and draw strokes from her best side. She was quite adept at doing this even with the handicap. There was plenty of water now; rapid #19 with its long center run put us in an exuberant mood for some aqueous adventure.

CI TECH., 450M. EASY RUN
MOSTLY CENTER, RT. @ END.

INTERESTING MARSH & CREEK
WORTH EXPLORING

BEACH WITH UPPER LEDGE

▲E

18 Ⓡ

CI, 50M. KEEP
RT. OF CENTER

m ▲

19 Ⓡ

(140) B.D.

WADE OR
RUN
150M.

DAM: PORTAGE 40M.

(135)

6

E▲

Lac

St.

Patrice

TR: 31/K 6

68

map 6

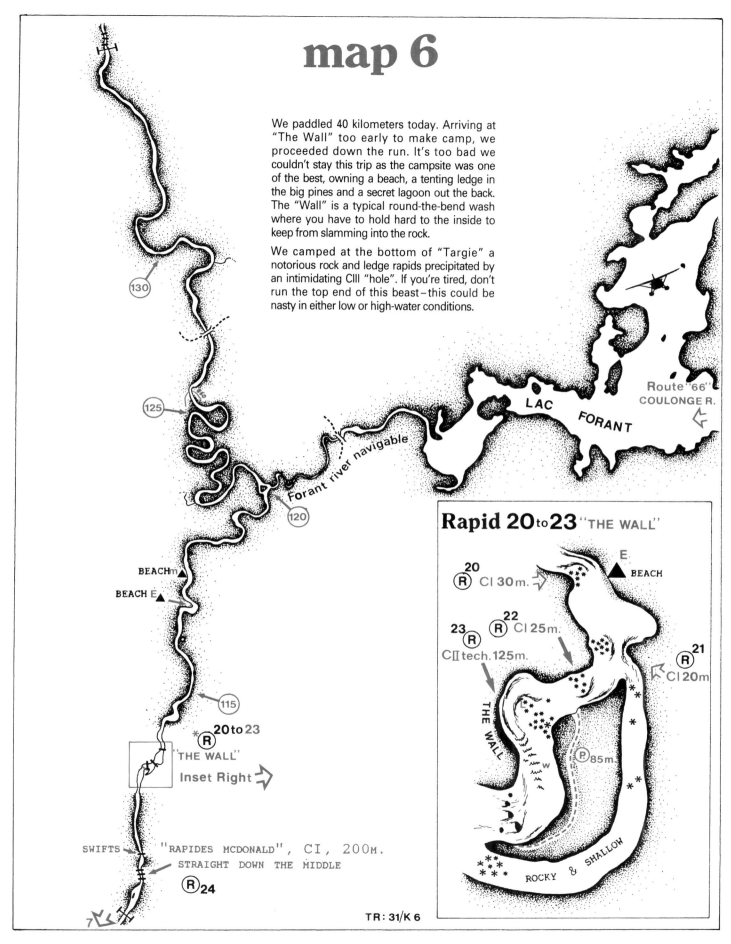

We paddled 40 kilometers today. Arriving at "The Wall" too early to make camp, we proceeded down the run. It's too bad we couldn't stay this trip as the campsite was one of the best, owning a beach, a tenting ledge in the big pines and a secret lagoon out the back. The "Wall" is a typical round-the-bend wash where you have to hold hard to the inside to keep from slamming into the rock.

We camped at the bottom of "Targie" a notorious rock and ledge rapids precipitated by an intimidating CIII "hole". If you're tired, don't run the top end of this beast – this could be nasty in either low or high-water conditions.

130

125

Forant river navigable

120

LAC FORANT

Route "66" COULONGE R.

BEACH m

BEACH E

115

* (R) 20 to 23

"THE WALL"

Inset Right

SWIFTS "RAPIDES MCDONALD", CI, 200m.
STRAIGHT DOWN THE MIDDLE

(R) 24

7

TR: 31/K 6

Rapid 20 to 23 "THE WALL"

20
(R) CI 30 m.

E
▲ BEACH

22
(R) CI 25 m.

23
(R)
CII tech. 125 m.

21
(R)
CI 20 m

THE WALL

w

(R) 85 m.

ROCKY & SHALLOW

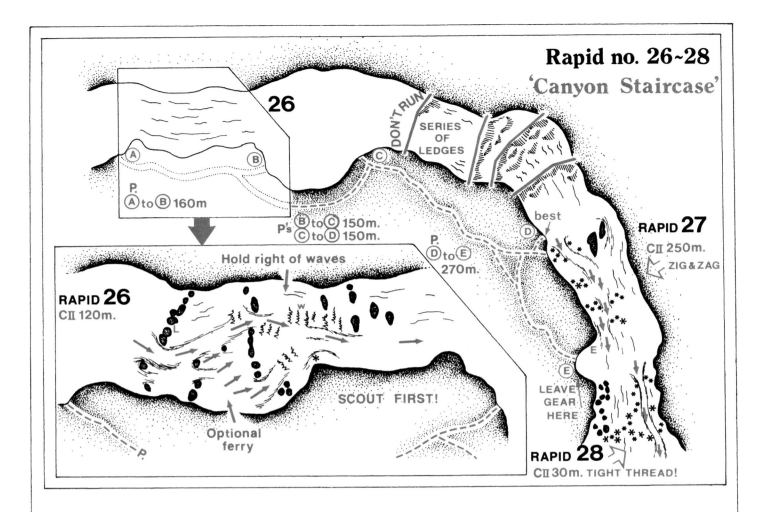

CANYON STAIRCASE

We woke up excited, knowing that the big day was beckoning us; and before the day was out, we would have only paddled about 15 kilometers with all the scouting, portaging and rapid play along this scenic stretch. The actual staircase was a series of granite steps surrounded by high, rocky walls. As long as you carry around this part then the rest can be played without too much risk. The plethora of tributary footpaths may cause havoc for first time visitors so it may be a good idea to keep a leash on everyone first trek across the portage to point "D" or "E" as shown on the inset map.

MOUNTAIN CHUTES (refer to Inset Map, page 70)

Probably one of the most entertaining runs of the Noire, it also owns the longest and most ridiculous portage trails. The well-worn portage takes a circuitous route to the summit of a hill and then down to a very steep pitch-off at the end. For the more daring, or should I say adept paddlers, this 1,000 meter portage can be whittled down to a single 200 meter carry around the sucking vortex of the chutes. You have to employ EXTREME CAUTION here, especially during high-water conditions because the entrance to the take out is directly in the down-current of the CIV at the head of the falls. You may want to pick your way slowly along the left shore–you don't want to dump out in the middle of this run!

Below the falls you'll find a long set of fun 'n games...if you've carried your gear across the long portage then you have to watch closely for the landing–you could easily scoot right by without even seeing your packs on the rocks and it's a hard paddle back up the current.

map 7

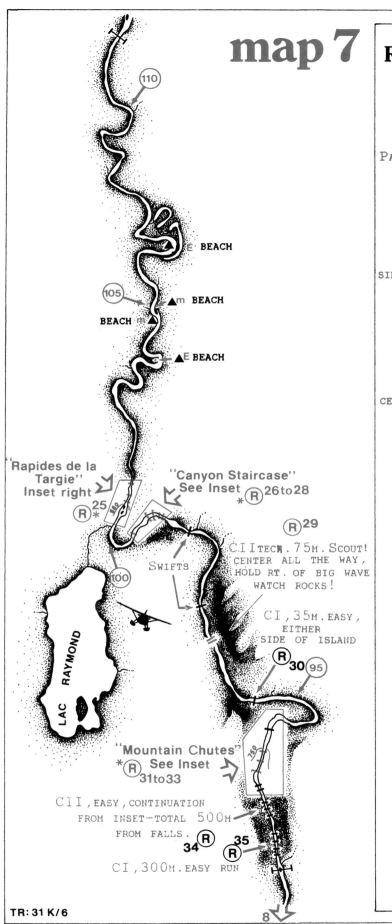

110

E BEACH

105 ▲m BEACH

BEACH m▲

▲E BEACH

"Rapides de la
Targie"
Inset right

R 25
*

"Canyon Staircase"
See Inset
* R 26to28

R 29

C II tech. 75 m. Scout!
Center all the way,
hold rt. of big wave
watch rocks!

100

Swifts

C I, 35 m. easy,
either
side of island

LAC RAYMOND

R 30 95

"Mountain Chutes"
* R See Inset
31to33

750

C II, easy, continuation
from inset—total 500 m
from falls.

34 R 35
R

C I, 300 m. easy run

8

Rapid no. 25 'Targie'
KEEP THE DUCT TAPE HANDY!

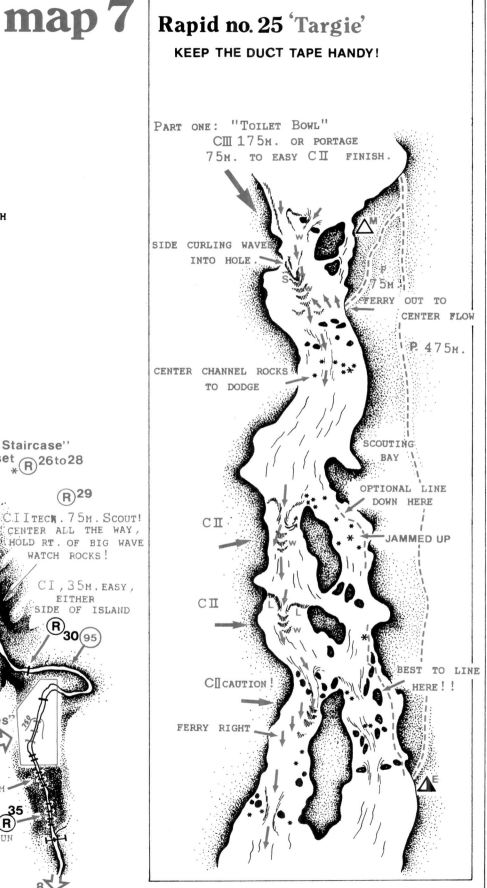

Part one: "Toilet Bowl"
C III 175 m. or portage
75 m. to easy C II finish.

△M

Side curling wave
into hole.

S
w
P
75 m.

Ferry out to
center flow

P. 475 m.

Center channel rocks
to dodge

Scouting
Bay

Optional line
down here

C II

Jammed up

C II
L L
w

Best to line
here!!

C II caution!

Ferry right

△E

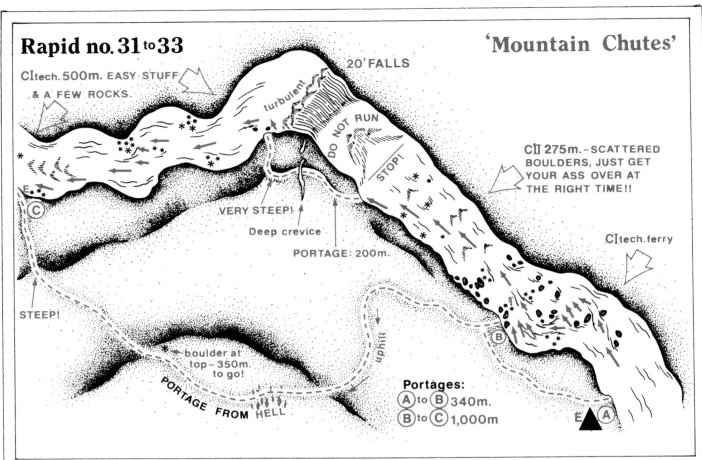

Rapid no. 31 to 33

'Mountain Chutes'

CI tech. 500m. EASY STUFF & A FEW ROCKS.

20' FALLS

turbulent

DO NOT RUN

STOP!

CII 275m. – SCATTERED BOULDERS, JUST GET YOUR ASS OVER AT THE RIGHT TIME!!

VERY STEEP!

Deep crevice

PORTAGE: 200m.

CI tech. ferry

E

C

STEEP!

boulder at top – 350m. to go!

PORTAGE FROM HELL

uphill

B

Portages:
A to B 340m.
B to C 1,000m

E A

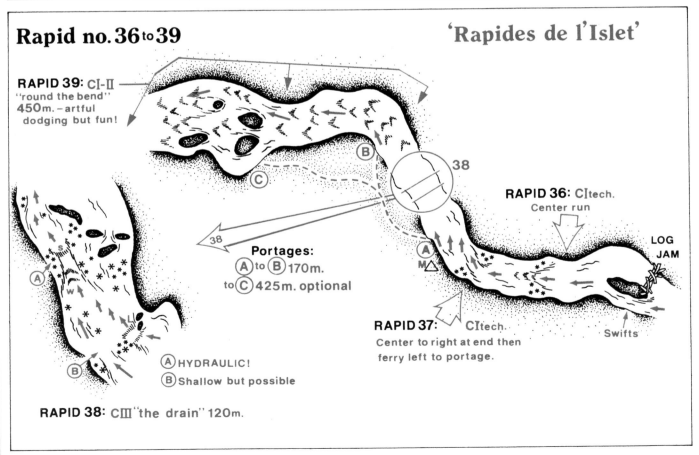

Rapid no. 36 to 39

'Rapides de l'Islet'

RAPID 39: CI-II "round the bend" 450m. – artful dodging but fun!

B

C

38

RAPID 36: CI tech. Center run

LOG JAM

A
M

38

Portages:
A to B 170m.
to C 425m. optional

A

w

s

B

A HYDRAULIC!
B Shallow but possible

Swifts

RAPID 37: CI tech. Center to right at end then ferry left to portage.

RAPID 38: CIII "the drain" 120m.

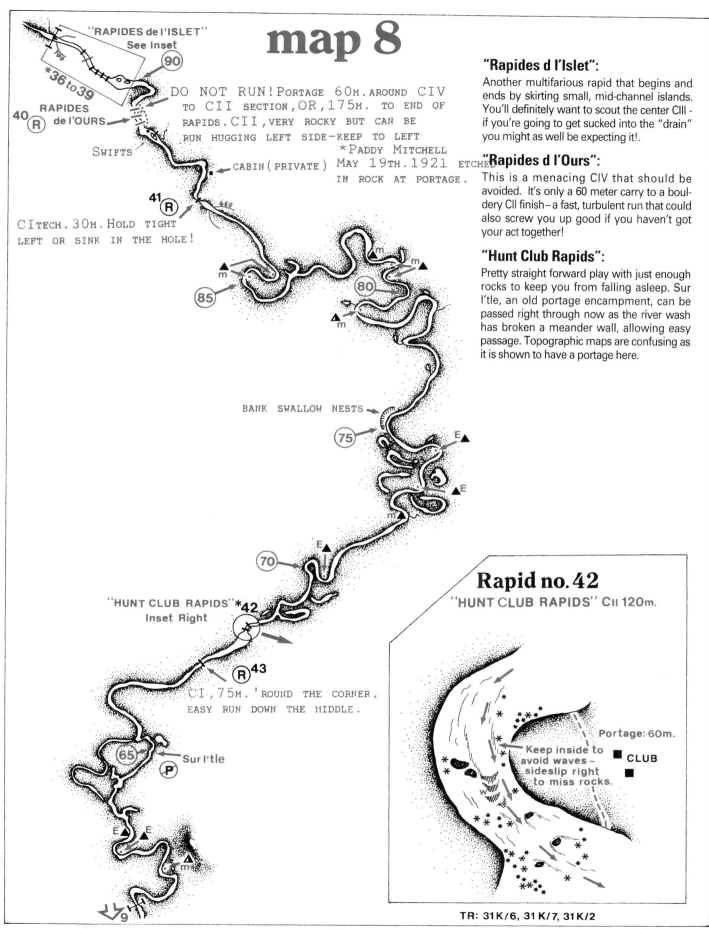

map 8

"RAPIDES de l'ISLET"
See Inset

90

*36 to 39

40 (R) RAPIDES de l'OURS

Swifts

DO NOT RUN! Portage 60m. around CIV
to CII section, OR, 175m. to end of
rapids. CII, very rocky but can be
run, hugging left side – keep to left
*Paddy Mitchell
CABIN (private) May 19th. 1921 etched
in rock at portage.

41 (R)

660

CI tech. 30m. Hold tight
left or sink in the hole!

85
m
m
m
80
m

BANK SWALLOW NESTS

75

E

E

m

70 E

"HUNT CLUB RAPIDS" *42
Inset Right

(R) 43

CI, 75m. 'round the corner,
easy run down the middle.

65 Sur l'tle

(P)

E E
m

9

"Rapides d l'Islet":

Another multifarious rapid that begins and
ends by skirting small, mid-channel islands.
You'll definitely want to scout the center CIII -
if you're going to get sucked into the "drain"
you might as well be expecting it!.

"Rapides d l'Ours":

This is a menacing CIV that should be
avoided. It's only a 60 meter carry to a bouldery CII finish – a fast, turbulent run that could
also screw you up good if you haven't got
your act together!

"Hunt Club Rapids":

Pretty straight forward play with just enough
rocks to keep you from falling asleep. Sur
l'tle, an old portage encampment, can be
passed right through now as the river wash
has broken a meander wall, allowing easy
passage. Topographic maps are confusing as
it is shown to have a portage here.

Rapid no. 42
"HUNT CLUB RAPIDS" CII 120m.

Portage: 60m.
■ CLUB
■

Keep inside to
avoid waves –
sideslip right
to miss rocks.

TR: 31K/6, 31K/7, 31K/2

Rapid no. 47　C̲II̲ tech. to C̲III̲ 200m.

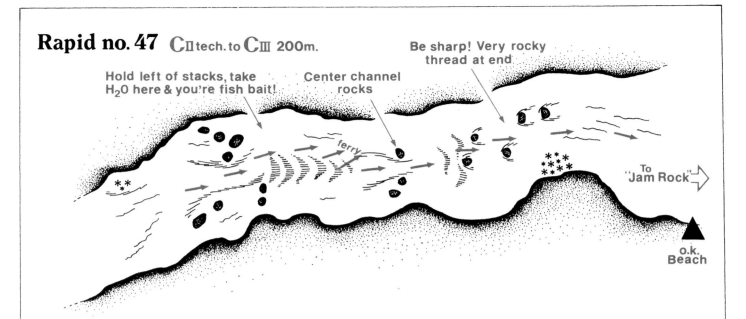

Hold left of stacks, take H₂O here & you're fish bait!

Center channel rocks

Be sharp! Very rocky thread at end

ferry

To "Jam Rock"

o.k. Beach

'Manitou Rapids'

Rapid no. 48

]tech. top 40m.
]bottom 175m.

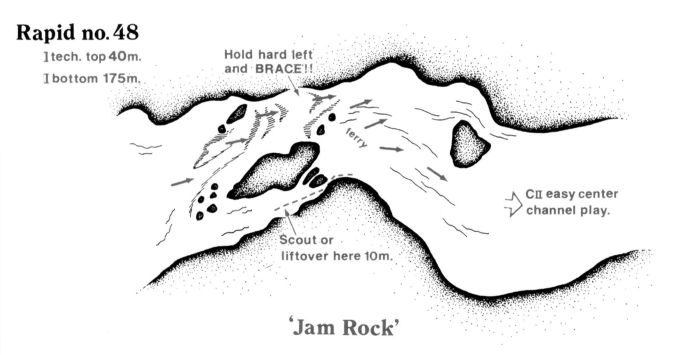

Hold hard left and BRACE!!

ferry

C̲II̲ easy center channel play.

Scout or liftover here 10m.

'Jam Rock'

Melissa's finger had been housed in its cocoon for three days now; we were afraid to look at it for fear that it had become infected, or worse...gangrenous. Another exciting day lay ahead of us; the current was strong and by the end of the afternoon we will have dropped another 125 vertical feet in elevation.

"Double Ferry" is more of a play-rapids...a teaser that baits you for the nefarious 50:50 rapids. There is an excellent campsite here and you may decide to spend an extra day

loafing. You'll want to carry your gear across and scout before running. This one is a lot similar to Wavy Rapids on the Missinaibi River – a straight forward, deep-channelled sluice with a roller-coaster ending...great to surf in from below on an upstream ferry. The rapid is called 50:50 after the hunt club perched across the chutes; also because you have a 50:50 chance of making it down right-side up. You'll also half-fill your canoe on the second set of stacks at the bottom.

At mileage "45" you could actually feel the drop of the river as you hurl through "Manitou" and "Jam Rock" rapids – both excellent runs, successfully played if you manage to escape the heavy rollers at the top.

From here the fun begins...the "Boulder Raceway" to the Black River Inn, a 14 kilometer stretch of continuous CI's, dappled with bouldery rapids that'll turn your upper lip into a permanent grin.

map 9

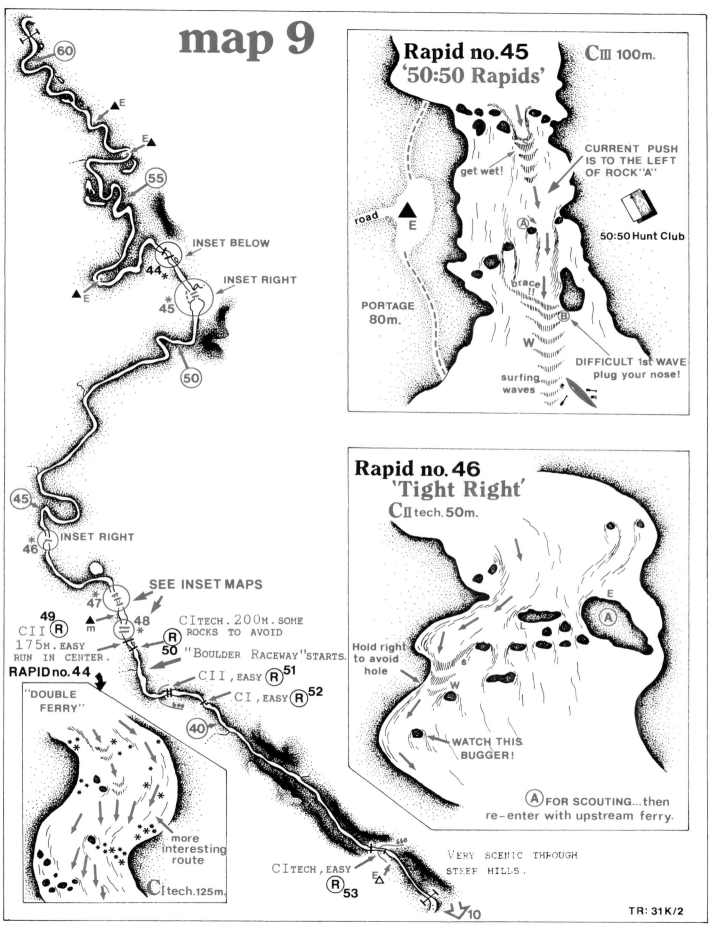

60

E
E

55

INSET BELOW

44 *

INSET RIGHT

45 *

50

45

* INSET RIGHT
46

* SEE INSET MAPS
47

49 (R)
CII
175M. EASY
RUN IN CENTER.

m

48 *

50 (R)

CI TECH. 200M. SOME
ROCKS TO AVOID
"BOULDER RACEWAY" STARTS.

CII, EASY (R) 51

CI, EASY (R) 52

40

RAPID no.44

"DOUBLE FERRY"

more interesting route

CI TECH. 125M.

CI TECH, EASY (R) 53

E

VERY SCENIC THROUGH STEEP HILLS.

10

Rapid no.45 ' 50:50 Rapids'

CIII 100m.

get wet!

CURRENT PUSH IS TO THE LEFT OF ROCK "A"

50:50 Hunt Club

road
E

A

PORTAGE 80m.

brace !!

B

W

DIFFICULT 1st WAVE plug your nose!

surfing waves

Rapid no. 46 'Tight Right'

CII tech. 50m.

E

A

L

Hold right to avoid hole

s

W

WATCH THIS BUGGER!

A FOR SCOUTING... then re-enter with upstream ferry.

TR: 31K/2

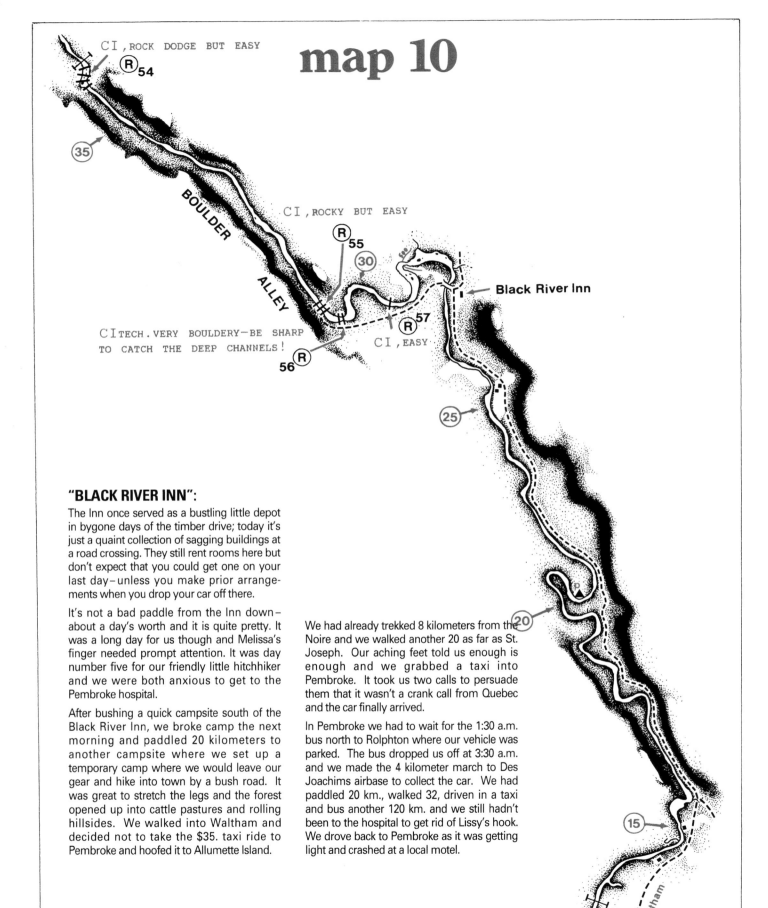

map 10

CI, ROCK DODGE BUT EASY

(R)54

(35)

BOULDER

ALLEY

CI, ROCKY BUT EASY

(R)55

(30)

Black River Inn

CI TECH. VERY BOULDERY—BE SHARP
TO CATCH THE DEEP CHANNELS!

(R)57

CI, EASY

56 (R)

(25)

(20)

(15)

Waltham

11

"BLACK RIVER INN":

The Inn once served as a bustling little depot in bygone days of the timber drive; today it's just a quaint collection of sagging buildings at a road crossing. They still rent rooms here but don't expect that you could get one on your last day–unless you make prior arrangements when you drop your car off there.

It's not a bad paddle from the Inn down–about a day's worth and it is quite pretty. It was a long day for us though and Melissa's finger needed prompt attention. It was day number five for our friendly little hitchhiker and we were both anxious to get to the Pembroke hospital.

After bushing a quick campsite south of the Black River Inn, we broke camp the next morning and paddled 20 kilometers to another campsite where we set up a temporary camp where we would leave our gear and hike into town by a bush road. It was great to stretch the legs and the forest opened up into cattle pastures and rolling hillsides. We walked into Waltham and decided not to take the $35. taxi ride to Pembroke and hoofed it to Allumette Island.

We had already trekked 8 kilometers from the Noire and we walked another 20 as far as St. Joseph. Our aching feet told us enough is enough and we grabbed a taxi into Pembroke. It took us two calls to persuade them that it wasn't a crank call from Quebec and the car finally arrived.

In Pembroke we had to wait for the 1:30 a.m. bus north to Rolphton where our vehicle was parked. The bus dropped us off at 3:30 a.m. and we made the 4 kilometer march to Des Joachims airbase to collect the car. We had paddled 20 km., walked 32, driven in a taxi and bus another 120 km. and we still hadn't been to the hospital to get rid of Lissy's hook. We drove back to Pembroke as it was getting light and crashed at a local motel.

TR: 31 K/2, 31 F/15

76

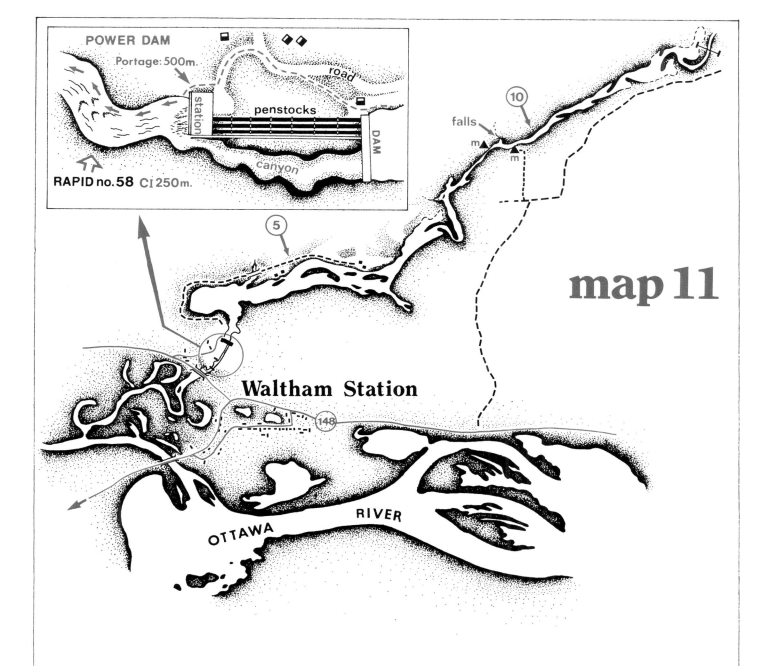

POWER DAM

Portage: 500m.

road

penstocks

station

DAM

canyon

RAPID no.58 Ci 250m.

⑤

⑩

falls

m

m

map 11

Waltham Station

⑭⑧

OTTAWA RIVER

There was happy ending to the story– Melissa finally had the hook removed at the Pembroke General and the finger was fine. We actually did a pretty commendable job in keeping it together. Our gear was rescued from the Noire campsite and we finished the trip by exploring the Waltham dam at Grande Chute. The "Pontiac Corp." of Toronto built the dam in 1950 for the "Pembroke Electric Light Co. Ltd.", which supplies power to area villages and the town of Pembroke.

The United Church and cemetery located at the station village is worth a visit. Buried here are mostly Perry's, Robinson's and Watt's...a lot of young women, 20 to 30 years of age, who probably fell ill with tuberculosis or died during childbirth. Many residing in the grave-yard were born in the 1700s and deaths are recorded as far back as the 1880s. Time is eternal here, and a place of purpose for those who lived and died along the Black River in the Province of Quebec.

Scenes Along the Noire

Cemetery at Waltham Dam

Shavings pile along the bank of the Upper Noire...old logging camps and mills are being steadily consumed by the burgeoning undergrowth

Rivière Coulonge

INFORMATION TO KNOW:

Classification: Novice Intermediate

Total Distance: 270 km. (Hwy#117, La Verendrye Park to Ottawa R.)

Practical Distance: 250 km. (Lac Barrage campsite to Grande Chute)

Vertical Drop: 700 feet (excluding Grande Chute) 3.1'/km.

Days Required: 12 to 14

Number of Campsites: 1 per 3km. (Total: 81)

Number of Runnable Rapids: 69 (70% CI's)

Distance total: 12km. or 4.5% of total river length.

Total Swifts: 40 km.

Total Distance Fast-Water: 52 km. or 19.5% of total river length.

PORTAGES:

Novice Intermediate: 19 portages (3,557 meters)

Creative Intermediate: 19 portages (2,039 meters) 42% reduction

Attributes: Compared with the Noire and Dumoine, the Coulonge has the highest percentage total fast-water overall; a more diverse geography; easy emergency evacuation capability and provides the most practical car-jockey logistics for drop and pick-up. It has a good combination of lake travel with river paddling, and lakes that can be accessed via tertiary creeks. Option to cross-over to the Noire by way of "Route 66". Many scenic chutes and falls.

Negative Factors: Visible effects from man's impact by the number of road crossings and recent logging activity.

*Note: The last timber drive was in 1984 and the river is reverting back rather quickly to an "acceptable" standard. The cost of flying in to the headwaters is more expensive than either the Noire or Dumoine.

Whitewater Characteristics: Predominantly ledge-type descents that require precise line-up for entry. Good, deep-channel runs and ample opportunity for up or downstream ferry's and eddy-turns. Wide variety of rapid layouts that make it interesting.

High-Water Notes: The Coulonge could present itself as the most dangerous of Quebec's "Triple Play" because of the difficult chutes that normally require creative running. The temptation to run rather than portage could create stress from peer-pressure to take undue chances. High-water in-creases the risk at these chutes and necessitates extra distance portaging without the option to run–at least for us mortals.

Low-water Notes: The river becomes sluggish and shallow in sections making wading and liftovers necessary–deep channels still exist and the rapids actually become more interesting. Instead of portaging, the more adept paddlers have the option to "play" through particular sections of potentially hazardous chutes.

Access: Fly-In Charter Service:

Base: Bradley Air Service, Des Joachims (D'Swisha) P.Q.

Chief pilot: Ron Bowes.
Telephone (613) 586-2374

Off-season: (613) 839-3340 For location see Map 1, Rivière Dumoine.

Destination Points: showing most popular lakes by price
Lac Ward: 12 day trips
Lac Pomponne: 10-12 day trips ($356. 1992)
Lac Bryson: 6-7 day trips ($238. 1992)
Lac Wright: 5-6 day trips
Lac Jim: 3 day trips (road accessible)

Note: Above prices are based on total flight cost for two persons, gear and canoe, one-way only. Do not leave your vehicle un-attended at Grande Chute. It is recommended that you make arrangements with one of the local residents that live nearby and offer remuneration for their services. The same arrangement should be made if you plan to take out at the bridge at mileage 20.

Drive-In: For those with two vehicles it is a pleasant 280 km. drive to the Grande/Barrage public campsite in La Vérendrye – access via highways 148, 301, 105 and 117. Turn left at signpost Road # 28 and drive 11 km. along a good gravel road to the start point for two-week canoe trips. The access to Lac Pomponne for 10-12 day trips is off hwy. 117 at signpost Road # 20. Be prepared though for a long, dusty ride on a gravel road. It's worth the extra two days paddle through the park!

RIVIERE COULONGE DIARY

Parc de la Vérendrye:

The park acquired its name from the Canadian explorer, Pierre Gauthier de Varennes de La Verendrye, who's travels in 1731 to 1743 eventually led him to the Rocky Mountains. This 13,615 sq. km. reserve with its 4,000 lakes and rivers is known today as reserve faunique La Verendrye. The huge Cabonga and Dozois reservoirs control the headwaters of the Ottawa and Gatineau rivers; the Dumoine and Coulonge river headstreams originate within the park as well.

The 60 km. paddle to Lac Pomponne is anything but boring. Those who decide to leave this stretch of lakes out of their itinerary are really missing one of the highlights of the trip. The landscape resembles Temagami rock and pine–except not as abrupt or harsh. Campsites are established on bedrock points or shelves, or on sandy beaches hemmed-in by natural rock levee's.

Before 1984, the year of the last log drive down the Dumoine, these lakes were all flooded by control dams. The dams are still very much intact but the gates are now wide open allowing the water levels to assume traditional heights. The young growth of poplar and birch visible along the once submerged shoreline is indicative of the natural regenerative processes at work. The gently undulating hills support a mixed forest with ample second-growth pine to give the nuance of a convalescent landscape. The irregular configuration of islands and deep channels afford protection from prevailing west or southwest winds; even on Lac Nichcotea you can stay on the leeward side of the small islands as you dash across to the west bay.

Surprising as it may seem, it is seldom that busy here–even in the summer. It's hard to judge the status of the water levels, too, through the park because of the obvious restoration of the shoreline. It isn't until you actually reach mileage 170 that you start to get a feel for river height.

One of my favourite campsites through the park is located on an island on Lac Giroux at mileage 229, perched atop a high pine bank overlooking a rather expansive sand beach. There are innumerable other choice sites that offer both sand or bedrock personalities or a combination of both.

No Shortage of Excitement

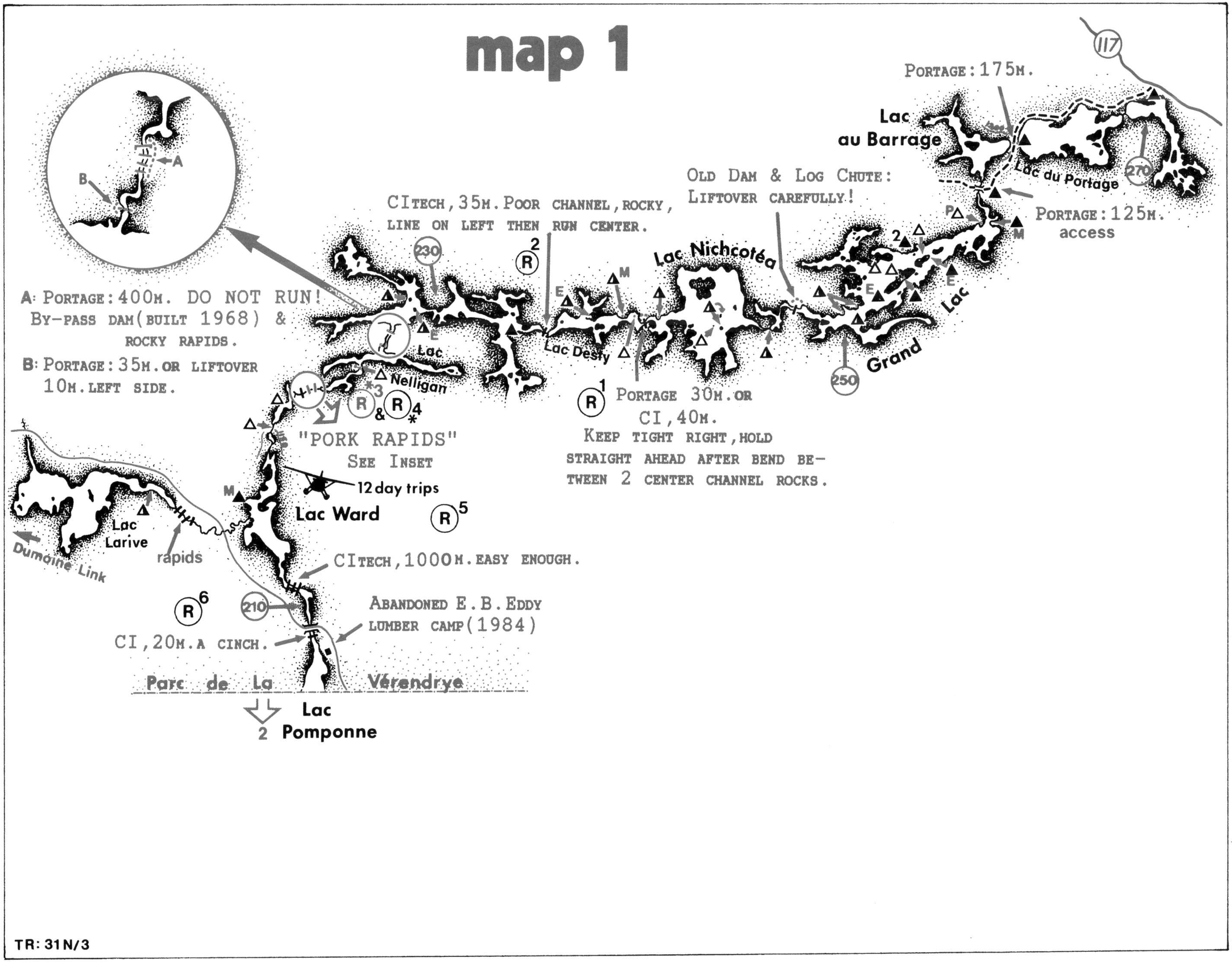

map 1

A: Portage: 400m. Do Not Run! By-pass Dam (built 1968) & Rocky Rapids.

B: Portage: 35m. or Liftover 10m. left side.

CI Tech, 35m. Poor channel, rocky, line on left then run center.

Old Dam & Log Chute: Liftover carefully!

Lac au Barrage

Portage: 175m.

Portage: 125m.

Lac du Portage access

(117)

(270)

(250) Grand Lac

Lac Nichcotéa

(250)

R(2)

Lac Désy

R(1) Portage 30m. or CI, 40m. Keep tight right, hold straight ahead after bend between 2 center channel rocks.

Lac Nelligan

"Pork Rapids" See Inset

12 day trips

R(3) & R(4)

Lac Ward

R(5)

CI Tech, 1000m. Easy enough.

(210)

R(6) CI, 20m. A cinch.

Abandoned E.B. Eddy Lumber Camp (1984)

Parc de la Vérendrye

Lac 2 Pomponne

Dumoine Link

Lac Larive

rocky rapids

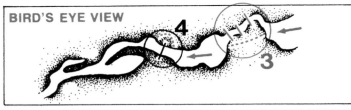

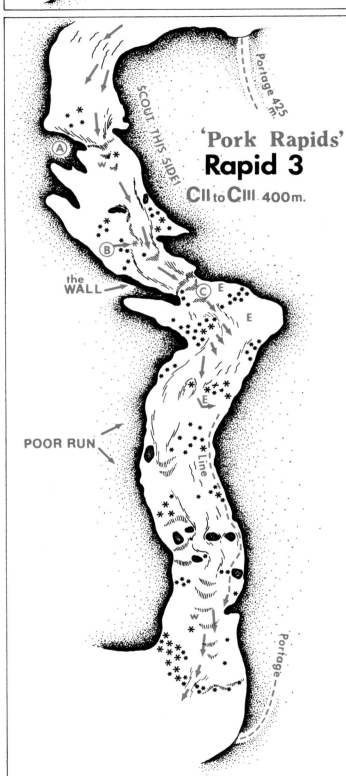

Portage 425 m.

SCOUT THIS SIDE!

'Pork Rapids'
Rapid 3
CII to CIII 400m.

(A)

W

(B)

the WALL

(C) E

E

E

POOR RUN

Line

W

Portage

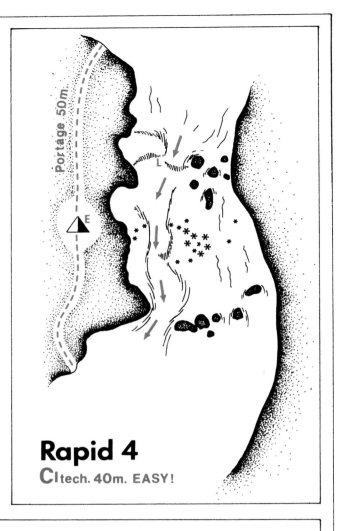

Portage 50m.

L

E

Rapid 4
CI tech. 40m. EASY!

This is not considered an easy run and The Wall can finish you off if you've already taken water at point "A" where there's a two foot ledge to drop over. Watch rock "B"...it could ruin more than your day. There's a small souse at "C", hold hard left, brace and then eddy out to the left to bail.

You can easily scout along the left shore during normal water levels and you can position a spotter across from the Wall. If someone is going to dump it'll be here. You can proceed another 75 meters but I suggest lining the bank after this to avoid a confusion of boulders and thin channels. The last leg is shallow but can be run with easy play to the center hole. If you're looking for a place to camp–rapid #4, just ahead, has an ideal site where huge square-timbers have been arranged around a commendable fire-pit.

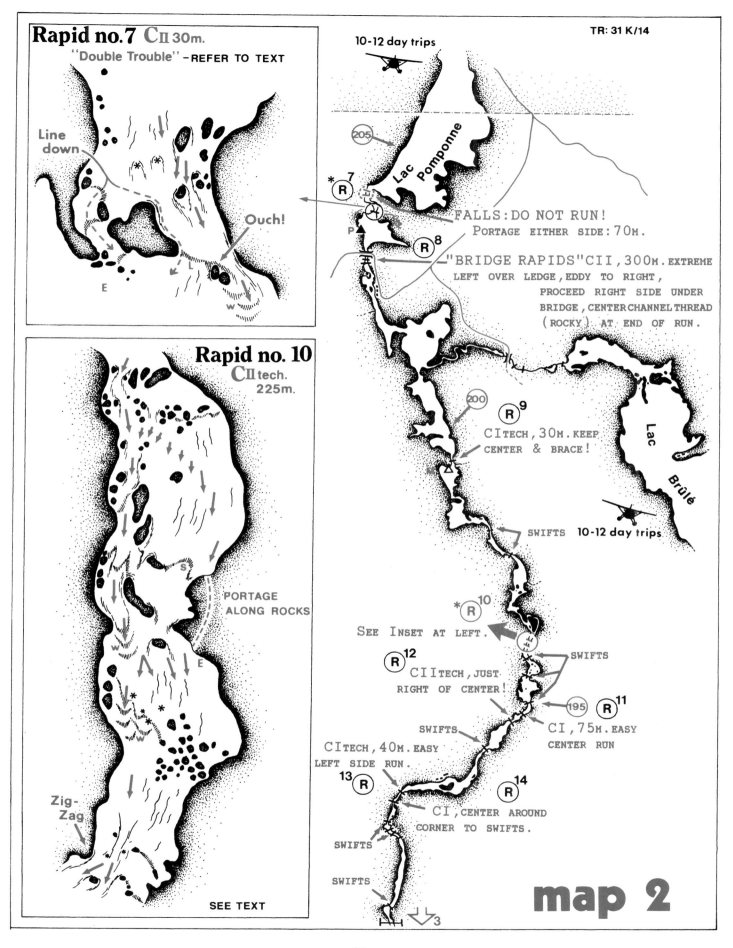

Rapid no. 7 C$_{II}$ 30m.
"Double Trouble" – REFER TO TEXT

Line down

Ouch!

E

L

W

10-12 day trips

Lac Pomponne

205

*7 R

P

R 8

FALLS: DO NOT RUN!
PORTAGE EITHER SIDE: 70M.

"BRIDGE RAPIDS" CII, 300M. EXTREME
LEFT OVER LEDGE, EDDY TO RIGHT,
PROCEED RIGHT SIDE UNDER
BRIDGE, CENTER CHANNEL THREAD
(ROCKY) AT END OF RUN.

200

R 9

CI TECH, 30M. KEEP
CENTER & BRACE!

M

Lac Brûlé

SWIFTS

10-12 day trips

Rapid no. 10
C$_{II}$ tech.
225m.

PORTAGE
ALONG ROCKS

S

W

E

Zig-Zag

SEE TEXT

*R 10

SEE INSET AT LEFT.

R 12

CII TECH, JUST
RIGHT OF CENTER!

SWIFTS

SWIFTS

195   R 11

CI, 75M. EASY
CENTER RUN

CI TECH, 40M. EASY
LEFT SIDE RUN.

13 R

R 14

CI, CENTER AROUND
CORNER TO SWIFTS.

SWIFTS

SWIFTS

map 2

3

83

Lac Pompone to "Stonewall Rapids"

E.B. Eddy abandoned Camp 206 in 1984. They just left everything and simply vanished. Machinery, boats, kitchen equipment, office supplies, work invoices – everything... scattered across a couple of acres of parched, oil-drenched and shack-littered shoreline. To keep vandals out a truck-bed was overturned in the creek, 200 meters down the access road...but then nothing keeps out the all-terrain vehicle nowadays. The camp had already been seriously pillaged over the past few years and now swallows and squirrels and other woodland critters roamed freely in and out of the vacant shells while the wind played a solitary tune through the dismembered gasoline pumps. You can camp here, if you wanted to...it's exposed but interesting enough to warrant an inspection and a couple of photographs.

The extent of wasted forest greets you at the bottom of Pomponne where the river tumbles over a ledge forming a small falls that has to be portaged. Cut timber, washed over the banks of the falls during spring run and never recovered, now lay drying like bleached bones piled high like mammoth

pick-up stix, only no-one was ever going to pick them up. It would make an interesting survey to inventory the value of the trees that never made it to the mill.

Rapid #7: "Double Trouble" is a short, but wiley run. This early into the trip you may want to line here – the flow washes against twin boulders at the bottom and it could be tricky work for green-hands to keep their canoe out of trouble.

Below here, campsites are few and far between so plan your trip carefully along this stretch. "Tall-pine Rapids" affords the next best stop-over; and if that's taken, there's a mid-size island campsite at mileage 181.

Rapid #10: This is a challenging CII technical with plenty of action. It can be approached in two ways: a right-side play all the way, or, ferry left and carry over the rocks to avoid the heavy stuff. The latter option may appeal to those who like to save their high-cards until the end of the game.

Starting at mileage 185 there is a lot of river activity and if it's near the end of the day you're probably already feeling the pangs of

fatigue – keep sharp, you have some work to do yet! The "Keel Hauler" is an interesting diagonal drop over a small ledge, a tight thread and a quick pivot right to escape the embrace of a rock island. Below rapid #19 you'll come to a serious CIII technical. My advice is to swallow your pride and pass this one by – the meek shall inherit the river. This rapid is not even included in the genre of runnables.

"TALL-PINE RAPIDS":

The top is intimidating and may get you off to a bad finish if you fail to read the signs. For those mortals with a flair for clean, easy runs, you can line down the island as indicated on the map to point "A". From here it's a simple ferry into the main run with lots of wave action as far as the campsite across the pond at the bottom. "Stonewall Rapids" can be scouted from the campsite by an adjoining logging trail. The rapids get their name from the rock embankments that were built-up to prevent logs from spilling over into the bush. For the next 20 kilometers you'll find it easy sailing, with several CI's and swifts as far as the falls at Batardeaux.

Creative play and gunnel-grab between the chutes

84

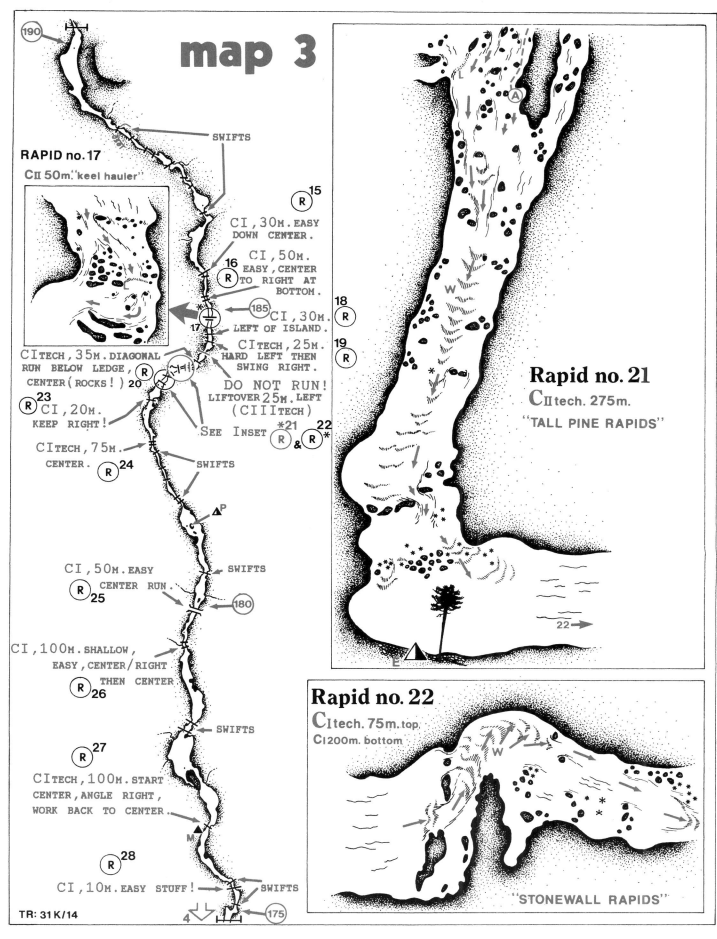

map 3

RAPID no. 17

C II 50m. "keel hauler"

190

SWIFTS

15
R

CI, 30M. EASY
DOWN CENTER.

CI, 50M.
EASY, CENTER
TO RIGHT AT
BOTTOM.

16
R

185

18
R

CI, 30M.
LEFT OF ISLAND.

17

CI TECH, 25M.
HARD LEFT THEN
SWING RIGHT.

19
R

CI TECH, 35M. DIAGONAL
RUN BELOW LEDGE,
CENTER (ROCKS!) 20

R

DO NOT RUN!
LIFTOVER 25M. LEFT
(CIII TECH)

23
R

CI, 20M.
KEEP RIGHT!

SEE INSET *21
R & 22 R *

CI TECH, 75M.
CENTER.

R 24

SWIFTS

△P

Rapid no. 21

C II tech. 275m.

"TALL PINE RAPIDS"

CI, 50M. EASY
CENTER RUN.

R 25

SWIFTS

180

CI, 100M. SHALLOW,
EASY, CENTER/RIGHT
THEN CENTER

R 26

SWIFTS

R 27

CI TECH, 100M. START
CENTER, ANGLE RIGHT,
WORK BACK TO CENTER.

▲M

R 28

CI, 10M. EASY STUFF!

SWIFTS

4

175

TR: 31 K/14

E

22

Rapid no. 22

C I tech. 75m. top,
C I 200m. bottom

W

"STONEWALL RAPIDS"

85

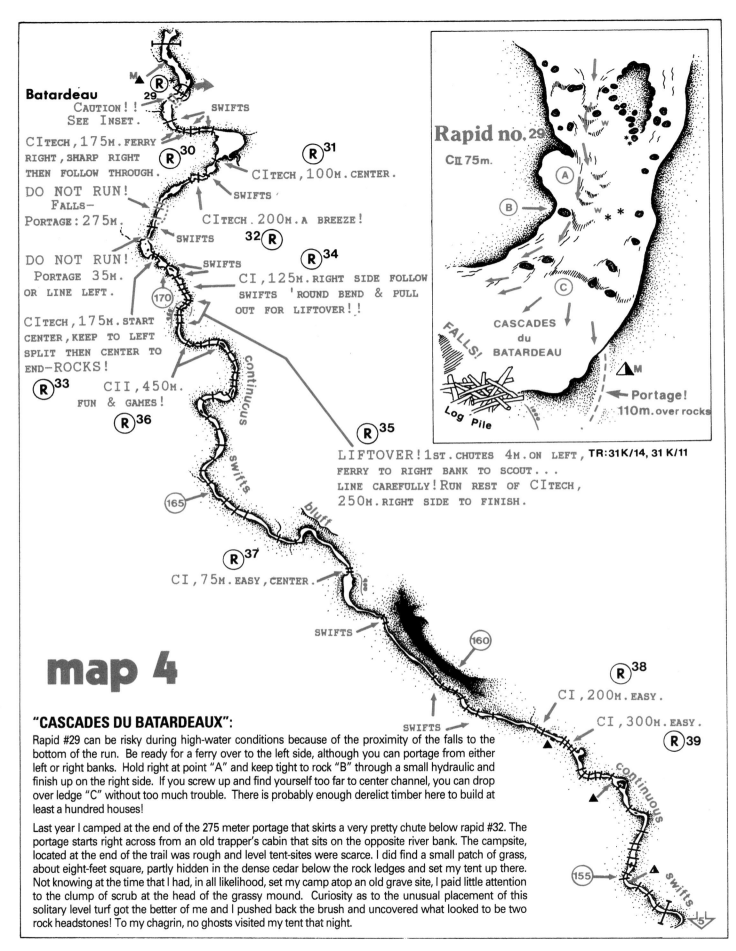

Batardeau

CAUTION!! SEE INSET.

R30 CI TECH, 175M. FERRY RIGHT, SHARP RIGHT THEN FOLLOW THROUGH.

R31 CI TECH, 100M. CENTER.

DO NOT RUN! FALLS— PORTAGE: 275M.

CI TECH. 200M. A BREEZE!

DO NOT RUN! PORTAGE 35M. OR LINE LEFT.

R32 SWIFTS

R34 CI, 125M. RIGHT SIDE FOLLOW SWIFTS 'ROUND BEND & PULL OUT FOR LIFTOVER!!

(170)

CI TECH, 175M. START CENTER, KEEP TO LEFT SPLIT THEN CENTER TO END—ROCKS!

R33 CII, 450M. FUN & GAMES!

R36

continuous swifts

(165)

bluff

R35 LIFTOVER! 1ST. CHUTES 4M. ON LEFT, **TR:31K/14, 31 K/11** FERRY TO RIGHT BANK TO SCOUT... LINE CAREFULLY! RUN REST OF CI TECH, 250M. RIGHT SIDE TO FINISH.

R37 CI, 75M. EASY, CENTER.

SWIFTS

(160)

SWIFTS

Rapid no. 29 CII 75M.

A
B
W
*
C
CASCADES du BATARDEAU

FALLS! Log Pile

▲M

← Portage! 110m. over rocks

map 4

R38 CI, 200M. EASY.

CI, 300M. EASY. **R39**

continuous

(155) ▲ swifts

"CASCADES DU BATARDEAUX":

Rapid #29 can be risky during high-water conditions because of the proximity of the falls to the bottom of the run. Be ready for a ferry over to the left side, although you can portage from either left or right banks. Hold right at point "A" and keep tight to rock "B" through a small hydraulic and finish up on the right side. If you screw up and find yourself too far to center channel, you can drop over ledge "C" without too much trouble. There is probably enough derelict timber here to build at least a hundred houses!

Last year I camped at the end of the 275 meter portage that skirts a very pretty chute below rapid #32. The portage starts right across from an old trapper's cabin that sits on the opposite river bank. The campsite, located at the end of the trail was rough and level tent-sites were scarce. I did find a small patch of grass, about eight-feet square, partly hidden in the dense cedar below the rock ledges and set my tent up there. Not knowing at the time that I had, in all likelihood, set my camp atop an old grave site, I paid little attention to the clump of scrub at the head of the grassy mound. Curiosity as to the unusual placement of this solitary level turf got the better of me and I pushed back the brush and uncovered what looked to be two rock headstones! To my chagrin, no ghosts visited my tent that night.

map 5

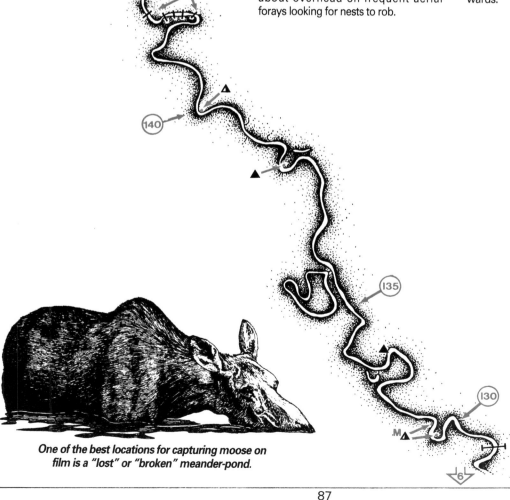

"THE RIVER SLOWS DOWN"

At least along the meanders you can always find a campsite on a beach...if you like pitching your camp on sand then you have a plethora of choices for the next 25 kilometers. Beach camps are fine places to read the signatures in the sand of the many animals and birds that frequent the river and adjoining marsh-lands.

Spotted Sandpipers or teeter-tails, named for the peculiar habit of bobbing their rear-ends up and down, are frequently seen scavenging for insects along the shores. Great Blue Herons, Barred Owls, Black Ducks and Mergansers often make sudden appearances as the canoe slips silently around a bend, like opening a new page to a storybook at every turn, something new is happening almost at every paddle-stroke. Bank Swallows and Kingfishers are sure to scold you for paddling too close to their nests while ravens circle about overhead on frequent aerial forays looking for nests to rob.

A wolf had approached to within a few meters of the tent one night while our group had set up camp on a beach point. Black bear, mink, otter and beaver tracks tell a story of daily occupations and nocturnal wanderings - the tiny footfall depressions in the moist sand left by the white-footed mouse, ending abruptly in a silent explosion of talon and wingtip percussions on the naked beach—a signature of death for the unsuspecting.

You won't find any beaver lodges along the river here; the water level fluctuates too much. They keep to the upper ponds and marshes, flooded creeks and broken or dead meanders. Snapping turtles often climb up on to the sandy slopes to bake in the hot sun or to lay their eggs.

You'll notice on the elevation chart on page 42, how the Coulonge levels off from mileage 160 to 125 and then begins to gradually descend afterwards.

One of the best locations for capturing moose on film is a "lost" or "broken" meander-pond.

TR: 31 K/11

87

map 6

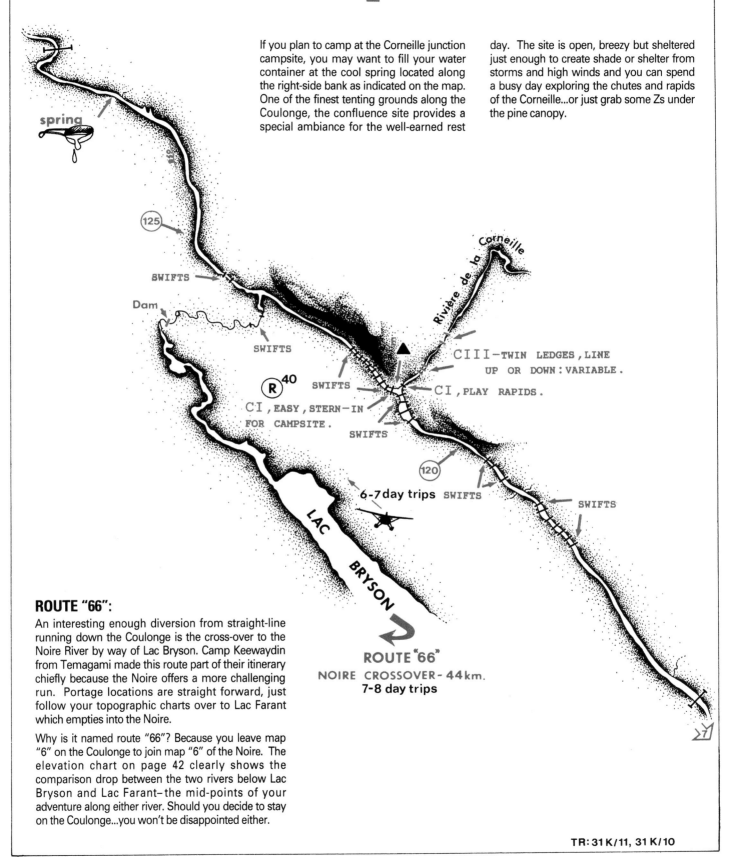

If you plan to camp at the Corneille junction campsite, you may want to fill your water container at the cool spring located along the right-side bank as indicated on the map. One of the finest tenting grounds along the Coulonge, the confluence site provides a special ambiance for the well-earned rest day. The site is open, breezy but sheltered just enough to create shade or shelter from storms and high winds and you can spend a busy day exploring the chutes and rapids of the Corneille...or just grab some Zs under the pine canopy.

spring

125

SWIFTS

Dam

SWIFTS

ⓇR 40

SWIFTS

CI, EASY, STERN-IN
FOR CAMPSITE.

SWIFTS

Rivière de la Corneille

CIII—TWIN LEDGES, LINE
UP OR DOWN: VARIABLE.

CI, PLAY RAPIDS.

120

6-7 day trips SWIFTS

SWIFTS

LAC BRYSON

ROUTE "66"
NOIRE CROSSOVER- 44km.
7-8 day trips

ROUTE "66":

An interesting enough diversion from straight-line running down the Coulonge is the cross-over to the Noire River by way of Lac Bryson. Camp Keewaydin from Temagami made this route part of their itinerary chiefly because the Noire offers a more challenging run. Portage locations are straight forward, just follow your topographic charts over to Lac Farant which empties into the Noire.

Why is it named route "66"? Because you leave map "6" on the Coulonge to join map "6" of the Noire. The elevation chart on page 42 clearly shows the comparison drop between the two rivers below Lac Bryson and Lac Farant–the mid-points of your adventure along either river. Should you decide to stay on the Coulonge...you won't be disappointed either.

TR: 31 K/11, 31 K/10

map 7

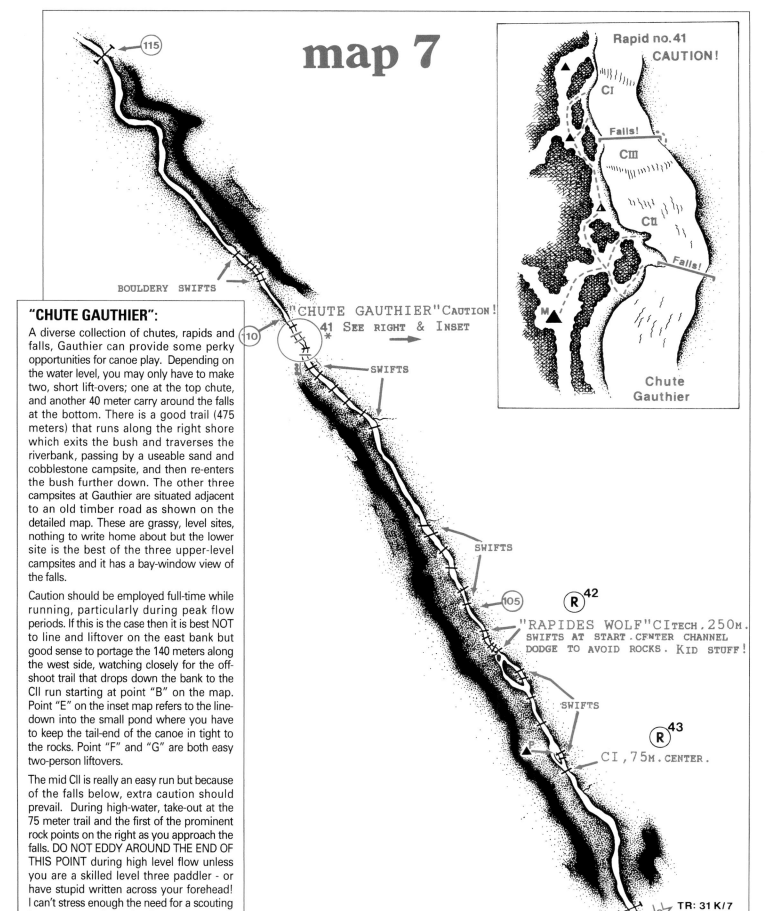

115 ←

Rapid no. 41
CAUTION!

CI

Falls!

CIII

CII

Falls!

M

Chute
Gauthier

BOULDERY SWIFTS

"CHUTE GAUTHIER" Caution!
41 See right & Inset
*

10 →

"CHUTE GAUTHIER":

A diverse collection of chutes, rapids and falls, Gauthier can provide some perky opportunities for canoe play. Depending on the water level, you may only have to make two, short lift-overs; one at the top chute, and another 40 meter carry around the falls at the bottom. There is a good trail (475 meters) that runs along the right shore which exits the bush and traverses the riverbank, passing by a useable sand and cobblestone campsite, and then re-enters the bush further down. The other three campsites at Gauthier are situated adjacent to an old timber road as shown on the detailed map. These are grassy, level sites, nothing to write home about but the lower site is the best of the three upper-level campsites and it has a bay-window view of the falls.

Caution should be employed full-time while running, particularly during peak flow periods. If this is the case then it is best NOT to line and liftover on the east bank but good sense to portage the 140 meters along the west side, watching closely for the off-shoot trail that drops down the bank to the CII run starting at point "B" on the map. Point "E" on the inset map refers to the line-down into the small pond where you have to keep the tail-end of the canoe in tight to the rocks. Point "F" and "G" are both easy two-person liftovers.

The mid CII is really an easy run but because of the falls below, extra caution should prevail. During high-water, take-out at the 75 meter trail and the first of the prominent rock points on the right as you approach the falls. DO NOT EDDY AROUND THE END OF THIS POINT during high level flow unless you are a skilled level three paddler - or have stupid written across your forehead! I can't stress enough the need for a scouting here–you can always hoof your gear across to the campsite and then walk back surveying the layout for the empty run down with the canoes and a light load.

SWIFTS

SWIFTS

105 ←

R 42

"RAPIDES WOLF" CI tech. 250m.
SWIFTS AT START. CENTER CHANNEL
DODGE TO AVOID ROCKS. KID STUFF!

SWIFTS

R 43

CI, 75m. CENTER.

P

8 ⟶

TR: 31 K/7

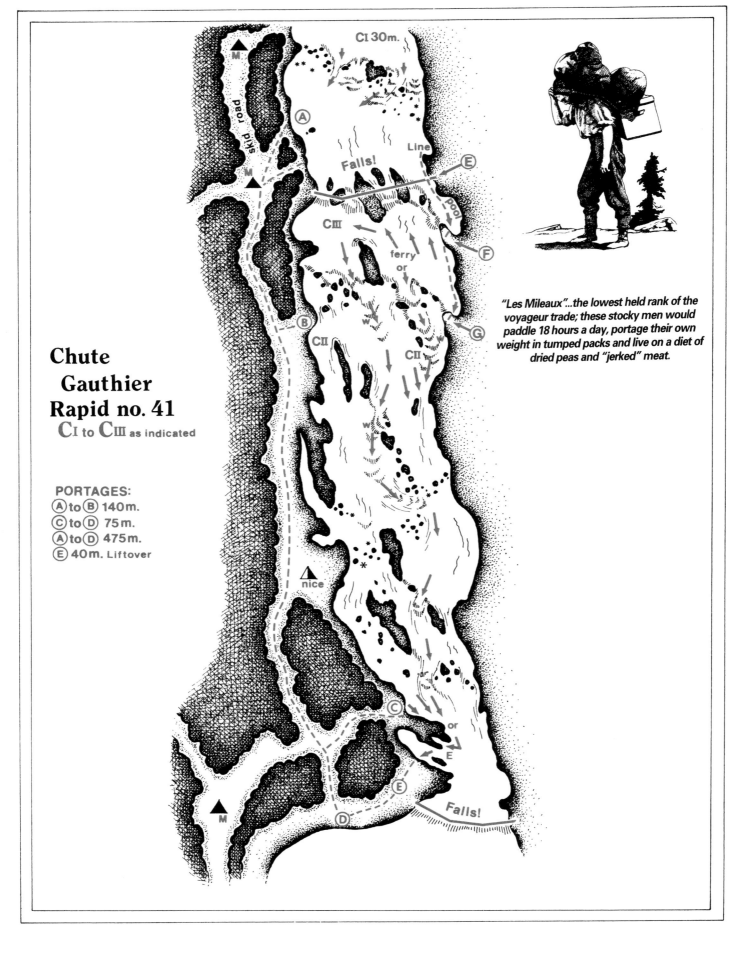

Chute Gauthier Rapid no. 41
CI to CIII as indicated

PORTAGES:
- (A) to (B) 140m.
- (C) to (D) 75m.
- (A) to (D) 475m.
- (E) 40m. Liftover

CI 30m.

Falls!

Line

CIII

ferry

or

CII

CII

nice

or

E

Falls!

skid road

"*Les Mileaux*"...the lowest held rank of the voyageur trade; these stocky men would paddle 18 hours a day, portage their own weight in tumped packs and live on a diet of dried peas and "jerked" meat.

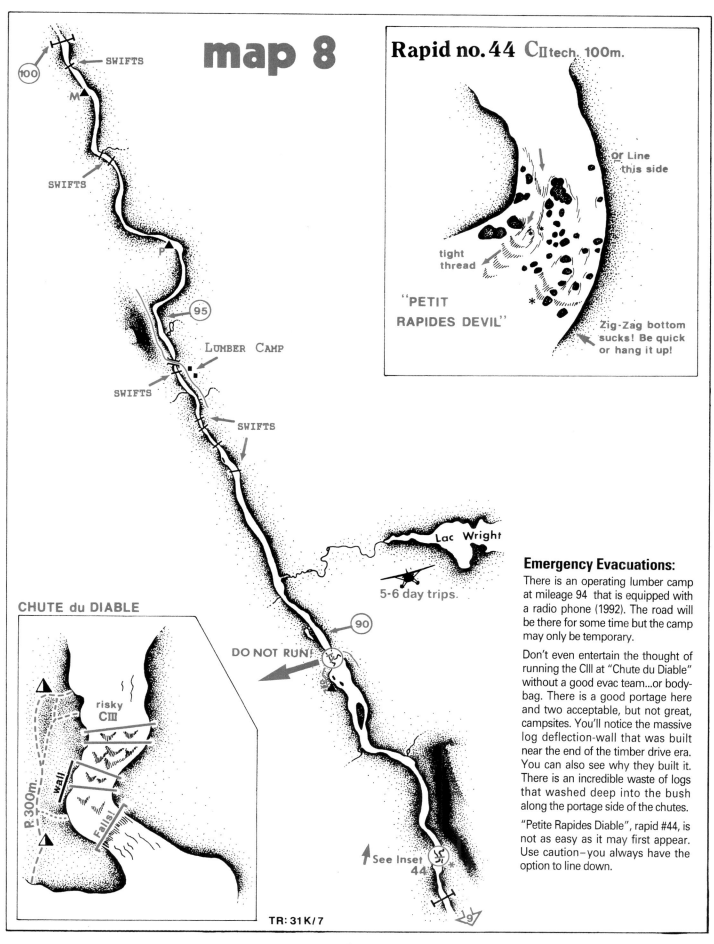

map 8

SWIFTS

100

M

SWIFTS

P

95

LUMBER CAMP

SWIFTS

SWIFTS

Rapid no. 44 C II tech. 100m.

Or Line
this side

tight
thread

"PETIT
RAPIDES DEVIL"

Zig-Zag bottom
sucks! Be quick
or hang it up!

Lac Wright

5-6 day trips.

90

CHUTE du DIABLE

DO NOT RUN!

risky
C III

R. 300m.

wall

Falls!

See Inset
44

9

TR: 31K/7

Emergency Evacuations:

There is an operating lumber camp at mileage 94 that is equipped with a radio phone (1992). The road will be there for some time but the camp may only be temporary.

Don't even entertain the thought of running the CIII at "Chute du Diable" without a good evac team...or body-bag. There is a good portage here and two acceptable, but not great, campsites. You'll notice the massive log deflection-wall that was built near the end of the timber drive era. You can also see why they built it. There is an incredible waste of logs that washed deep into the bush along the portage side of the chutes.

"Petite Rapides Diable", rapid #44, is not as easy as it may first appear. Use caution—you always have the option to line down.

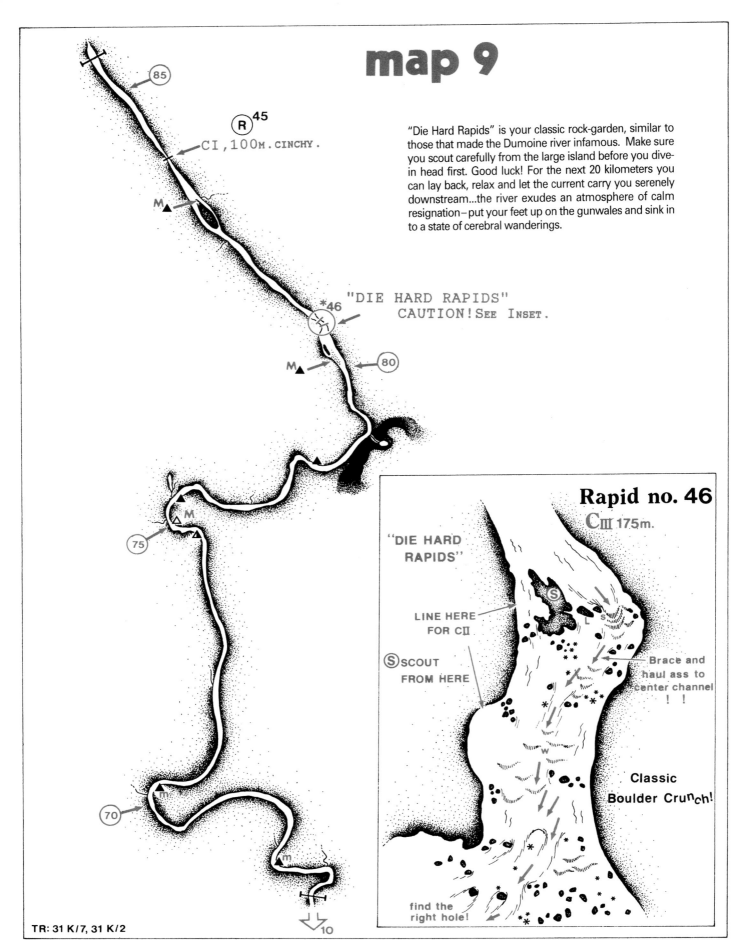

map 9

(85)

(R)⁴⁵
CI,100M.CINCHY.

M▲

"DIE HARD RAPIDS"
CAUTION! See Inset.

*46

M▲ (80)

M

(75)

(70) m

m

"Die Hard Rapids" is your classic rock-garden, similar to those that made the Dumoine river infamous. Make sure you scout carefully from the large island before you dive-in head first. Good luck! For the next 20 kilometers you can lay back, relax and let the current carry you serenely downstream...the river exudes an atmosphere of calm resignation – put your feet up on the gunwales and sink in to a state of cerebral wanderings.

Rapid no. 46
C_{III} 175m.

"DIE HARD RAPIDS"

LINE HERE FOR CII

(S) SCOUT FROM HERE

(S)

L s

Brace and haul ass to center channel ! !

w

Classic Boulder Crunch!

find the right hole!

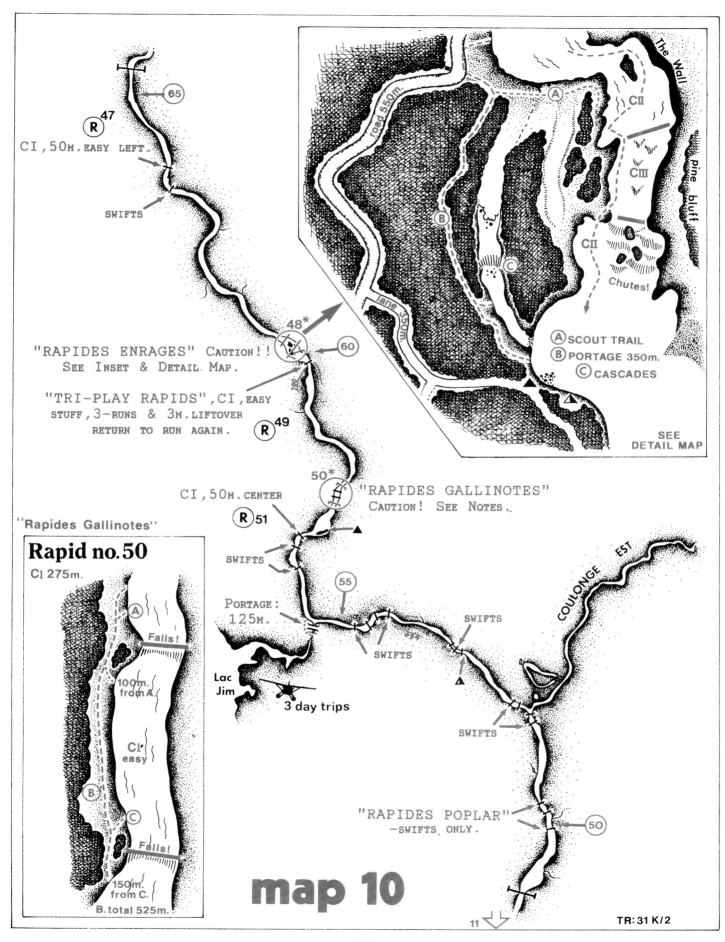

Rapid no.50

CI 275m.

Ⓐ

Falls!

100m. from A.

CI easy

Ⓑ

Ⓒ

Falls!

150m. from C.

B. total 525m.

"Rapides Gallinotes"

65

Ⓡ⁴⁷

CI, 50M. EASY LEFT.

SWIFTS

48*

"RAPIDES ENRAGES" CAUTION!! SEE INSET & DETAIL MAP.

60

"TRI-PLAY RAPIDS", CI, EASY STUFF, 3-RUNS & 3M. LIFTOVER RETURN TO RUN AGAIN.

Ⓡ⁴⁹

50*

CI, 50M. CENTER

"RAPIDES GALLINOTES" CAUTION! SEE NOTES.

Ⓡ 51

SWIFTS

55

PORTAGE: 125M.

SWIFTS

SWIFTS

SWIFTS

Lac Jim

3 day trips

SWIFTS

COULONGE EST

"RAPIDES POPLAR" —SWIFTS, ONLY.

50

map 10

11

Detail map:

road 550m.

lane 350m.

700

west 350m.

Ⓐ

The Wall

CII

CIII

pine bluff

Ⓑ

Ⓒ

CII

Chutes!

Ⓐ SCOUT TRAIL

Ⓑ PORTAGE 350m.

Ⓒ CASCADES

SEE DETAIL MAP

TR: 31 K/2

"RAPIDES GALLINOTES":

This is an easy double carry with a placid CI in between. There is an intriguing rock mosaic along the shore here, certainly worth investigating. You'll see a crossing of two compressed rock-veins; one quartz, the other some molten magna of volcanic rock, both coming together at a pothole–a depression made from water flowing in a circular pattern, usually pushing stones around for a few million years.

Out of curiosity I began pulling stones, sand and rocks out of the watery hole eventually coming upon a vintage pop bottle that was probably turfed by some logger in 1940 or something. It wasn't quite the artifact I was hoping to find...like an astrolabe maybe, however the excitement of the moment gave way to a rather anti-climactic volley of laughter from all.

The falls are badly molded, and well worth a couple of camera snaps. During high-water you may have to approach the portage landings with extra care and make sure your upstream end is in tight before beaching. The river continues to drop steadily, past the confluence of the East Coulonge, through the disappointing "Rapides Poplar" which are nothing more than glorified swifts...an extremely picturesque part of the voyage through steep-sided hills of pine and hardwood.

Chutes du Diable

A quiet campsite...Big Pine Rapids

94

Rapid no. 48

CII to CIII as indicated

'Rapides Enrages'

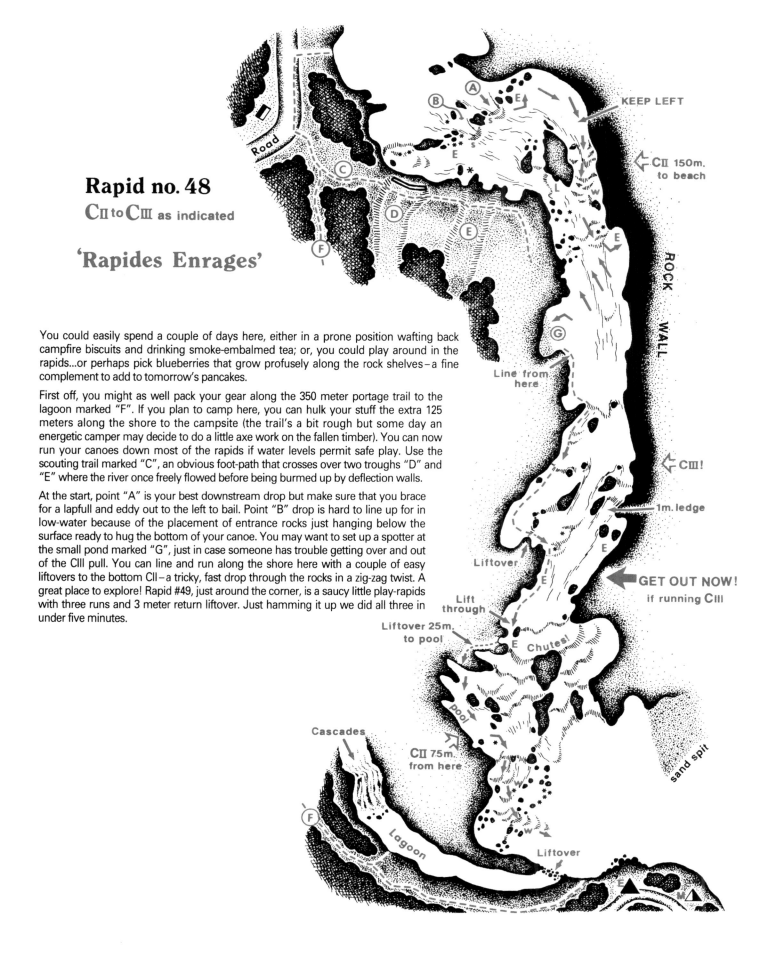

You could easily spend a couple of days here, either in a prone position wafting back campfire biscuits and drinking smoke-embalmed tea; or, you could play around in the rapids...or perhaps pick blueberries that grow profusely along the rock shelves – a fine complement to add to tomorrow's pancakes.

First off, you might as well pack your gear along the 350 meter portage trail to the lagoon marked "F". If you plan to camp here, you can hulk your stuff the extra 125 meters along the shore to the campsite (the trail's a bit rough but some day an energetic camper may decide to do a little axe work on the fallen timber). You can now run your canoes down most of the rapids if water levels permit safe play. Use the scouting trail marked "C", an obvious foot-path that crosses over two troughs "D" and "E" where the river once freely flowed before being burmed up by deflection walls.

At the start, point "A" is your best downstream drop but make sure that you brace for a lapfull and eddy out to the left to bail. Point "B" drop is hard to line up for in low-water because of the placement of entrance rocks just hanging below the surface ready to hug the bottom of your canoe. You may want to set up a spotter at the small pond marked "G", just in case someone has trouble getting over and out of the CIII pull. You can line and run along the shore here with a couple of easy liftovers to the bottom CII – a tricky, fast drop through the rocks in a zig-zag twist. A great place to explore! Rapid #49, just around the corner, is a saucy little play-rapids with three runs and 3 meter return liftover. Just hamming it up we did all three in under five minutes.

95

map 11

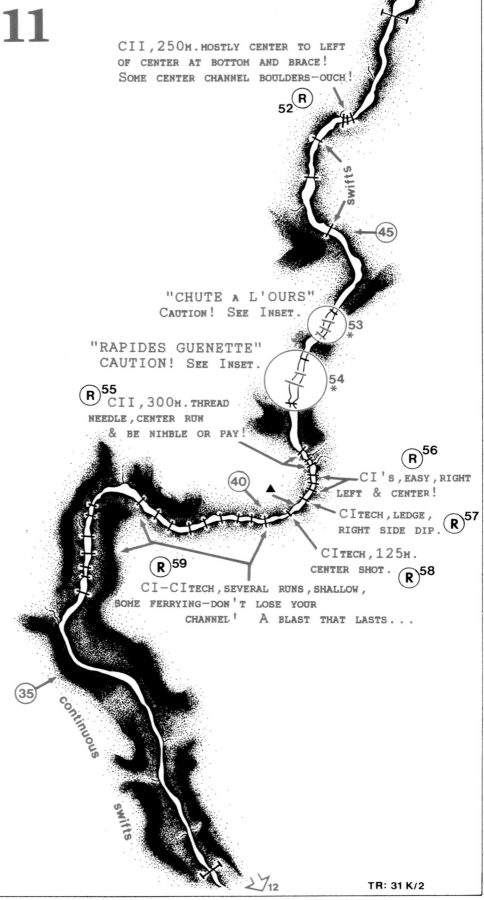

CII, 250M. MOSTLY CENTER TO LEFT
OF CENTER AT BOTTOM AND BRACE!
SOME CENTER CHANNEL BOULDERS—OUCH!

52 (R)

swifts

(45)

"CHUTE A L'OURS"
CAUTION! SEE INSET.

53
*

"RAPIDES GUENETTE"
CAUTION! SEE INSET.

54
*

(R) 55
CII, 300M. THREAD
NEEDLE, CENTER RUN
& BE NIMBLE OR PAY!

(40)

(R) 56

CI'S, EASY, RIGHT
LEFT & CENTER!

CI TECH, LEDGE,
RIGHT SIDE DIP.

(R) 57

CI TECH, 125M.
CENTER SHOT.

(R) 58

(R) 59

CI-CI TECH, SEVERAL RUNS, SHALLOW,
SOME FERRYING—DON'T LOSE YOUR
CHANNEL! A BLAST THAT LASTS...

(35)

continuous

swifts

12

TR: 31 K/2

"RAPIDES GUINETTE":

Midway down the run, on a prominent rocky point that juts out on the west-side bank you'll find a good campsite and a commemorative shrine to Alex Guinette, a riverman that gave up his life in the rapids. The top of this run is a straightforward CI that branches off to give you the option of following the right bank through to the CII technical; or, ferry left to point "A" and liftover the rocks for three meters to avoid the cascading ledge "E". Point "C" indicates where the flow picks you up suddenly and hurls you toward this boulder...you'll notice splotches of canoe paint on this one where canoeists got caught with their paddles out of the water!!

The cross-river ledge below the campsite should be avoided. You may be lucky to find a hole in high-water but in normal conditions you'll just drop over and get hung up. Liftover and start the CII run clean and neat with a side-slip left to center channel and a run through a gauntlet of rocks. Point "D" defines an optional route for lining through or a tight, rocky squeeze-play along the shallows.

There is a triple ledge to contend with from here; not difficult if you line up properly—just try and stay out of the small hydraulics and ease right to avoid the wave action on each run...or line along the far west bank. Tilley hats-off to Alex Guinette—a mighty fine set of rapids!

There is a five kilometer run of CI's and CII's as far as mileage 35; none are difficult but you still need a quick eye to spot the rocks that seem to pop up in the craziest places. Watch too that you avoid wrong line-up on the ledges—a lot of fun for your money.

Just after rapid #57 you'll find an excellent campsite in the pines—a good alternative site to the one at Guinette with a lot more room.

Rapid no. 53

'Chute a L'Ours'

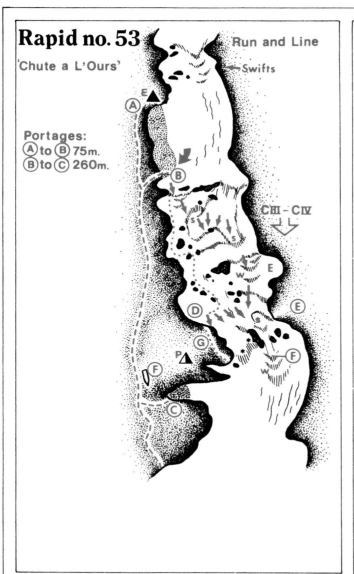

Run and Line
→ Swifts

Portages:
(A) to (B) 75m.
(B) to (C) 260m.

CIII – CIV

Rapid no. 54

'Rapides Guenette'

Classification as
Indicated
TOTAL RUN: 1km.

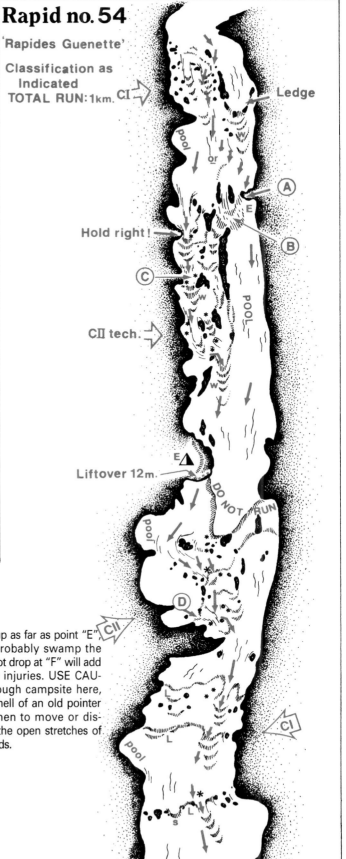

CI →
Ledge
(A)
E
(B)

Hold right!

(C)

POOL

CII tech. →

Liftover 12m.
E

DO NOT RUN

pool

(D)

CII →

CI →

pool

swifts

"CHUTES A L'OURS":

There is a classic pine campsite at the head of the rapids below the swifts – or a good lunch spot to rest before the portage. If you are moving through during high-water, take the easy 260 meter portage starting at point "B" to "D" (as shown by the dotted line on the map – not arrows!) Then a short liftover to clear a particularly nasty CIV. The CIII run (marked with arrows), should only be done by seriously advanced or demented paddlers. If you end up as far as point "E", then the hole will probably swamp the canoe and the four foot drop at "F" will add insult to your many injuries. USE CAUTION! There is a rough campsite here, located behind the shell of an old pointer boat used by rivermen to move or disentangle logs along the open stretches of river between the rapids.

map 12

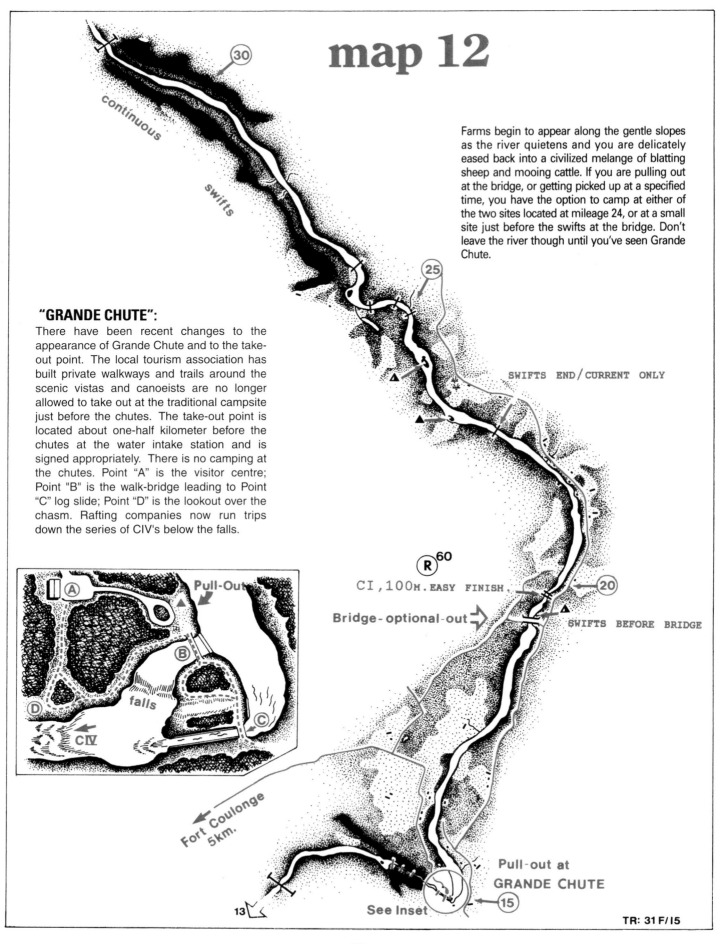

Farms begin to appear along the gentle slopes as the river quietens and you are delicately eased back into a civilized melange of blatting sheep and mooing cattle. If you are pulling out at the bridge, or getting picked up at a specified time, you have the option to camp at either of the two sites located at mileage 24, or at a small site just before the swifts at the bridge. Don't leave the river though until you've seen Grande Chute.

continuous

swifts

30

25

"GRANDE CHUTE":

There have been recent changes to the appearance of Grande Chute and to the take-out point. The local tourism association has built private walkways and trails around the scenic vistas and canoeists are no longer allowed to take out at the traditional campsite just before the chutes. The take-out point is located about one-half kilometer before the chutes at the water intake station and is signed appropriately. There is no camping at the chutes. Point "A" is the visitor centre; Point "B" is the walk-bridge leading to Point "C" log slide; Point "D" is the lookout over the chasm. Rafting companies now run trips down the series of CIV's below the falls.

SWIFTS END/CURRENT ONLY

R 60

CI,100M. EASY FINISH

Bridge-optional-out ➡

SWIFTS BEFORE BRIDGE

20

Pull-Out

A

B

C

D

falls

CIV

Fort Coulonge 5km.

Pull-out at GRANDE CHUTE

13

See Inset

15

TR: 31 F/15

map 13

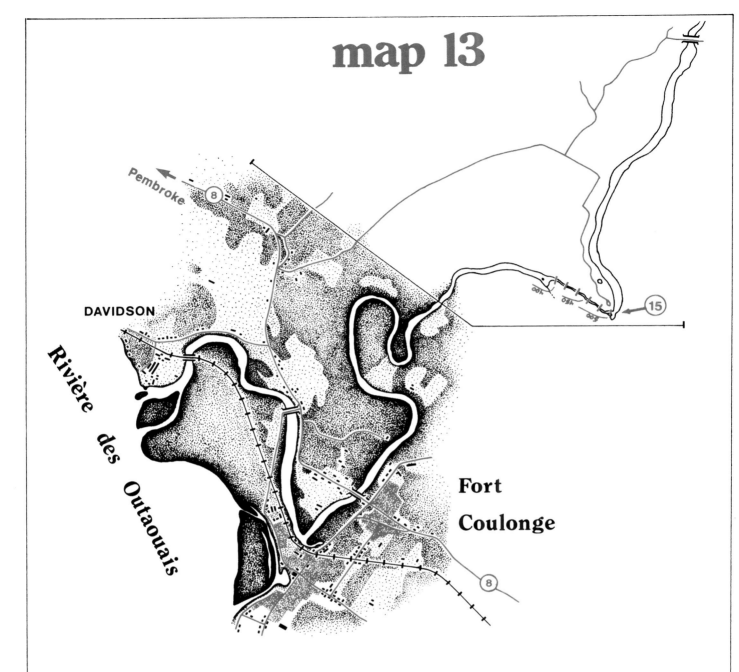

Pembroke

DAVIDSON

Rivière des Outaouais

Fort Coulonge

THE ADVENTURE ISN'T OVER YET

A valid complaint that local Quebecois have against canoeists is that they generally do not spend any money. If we were to contribute more to local economies we would certainly have a stronger voice when it came to issues of land management and environmental concerns that may affect the integrity of the river experience.

Please, patronize the small village shopkeeper throughout the Ottawa Valley; Fort Coulonge, Waltham Station, Chapeau ...the residents are extremely warmhearted and helpful. While you're in the area you may want to visit Grande Chute dam on the Noire, Mont Dube north of Chapeau or even play in the rapids at Morrison Island–the voyageurs once ran their canot de maitre down the east rapids here.

TR: 31 F/15

Memorial to a dead riverman...Guinette Rapids

Camp at Guinette Rapids

Log flume at Grande Chute

– Section IV –

Afternotes

" ...the pretty rosebuds that blossom in the gardens of Mattawa, those full-blown flowers that adorn the walk of human life. Can I forget the witchery of their soft dark eyes... "

**—Colin Rankin, factor, H.B.C. post in Mattawa
tribute to native women**

The Politics of Wilderness

Rivers provide us with the last vestiges of wilderness and seclusion simply because we have managed to invade the privacy of nature everywhere else with a network of roads and development. The intrusion into once secret places remains unchecked by those sitting in the management position who yield the fruit of our resources to those who portend to generate the most economic gain.

When it comes down to the crunch, how much are we willing to do to protect the integrity of that wilderness? Will we voluntarily chain ourselves to road-building bulldozers, tree-crunching skidders...blockade access or strap ourselves to giant pines? Not likely. In the least we'll buy a membership into a canoeing club or organization, maybe write a letter to a non-plussed politician but sure enough we'll complain incessantly amongst ourselves about a new river crossing, clear-cut logging operation that wiped out a portage or the development of another riverside strip-mine. Meanwhile it's business as usual for our corporate and government hierarchy and the quality of the pristine river experience erodes, and...instead of fighting to protect it from further degradation we lose interest and move on.

The politics of wilderness is about social and economic manipulation by this country's industrialists. They have had carte blanche access to our resources made available through the unquestioned authority of those governing our wild places. Multiple-use of crown-land is promoted under the democratic theory that equally allows the seekers of wilderness and quietude to co-habitate with the chainsaw wielding logger, the all-terrain vehicle sportsman and the R.V. camper. Tying up tracts of land for "single use" preserves for self-propelled recreation is undemocratic. Oddly enough our government is striving towards creating single-use of all remaining wild areas by employing multiple-use strategy which eventually will relinquish all crown lands to extractive or high-impact user groups. Even provincial parkland is threatened by policy change and re-classification which allows access by hard-use groups. What do we do about it–virtually nothing save for a handful of dedicated individuals. We are nothing but grumbling couch-potato activists when it comes to speaking out for a worthy enough cause–like saving wilderness rivers.

It has been the general rule of thumb that if a river has a low or negative self-propelled recreational flow (canoeists), then the doors are wide open for resource exploitation, extractive-based recreation (hunting) and minimal shoreline reserve status.

On the other hand, an acknowledged "recreational" class river always receives preferential treatment. Thirty meter shore reserves may be increased to one-hundred and twenty, access may be curtailed and policy implemented to at least conserve wilderness values. Canoeing then, as an economic contributor, assumes a place alongside of the other forest-user groups. However, in doing so we are forced to abandon the emotional or psychological plea to save wild places. We compromise our own integrity to appease forest managers and become "politically correct."

In 1978, I published the "Temagami Canoe Routes" book through the Ontario Ministry of Natural Resources. This project was undertaken certainly not with the intent to exploit the region for some purported economic gratuities, but to establish an inventory of canoe trails, enforce protective buffers and to

Iron-ore pit in Temagami – Sherman Mine ... an environmental nightmare

disperse traffic from the increasingly popular Lady Evelyn River Waterway Park. The book provided 65% additional regional canoe routes and established at least minimal protection status along waterways that were being threatened by logging interests. It also resulted in the protection of much of Temagami's ancient "nastawgan" or native travel routes, established hiking trails through old-growth pineries and opened a whole new field of opportunity for exploring canoeists.

Temagami clear-cut logging...now called "multiple-specie harvesting."

There are always trade-offs. In order to protect our wilderness rivers we inevitably must make them known to the canoeing public. There is no grey-area of choice here. Hopefully, through a responsible approach to wilderness travel we won't succumb to the depths of ignorance and reckless abandon...love our rivers "to death" with callous indifference to environmental or wilderness ethics.

Knowledge is power... the more we understand about our rivers, the greater the opportunity we create to enjoy their attributes in a sustainable fashion. We also prove to the powers in control that the river is worth more left alone than sheered of forest or dammed for power.

In the past we have relied on sub-standard information about rivers composed by non-professional canoeists, usually based on aerial surveys and a lot of guesswork. Most information provided by government offices falls into this category. Data is antiquated, inaccurate and outright dangerous in a lot of cases.

Most natural resources district authorities did not acknowledge the importance of recreational canoeing until recently. Budgets for crown-land maintenance are still only applied

River crossings...most are not necessary

to parks only and that leaves rivers or canoe routes outside these preserves to fend for themselves. The free-for-all land grab is dominated by whichever user-group makes the most noise, controls the fourth estate or dumps the biggest contribution into political coffers.

Canoeists are pacifists – an admirable quality induced by our reverence for quiet places, peaceful co-existence with nature and solitude. North Americans are in fact, spending more money and time observing nature instead of terminating it, but...the political pecking order has subjugated those preservable and sustainable activities below those of traditional use and abuse impact sports.

Why? Because we don't have the powerful groups like the NRA or the Ontario Federation of Anglers and Hunters speaking out for us. Surely if the government collected licence fees from canoeists as they do from anglers and hunters, the subsequent revenue may contribute to a better understanding of the need to preserve wilderness areas.

The canoeing industry does generate millions of dollars; a mere pittance is collected by governments through the issuing of travel permits. This is one reason why canoeing has never been heralded as an industry per se, but more of an "invisible" past-time for southern tourists . Canoeists don't loiter in obvious places long enough to be considered an economic contributor...locally or otherwise.

In 1979, during the fight to create the Lady Evelyn-Smoothwater Wilderness Park in Temagami, the mayor of Haileybury was quoted in a local paper as saying, "canoeists leave five cents and a trail of beer cans." This neanderthal mentality was born out of our subtleness as "tourists", rendering us unimportant and certainly ineffectual when it comes to formulating a political view.

Our only solace is to make it obvious that we are out there enjoying these rivers in an economically viable way. We'll keep the real reason for river tripping to ourselves...the magic and mystery, the challenge and reward – that way we can preserve both the integrity of our own values and the sanctity and completeness of the river environs.

Trip Log

Check List

Menu Chart – 2 weeks

BREAKFAST	LUNCH	DINNER

DAY 1

BREAKFAST	LUNCH	DINNER

DAY 2

BREAKFAST	LUNCH	DINNER

DAY 3

BREAKFAST	LUNCH	DINNER

DAY 4

BREAKFAST	LUNCH	DINNER

DAY 5

BREAKFAST	LUNCH	DINNER

DAY 6

BREAKFAST	LUNCH	DINNER

DAY 7

BREAKFAST	LUNCH	DINNER

DAY 8

BREAKFAST	LUNCH	DINNER

DAY 9

BREAKFAST	LUNCH	DINNER

DAY 10

BREAKFAST	LUNCH	DINNER

DAY 11

BREAKFAST	LUNCH	DINNER

DAY 12

BREAKFAST	LUNCH	DINNER

DAY 13

BREAKFAST	LUNCH	DINNER

DAY 14

River Notes

Upper Ottawa Valley "Time Table"

1534-5: Jacques Cartier explores Gulf of St. Lawrence and claims new land for France.

1609: Hurons first learned of French coming up St. Lawrence; sent "Atironta", headman of the Arendarhonon tribe to make alliance and help fight Iroquois. Battle of Lake Champlain, unprovoked attack on Iroquois by Champlain who quickly learn that wood-slat armour does not repel musket shot!

1610: Battle of Richilieu River keeps Iroquois quiet until 1634.

1610-11: Henry Hudson spends winter on Hudson's Bay-crew mutinies in spring and set him afloat.

1610-23: Explorations up Ottawa River by Etienne Brule.

1613-15: Champlain explores Ottawa and Mattawa Rivers and produces first map.

1616: Nipissing Indians offer to take Champlain to James Bay where they have been trading with the Cree for some time (via the Missinaibi and Abitibi Rivers); Algonquins dissuade Champlain from going.

1620-30: Tessouat, powerful chief of the Kici-si-bi Algonquin, exact tolls at Morrison's Island. Jean Nicolet lives with the Nipissing natives.

1630's: Jesuits begin to move in and control fur trade for their own economic benefit and convert heathens to Christianity.

1633: Brule murdered by the Huron.

1634: Explorations by Nicolet as far west as Wisconsin.

1635: Champlain dies, exploration slackens while Iroquois increase hostilities.

1647-50: Ferocious Iroquois wars, Hurons destroyed and Algonquins and Nipissings driven out of Ottawa Valley.

1654: Iroquois Peace Treaty, Ottawa Valley still under Iroquois control and remains uninhabited. "Coureur de bois" now serve as middlemen for the fur-trade because of severed trade link with Huron and Ojibway.

1658-63: Explorations by Radisson and Grosselliers.

1660: Ojibway and Huron refugees oust Iroquois from central Ontario; 700 canoes gather on Lake Huron prior to battle. Nipissings return to Mattawa River.

1669-70: Galinee and Casson, two suplican priests, produce map of the Ottawa River.

1670: Hudson's Bay Company formed in England.

1673: Explorations by Marquette and Joliet.

1679-80: Fort Coulonge established by the d'Ailleboust family. Chevalier du Troyes establishes Lake Temiskaming trading post at the mouth of the Montreal River.

1686: French military expedition under du Troyes passes through Lake Temiskaming and goes on to capture all H.B.C. posts on Hudson's Bay.

1688: Party of Iroquois massacre garrison on Lake Temiskaming and post is abandoned.

1697: Le Moynes, a French trading family paddles up the Ottawa–Dumoine River finds a name.

1713: Treaty of Utrecht ends French/English war in Englands favour–H.B.C. given authority over James Bay region.

1720: Paul Guillet, French trader, establishes Fort Temiskaming.

1730: French trading post established at the mouth of the Dumoine River.

1731-43: Explorations of La Verendrye-first to view rockies.

1759-60: British defeat French at Quebec and Montreal-New France falls to English & British fur traders begin Montreal operations.

1761: Alexander Henry establishes Fort Coulonge as post.

1763: Treaty of Paris–British cede colony of New France to the French.

1763-85: Great fur rivalry between Montreal factors leads to formation of the "North West Company" or N.W.C.in 1779.

1783-93: Explorations by Alexander MacKenzie.

1800: Teme-Augama Anishnabai settle in Temagami.

1801-2: Winter of starvation in upper Ottawa Valley for natives.

1806: Napoleon blocks Englands timber trade with the Baltic–Pressure now to use Canadian forest reserves.

1810: Usborne family acquires pine reserves along Coulonge River.

1812-14: Napoleonic Wars and War of 1812 with the U.S.–Great Lakes first use of steam-powered ships.

1815: End of Napoleanic wars–British government gives tracts of land to veterans (mostly south of Pembroke).

1820's: Quebec tributaries (Dumoine, Noire, Coulonge, Kipawa) still unexplored. Gillies, Wright and Bryson, timber barons, send cullers in to inventory this region for pine.

1821: Amalgamation of H.B.C. and N.W.C. –Fur-trade routes wane in Valley while Hudson's Bay route is more efficiently serviced.

1823: Fort William established by H.B.C.

1824-5: Another winter of starvation in Upper Valley area due to poor hunting success.
Creation of the wood/canvas canoe.

1857: Peterborough Ontario organizes first "canoe regatta".
First wood/canvas canoe design introduced by John Edwards.
H.B.C. begins gradual retreat from Ottawa Valley.

1858: The "Walter's Axe Co." of Hull, P.Q. produces the famous "Ottawa Valley Axe".

1859: Legendary canoe brigades cancelled along Ottawa River -goods now shipped by rail and steamer.

1859-67: Lumber interests build Ottawa/-Brockville rail lines and several side tracks - now connects Arnprior directly with U.S. market.

1861: W. MacKay purchases 100 sq.miles of timber limits for $4.00/acre (sells limit to J.R. Booth in 1902 for $665,000.).
Pembroke Light Co. established and is first in Ontario to install electric street lighting from their own power source.

1866: Royal Canoe Club formed in London England, founded by John MacGregor and Warington Baden-Powell. First club devoted to canoeing in history.
Abrogation of the Reciprocity Treaty.

1867: Confederation of Canada established.

1868-76: Destructive fires from timber slash devastate Petawawa and Barron Rivers.

1869: New England States adopt recreational canoeing.

1870: Canada annexes H.B.C. territories ending monopoly that spanned the continent.
Logging commences along the Montreal River.
G. Bryson promotes Pontiac and Pacific Junction railway–Hull to Waltham Station and Noire River (later C.P.R.).
Heavy influence by timber barons on Canadian politics;
E.B. Eddy becomes federal member of Parliament and mayor of Hull.
Noah Timmins operates steamboat service from Deux Rivière to Mattawa until 1881.
J.R. Booth employs 6,000 at mills and in the bush.

1871: New York Canoe Club–first in North America.

1880's: Recreational canoeing blossoms in northeast U.S. and into Canada.
Oblate Father Paradis conceives idea of settling east shore of Lk. Temiskaming with French-Canadian farmers from the St. Lawrence and eliminate Ottawa rapids by lowering the lake level.
Beaver and moose populations decimated.

1881-2: C.P.R. reaches Mattawa and North Bay.

1883: First steamer on Lake Temiskaming–side-wheeling "Argo".

1885: Alexander Kirkwood, official for Provincial Department of Crown Lands initiates movement to create Algonquin Provincial Park.
System of fire-rangers established to protect crown lands. This conservation movement was sparked by Theodore Roosevelt and Gifford Pinchott who were working on a system of parks in the U.S.

1887: The "Meteor" is launched on Lake Temiskaming.

1889-90: E.M. White and Old Town Canoe Companies founded in Old Town, Maine.

1890s: Sportsmen's magazines and periodicals in U.S. begin to feature canoe expeditions into northern Ontario.

Imposition of the McKinley/Dingley Tariffs by Washington Republicans to protect U.S. forest industry - new markets were opening up in the U.S. northwest.

1891: Settlement increases with the building of several rail lines up the valley interior. C.P. builds rail line from Mattawa to Temiskaming (steamer depot for travel north).

1893: Algonquin Provincial Park established.

1895: Ontario Forstry Branch (O.F.B.) set up to manage forests; similar action taken in Quebec. P.Q. creates Laurentide Park, followed by the Kipawa Forest Reserve and La Verendrye. The latter which would protect the source waters of the Ottawa, Dumoine, Coulonge and Gatineau Rivers.

1895-1910: Birth of pulp mills - large scale exploitation stimulated by demands from U.S. publishers and newspaper chains.

1900: Ontario government survey identifies Lake Temiskaming potential for mining and farming–plans tossed about to build railway from North Bay to west Lake Temiskaming and on to James Bay.

E.B. Eddy mill burns down.

1901: Temagami Forest Reserve established to preserve area - worked until 1924.

1903: Cobalt silver rush.

1904: Keewaydin establishes first North American canoe camp for boys on Lake Temagami.

1905: T&NO rail service opens to Temagami and New Liskeard.

1906: Elk Lake silver rush.

1908: Gowganda silver rush.

1909: Ontario Provincial Police is formed.

1910: Almost all high-class red/white pine along the Ottawa Valley tributaries has been cut. Companies begin cutting spruce, balsam and jackpine.

Implementation of unions gives rise to violence at mills.

1912: L.L.Bean founds company in Freeport, Maine based on his popular boot design.

137 fire-rangers operating in the district of Temagami–birth of the "canoe-brigades" this time to spot and fight forest fires.

1913: Rail line completed to Elk Lake.

1914: Canada enters World War I and conscription begins.

1916: Worst fire in Canadian history kills 223 and destroys 1,320 sq.miles at Cochrane, Ontario.

1920s: Fort Matachewan H.B.C. post closed.

First "float-planes" in the bush.

Chestnut and Peterborough Canoe Co's bought out by the Canadian Watercraft Company.

1922: Haileybury fire kills 43 and destroys 6000 homes.

1924: Temagami Forest Reserve opened to logging.

1925: Keewaydin camp loses two canoeists under log jam on the La Cave rapids on the Ottawa River.

1928: First quality topographic maps produced from aerial surveys.

1930's: "Grey Owl", author and lecturer who found roots in the Temagami wilds, becomes icon of conservation and adventure. Famous quote...civilization says,"Nature belongs to man."–The Indian says,"No man belongs to nature."

Steel fire-towers erected for fire surveillance.

1932: T&NO railway now links Moosonee at James Bay.

1937-38: Concrete dam built across the Noire River at Waltham Station and Grand Chutes–improves power facility feeding Pembroke.

1939: Canada enters World War II and conscription commences.

1943: Ontario and Quebec sign agreement for water-power development along the Ottawa River.

1944-5: Construction begins on the Chalk River Nuclear Power

Research Station. Aug. 6, 1945, the Hon. C.D. Howe (minister of Munitions and Supply), announced that; "Canadian scientists and Canadian Institutions have played an intimate part and have been associated in an effective way with this great scientific development."

This, of course, refers directly to the H.Bomb which had just been dropped on Hiroshima, Japan. Secretly known as the "Petawawa Works", local residents believed it to be a synthetic rubber plant. Little did they know that it was playing with "X-metal" or uranium and "polymer"...better known today as "heavy-water". *See #12, "Hunting Territories" map.

1946-50: Dam at Des Joachims constructed creating 57 mile lake upstream. 11,000 acres of forest was cleared. Dam is 2,400 ft. long and 190 ft. high. 875,000 cu.yds. of concrete used (sufficient to build a 4ft. wide sidewalk from Quebec City to Vancouver. Fort Dumoine ruins now underwater.

1950s: Forest industry becomes mechanized, using skidders and bulldozers instead of horse-drawn sleighs.

Northern Ontario Power Co. builds power plants on the Montreal River to service the Cobalt mines. P.Q. builds dams above Lac des Quinze on the Ottawa to service mines at Rouyn and Noranda.

1952: Otto Holden dam built above Mattawa creating 30 mile lake upstream–La Cave rapids drowned.

1960s: Fire detection towers phased out–aerial surveillance takes over.

1965: Iron ore is mined in Temagami (Sherman Mine).

1970: Ontario government designates the Mattawa River as the first "Waterway Park" in the province.

1971: Ontario Hydro completes "Lower Notch" power station and floods the entire lower Montreal River.

1972: Ontario government proposes to build a ski resort on Maple Mountain, a native burial site. Environmentalists and natives fight to reject project.

Hydro Quebec commences construction of LG-2 power dams on Le Grande River - native Cree protest but not to loud.

1973: Temagami band registers legal land claim against Ontario government and goes to court.

Lady Evelyn River receives "Waterway Park" status.

1974: Quebec Cree surrender rights for cash from hydro project.

13 boys drown on Lake Temiskaming from St. John's school on their first day out.

1984: Ontario government establishes Lady Evelyn-Smoothwater "Wilderness Park" and Makobe "Waterway Park".

1985-90: Temagami logging companies battle with environmentalists and natives over fate of province's last remaining old-growth pine forests. Premier Bob Rae gets arrested at the Red Squirrel road blockade in 1989 - helps him win provincial election. Province spends 10 million to build road but closes it down after forming "Stewardship" treaty with the Temagami Anishnabai. They lose both provincial and federal court case but establish the "Wendabun Stewardship Authority", a co-operative agreement for land management with the Ontario government.

Government expands Temagami park systems to include the Sturgeon and Obabika and Pinetorch corridors.

1988: Mattawa River receives Canadian Heritage River status.

1993: New dam proposed for Noire and hydro-power development for the Coulonge. Outcome...?

Glossary of Terms

Alligator: An amphibious boat used to haul log booms down lakes and able to pull itself across land by the use of huge winches. (See "Alligator Point", Dumoine River–Lac Laforge).

Anishnabai: Alonkian Ojibway for "people".

Bark Mark: Logging company stamp on a log.

Barron River: Named after Augustus Barron in 1980 who was a member of the House of Commons.

Beaver: Single-engined bush plane built by De Havilland Aircraft reknowned as the "work horse" of the north.

Blaze: Axe-mark on a tree often used to indicate a portage trail.

Bowman's Portage: Last portage on the Dumoine River by-passing a falls named after Baxter Bowman, an early timber baron.

Calk Boots: Logger's boots equipped with spiked soles, used to jumping from log to log during the river drive.

Camboose Shanty: Derived from e French "Chantier" for lumber yard, a low-ceilinged log building with an open, central fire-pit of the 1880s–early 1900s logging era that housed the rivermen.

Canot de Maître: The "Montreal" canoe used for larger lake travel, weighing 600 lbs., 36 ft. in length, paddled by 10 to 12 men and carried a cargo of 3 tons.

Chalk River: Named for the milky appearance of the water or for the alder and poplar twigs that were charred and used to "chalk" square timber.

Chapeau: Town named after a hat-shaped rock in the he rapids of the "Cheval de la Culbute", north channel of the Ottawa River at Île des Allumettes.

Cobalt: First known as Cobalt Station, it was named in 1909 by provincial geologist Dr. Willet G. Miller, who "was impressed by the presence of the mineral cobalt in the local silver ore".

Contre maître: Camboose camp boss.

Courier de bois: French for "runners of the woods", took over as "middlemen" from the Indians after the Iroquois wars of the 1647-50s. Travelled the inland waters in search for furs.

Deadhead: Refers primarily to cut logs, now fixed to the bottom but still buoyant enough so that one end breaks the water surface.

Dead or Windfall: A tree lodged across a trail or stream, probably pushed over by heavy winds or snow cover.

Deep River: Town named after "La Riviére Creuse" by French voyageurs–the section of the Ottawa River from here to Des Joachims where the hills are very steep.

Des Joachims: Named after a brother or father of the wife of Chevalier de Troyes (Joachim de l'estang), or after Saint-Joachim, father o the Virgin Mary. Rapids were once known as "rapids Joachim de l'estang, Coloquial name, "D'Swisha".

Dumoine River: Named after famous French trading family–the Le Moynes, specifically one 17 year old Jean Baptiste Le Moyne, brother to Sieur d'Iberville. The founding of New Orleans was attributed to Jean years later.

Fourt Coulong/Coulonge River: Named after French trading family Nicolas d'Ailleboust de Monthet, Sieur de Coulonge.was both a part of a family name and of a seigneury that it owned.

Fort William: Named after William McGillivray (1764-1852), Chief of the N.W.C. from 1804 to 1821.

Gars de haches: Men employed to square the felled timber.

Green hands: Young men hired for the timber drive. They used pike poles or hand spikes to help them jump from log to log. Highest mortality rate of the drive.

Haileybury: Name conferred in 1873 by C.C. Farr–a graduate of Haileybury College in England.

Haystack: Known as a "standing wave" or "roller", they are created by submerged obstacles or fast-current meeting the slower-moving water at the base of a rapid.

Horserace, swifts, fun & games: Strong current not quite classed as Cl grade rapids.

Île Allumette: Two origins– 1) A Jesuit forgot his box of "Allumettes" (wooden splints tipped with sulphur, which he carried to make fire; 2) Island named for reeds that grow which were also used to make fire sticks.

Île du Calumet: As described by Alexander Henry in 1761; "this carrying place is long and arduous, consisting in a high steep hill, over which the canoe cannot be carried by fewer than 12 men – On the morning of the 14th, we reached a trading fort, or house, surrounded by a stockade, which had been built by the French, and at which the quantity of peltries received was once not inconsiderable" – speaking of Fort Coulonge.

Jam Dragger: A series of ropes attached to problem logs and james, and tied-off to shore (like modern "Z" drag). If this didn't work, rivermen were tied by the waist and sent in to chop it out. Safety depended on skill, agility and speed.

Matachewan: Cree word for "meeting of the currents", where the Montreal west and east come together.

New Liskeard: Named after the town of Liskeard in Cornwall, England. Post office dates from 1903 when "new" was added to Liskeard to avoid confusion with Liskard in Southern Ontario.

Noire River: French for "black river", named for the very dark colouration of the water.

North Canoe: Used for small-lake and river travel, weighing 300 lbs., paddled by 6 voyageurs and could carry 1 1/2 tons of cargo. Each voyageur, or "mileaux", would carry 3 loads of 180 lbs each across every portage.

Pembroke: Named after Sidney Herbert, son of the Earl of Pembroke (1810-61), Secretary of the Admiralty in 1843 when the name was adopted.

Pike Pole: Most common tool used by river drivers consisting of a 12-16 ft. pole with a gaffed spike at the end used to prod logs.

Piqueteurs: Lumber-jacks employed to fell trees beginning late September to mid-March. Logs were then hauled by horse-drawn sleigh to headwater lakes and piled for spring thaw.

Pointer: A shallow-draft boat with pointed bow and stern, powered by series of rowers. Built in Ottawa or Pembroke for the logging drives. They could be run down rapids or dragged over portages along log skids for rollers. Last used on the Coulonge River.

Sorters: When logs piled up, sometimes 300 m long, the key logs had to be removed. Different companies often intro respective booms for further movement downstream.

Sweeper: Tree fallen or lodged along a rapids posing serious safety threats to canoeists.

Timber cullers: Early forest surveyors or "cruisers" sent in to inventory stands of pine.

Turkeys: Men's packsacks or bed-rolls.

Upper Ottawa Improvement Company: Operated a series of slides and booms for the lumber companies between Temiskaming and Ottawa from 1867.

Works: Construction of slides, dams, booms to prevent log loss or damage particularly at rapids, chutes and falls. Remants of works can be seen on all Ottawa Valley rivers.

Bibliography

ADDISON, Ottelyn, "Early Days In Algonquin Park", McGraw-Hill Ryerson Ltd. 1974

BACK, Brian, "The Keewaydin Way - A Portrait: 1893-1983", Keewaydin Camp Ltd., Temagami, 1983

BEDORE, Bernie, "The Shanty", Mufferaw Enterprises, Arnprior, 1963

CASSIDY, G.L., "Arrow North: The Story of Temiskaming", Highway Book Shop Publishers, Cobalt, 1976

FINNIGAN, Joan, "Some of the Stories I Told You were True", Denwau Publishers & Co. Ltd., 1981

FOWKE, Edith and Richard Johnston (editors), "Folk Songs of Canada", Waterloo Music Co., 1954

GREENING, William E., "The Ottawa", McClelland & Stewart, 1961

HODGINS, Bruce, "Nastawgan", Betelgeuse Books, 1985

KENNEDY, Clyde C., "The Upper Ottawa Valley–a Glimpse of History", Renfrew County Council, Pembroke, Ont., 1970

LEGGET, Robert, "Ottawa Waterway, Gateway to a Continent", University of Toronto Press, 1975

MITCHELL, Elaine A., "Fort Temiskaming & the Fur Trade", University of Toronto Press, 1977

MORSE, Eric W., "Recreational Canoeing in Canada: its history and hazards", Canadian Geographical Journal, 1977

POSEN, Sheldon I., "The Chapeau Boys", Deneau Publishers & Co. Ltd., 1988

REID, Richard M., "Upper Ottawa Valley to 1855"

TRIGGER, Bruce G., "The Children of Aataentsic - A History of the Huron People to 1660", McGill-Queen's University Press, 1976

WATSON, Wreford J., "North America - its Countries and Regions", Longmans, Green & Co. Ltd., 1963

WILSON, Hap, "Temagami Canoe Routes", Northern Concepts, 1977. Reprinted & updated, Canadian Recreational Canoeing Association, 1992.

MANUSCRIPTS (Secondary Sources)

SPECK, F.G., "Family Hunting Territories & Social Life of Various Algonkian Bands of the Ottawa Valley", Geological Survey, Dept. of Mines, Government Printing Bureau, Ottawa, 1915

Canadian Heritage River System, "Mattawa River", Canadian Heritage Rivers Board, Ottawa K1A 0H3

Ministry of Natural Resources, "Mattawa River & Samuel de Champlain Provincial Parks", Box 147, Mattawa, Ont. P0H 1V0

ARCHIVES (Research Sources)

Camp Keewaydin Ltd., archival collection, Lake Temagami, Ontario

Champlain Trail Museum & the Ottawa Valley Historical Society

National Archives of Canada, Ottawa, K1A 0N3

Pembroke Hydro Museum, Pembroke, Ontario

Samuel de Champlain Provincial Park, Mattawa, Ontario

Schoolhouse Museum, Deep River, Ontario

Wabun Camp for Boys, Trip archives, Lake Temagami, Ontario

About the Author

A wilderness tripper for more than 30 years, Hap Wilson has written and illustrated several books about the Canadian wilderness since his first book, *Temagami Canoe Routes*, was published in 1978. His original maps and illustrations were featured in *Voyages: Canada's Heritage Rivers*, which won the Natural Resources Council of America award for best environmental book of 1995. His other field-friendly eco-guidebooks include *Wilderness Rivers of Manitoba, Missinaibi: Journey to the Northern Sky, Canoeing, Kayaking and Hiking Temagami,* and *Wild Muskoka,* all published by Boston Mills Press. His work appears frequently in U.S. and Canadian magazines, including *Canadian Geographic, Explore, Cottage Life, Outdoor Canada, Razor, Kanawa,* and *Canoe & Kayak.* Wilson has actively promoted conservation through ecology-based tourism for the past 30 years.

Wilson shares the trail with his wife, Stephanie, and their two children, Christopher and Alexa. When not out tripping, you can find them at their wilderness outpost on the Lady Evelyn River or at their studio-gallery home in Muskoka, Ontario.

You can contact Hap Wilson through his website: www.sunriseadventures.com

Stephanie Aykroyd

Acknowledgments

It's sometimes hard to fathom the amount of work that goes into composing travel guidebooks. The final product constitutes innumerable days on the trail, coupled with equal time at the drafting table. One of the primary constituents of the quintessential trail guide is the sponsor, who without their undying support (or gullibility) this book would not have made its way to the many backpacks and map pouches bound for the rivers highlighted here. Thanks go to the Canadian Recreational Canoeing Association who published the first editions of the book. To my corporate sponsors, *Johnson Worldwide* (Old Town Canoe, Camp Trails & Eureka Tents); *Harvest Foodworks;* Ron Bowes of *Bradley Air* & more recently, Daryl Vaillencourt of *Air Swisha;* the late Bob Gareh of *Lakeland Airways* in Temagami; the staff at the Pembroke museum who allowed me to rummage through the archives; the Pembroke Power & Light Company; the kind woman from Fort Coulonge who drove us all the way back to the air base at Swisha after we had forgotten the keys to our shuttle truck parked at Grande Chute; and to Gary, Art, Ed, Michelle and the *CITY TV* gang who punched a few haystacks on these rivers with me; Martin Cooper of *Archaeological Services* and John Dressler at Samuel Champlain Park; my ex-wife Trudy (yes, you were right); Melissa Thompson; Marie-Lynn Hammond for the beautiful song, and to the wonderful people I encountered throughout the valley region — my heartfelt thanks. Most importantly, I would like to thank my wife Stephanie for her support and guidance, and to Kirk Wipper for his sage wisdom.

Directory of Services

Swift Canoe & Kayak
Swift Canoe & Kayak was founded by paddlers for paddlers. The company is located in South River, Ontario – in the heart of Canoe Country. We are currently building 11 canoes and 10 kayak models, in Goldenglass, Expedition Kevlar, Ultralight Kevlar and Royalex. Our boats can be found throughout North America and as far away as Europe. Please contact us for a location near you.
www.swiftcanoe.com
Swift Canoe & Kayak
South River, Ontario
Tel: 1-800-661-1429
swift@swiftcanoe.com

Sunrise Adventures
Over thirty years experience in wilderness travel, Nature writing, photography and graphic art, Hap Wilson and Stephanie Aykroyd custom design adventures just about anywhere in Canada. *Sunrise Eco-Lodge* provides soulful adventures within the Lady Evelyn-Smoothwater Wilderness Park in the heart of Temagami's ancient forests.
www.sunriseadventures.com
Sunrise Adventures
1141 Crawford St.
Rosseau, Ontario, P0C 1J0
Tel: 705-732-8254
Fax: 705-732-8255
Email: sunrise@vianet.on.ca

Air Swisha
We operate Cessna, Beaver and Otter aircraft, servicing the Dumoine, Coulonge, Noire and Kipawa rivers. We also provide current river information and paddling tips from the pro's.
www.airswisha.com www.airkipawa.com
www.kipawaoutfitters.com
Air Swisha
Rapides-des-Joachims, QC
Tel: 613-586-2374
Fax: 819-627-9256
Toll free: 877-610-3474

Ostrom Outdoors
Makers of the toughest packs around. We design and manufacture canoe packs and accessories, including the popular coated 70D Packcloth canoe pack liner. Write for a free catalogue.
www.ostrompacks.com
Ostrom Outdoors
R.R.#1 Nolalu, Ontario, P0T 2K0
Toll free: 1-877-678-7661
Email: ostromab@tbaytel.net

Temagami Outfitting Company
Paddling Temagami in style, choose the finest Kevlar canoes and kayaks that are lightweight and affordable to rent. We are centrally located to all area access points and offer shuttle services, route planning, complete outfitting, maps and accommodation.
www.icanoe.ca
Temagami Outfitting Company
Temagami, Ontario, P0H 2H0
Tel: 705-569-2595
Fax: 705-569-2598
Email: info@icanoe.ca

North Bay Canoe & Kayak
Traditional craftsmanship by paddlers serving paddlers. Sales and rentals, gear and accessories, guided trips, repairs and supplies, restorations, clinics and courses.
www.nbcanoe.com
North Bay Canoe & Kayak
34 Johnson Rd. Corbeil, Ontario
Toll-free: 1-800-927-1290
Email: canoe@efni.com

Algonquin Outfitters
Outdoor Adventure store specializing in, canoe and kayak sales and rentals, guided day trips, canoe trip outfitting and much more. Open year round.
www.algonquinoutfitters.com
Algonquin Outfitters
Oxtongue Lake – Hwy # 60
Tel: 705-635-2243
Huntsville – Main St. at Brunel
Tel: 705-787-0262
Email: info@algonquinoutfitters.com

Trailhead/Blackfeather
Outfitting and guiding in the Ottawa River valley since 1969. Sales of equipment and clothing for canoeists, rentals, guided trips and instructional courses. Specializing in Dumoine River trips with rental fleet located at the Swisha air-base.
www.trailhead.ca
Trailhead
1960 Scott St.
Ottawa, Ontario, K1Z 8L8
Tel: 613-722-4229
Fax: 613-722-0245
Email: scottst@trailhead.ca

Johnson Outdoors Canada/Eureka Tent
Manufacturing quality tents since 1895. Firsthand experience of designing tents for the most extreme conditions is helping us produce exciting new styles made to meet any challenge in the outdoors. Check out our new lines of canoe packs and dry bags.
www.eurekatentscanada.com
Johnson Outdoors Canada
4180 Harvester Rd.
Burlington, Ontario, L7L 6B6
Tel: 905-634-0023
Fax: 905-634-0261
Email: sales@eurekatentscanada.com

Valley Ventures
Dumoine, Petawawa, Noire, Coulonge Rivers, including canoe trips to the far north. Custom trips, complete and partial outfitting, drive in shuttles (including the Dumoine River), full-service accommodation at the Eddy Inn, experienced and expert service.
www.magma.ca/-vent
Valley Ventures
Deep River, Ontario
Tel: 613-584-2577
Fax: 613-584-9016
Email: vent@magma.ca